AUTISM
& READING
COMPREHENSION

Ready-to-Use Lessons for Teachers

Joseph Porter, M.Ed.

AUTISM & READING COMPREHENSION
Ready-to-use Lessons for Teachers

All marketing and publishing rights guaranteed to and reserved by

FUTURE HORIZONS INC.

721 W. Abram Street, Arlington, Texas 76013

(toll-free) 800-489-0727, (local) 817-277-0727, (fax) 817-277-2270

Email: info@FHautism.com, www.FHautism.com

Publisher's Cataloging-In-Publication Data
(Prepared by The Donohue Group, Inc.)

Porter, Joseph, 1962-
  Autism & reading comprehension : ready-to-use lessons for teachers / Joseph Porter.

  p. : ill. ; cm.

  Includes bibliographical references and index.
  ISBN: 978-1-935274-15-5

  1. Autistic children--Education. 2. Reading comprehension--Study and teaching (Elementary)--Problems, exercises, etc. I. Title. II. Title: Autism and reading comprehension

LC4717.5 .P67 2011
371.94

TABLE OF CONTENTS

TABLE OF CONTENTS

AUTISM & READING COMPREHENSION
© 2011 by Joseph Porter, M.Ed. Future Horizons, Inc.

INTRODUCTION

When it comes to being a new teacher, there's probably nothing more frightening and overwhelming than facing a room full of children with autism, all under the age of ten.

Trust me. I lived it.

During those first few weeks, I would have given my right hand—the one I squeezed my stress ball with—in exchange for any kind of accessible, teacher-friendly material. Every book I picked up was either an overwhelming, science-journal-type of tome or a book full of therapy-style exercises designed exclusively for one-on-one instruction. These resources are valuable in their own way, but when you're a new teacher faced with the daunting task of managing and teaching a classroom of autistic students, you have precious little time or energy to process complicated, science-based articles or plan one-on-one lessons.

I think that teachers in autism classrooms should receive as much easy-to-process, no-nonsense help as possible. I created my own material, honing and fine-tuning it as I came to understand my students and their highly specific needs. This program, which includes worksheets and scripted lessons, was effective with my students, so I thought I'd share it with other teachers.

However, this is not to say that this is a one-size-fits-all curriculum. You should be aware that lower-functioning kids may have trouble with the more conceptual aspects of these lessons, such as "wh" questions, prepositional phrases, directional words, adjectives, feeling words, and prompts that require subjective thinking (e.g., "Tell me about the cat."). Many may also lack the organizational skills to copy from the board and transfer words from one paper to another. That's okay. Take it one step at a time, and structure the lessons as needed to foster success for your students.

I hope this manual helps you and your students not only to manage but also to learn and grow in productive, fun ways.

THE UNDERLYING PRINCIPLES OF THE PROGRAM

Autism and Reading Comprehension revolves around what I believe are the two most important elements in teaching individuals with autism to read: whole-group instruction and reading comprehension.

It seems to me that almost every book on teaching children with autism focuses on one-on-one instruction. For a new teacher, in my opinion, it's just not practical. You can plan whole-group instruction more easily than you can plan individual lessons. I believe one-on-one instruction isolates autistic children from their classmates and the rest of the school population. This seems to be the opposite of what we, as teachers, should be providing them. Whole-group instruction allows children to interact with their classmates and practice socially appropriate behavior, e.g., raising their hands before speaking, sharing materials, and listening to each other speak. This type of interaction should be coached and encouraged at every opportunity.

That's not to say that I feel that one-on-one instruction is superfluous or even secondary. We need focused, intensive, one-on-one instruction in the basic skills that make whole-group instruction possible. However, whole-group instruction (as well as mainstreaming and inclusion) should never be treated as a "second-best" approach. They are equal partners, one complementing the other.

Yet with any method of instruction, the goal is reading *comprehension*, not just word recognition. My first couple of years of teaching, I was thrilled at the progress (I believed) I was making with my students' reading skills. It took me a while to realize that they weren't really reading—they were simply calling the words, without understanding the meaning. Most children with autism are visual learners. They use these visual skills, often to the exclusion of other senses, when reading. One of my students read two pages about a black cat drinking milk, playing with yarn, and climbing the curtains. His word recognition and fluency were nearly flawless. Then I asked him, "What color is the cat?" He answered, echolalia-style, "What color is the cat?" Sometimes he repeated only the last word of my question: "Cat." This is one of the core challenges in teaching this population.

Then I began to wonder about the correlation between reading comprehension and "people comprehension." I thought that if I could successfully teach my students reading comprehension skills, they would learn how to communicate more successfully with people. Reading comprehension, in its simplest terms, is about paying attention to what you're reading—having an active relationship with the words on the page. If I could get the kids to listen to what they were reading, then I could get them to listen to people.

With children who have autism, dealing with people is difficult. I figured I'd start with inanimate words on the page and work my way up to people.

It worked.

Little by little, as a direct result of their success and confidence with the simple question-and-answer format of these worksheets, my students began responding appropriately to questions outside of the lessons, on the playground, in the lunchroom, and on field trips—as long as I asked the questions in the same, simple, direct manner as on the worksheets. It was clear, measurable progress.

These worksheets, and their accompanying lessons, also worked well with some of the younger ELL (English Language Learners) in my school.

It's critical to build and sustain students' confidence. If you start a program at too high a difficulty level, students will be intimidated and give up, failing before they've even begun. These worksheets start with easy questions. Then, once students are comfortable and confident within the format, you slowly increase the difficulty. You must take gradual, incremental steps to build their confidence and their skills.

Let's get to the nitty-gritty. Good luck. I hope this program helps you and your students as it helped me and mine.

OVERVIEW OF LESSONS

The Worksheets

There are two reading-comprehension worksheets for each of nine animals, totaling eighteen worksheets. Each worksheet has four variations. Each variation goes with a one-hour lesson. This is approximately 72 hours of instruction.

For more severely affected children, a thirty-minute or even fifteen-minute lesson may have to suffice. Even if students are able to attend for the full hour, it may be best to take a short break every fifteen minutes or so. Use your best judgment based on your students' needs and abilities. The children should be challenged but not agitated and panicky. Customize the lessons as needed, but try to maintain a consistent lesson structure.

The lessons provide lots of much-needed repetition. I suggest teaching these lessons every other day. Then supplement on the "off" days with art projects, music, books, and instructional videos related to the animal theme. In the back of this manual, you'll find an appendix with numerous suggestions for complementary activities for each animal theme.

Doing the same worksheet for four consecutive lessons is central to the success of the program. It gives students the predictability and routine they need so they can relax and learn. However, the colors of the objects change with each lesson. This helps the children to pay attention. This formula works for children with autism in many different settings. Establish a predictable framework, but change the details within that predictable framework. You'll be surprised how many different ways you can work this formula into your day.

For these worksheets, I've used animals, food, and prepositional phrases on purpose. My students love animals and food, and any academic exercise with these two things catches their attention and keeps them engaged. Prepositional phrases are particularly difficult for autistic students to grasp, so repetition helps. You can also teach these separately using concrete objects and flashcards. Mayer-Johnson (www.mayer-johnson.com/default.aspx) has many resources for teaching language and communication.

Sentence-Building Exercises

There are two sentence-building exercises for each animal theme. Each exercise is a one-hour lesson. This is approximately 18 hours of instruction.

It's hard for children who have autism to generate their own conversation. The sentence-building exercises concentrate on building your students' observation skills and corralling those observations into conversation. Not unlike the worksheet lessons, the conversation is transformed into written language. However, this time, the written language is plugged into a pair of graphic organizers and, ultimately, into actual sentences.

The goal of each sentence-building exercise is to build three sentences describing the animal in the picture and to illustrate those three sentences.

Schedule

The program covers one animal at a time. Here is a sample schedule:

<u>The Cat</u>

Monday – First variation of first reading comprehension worksheet
Tuesday – Supplemental activity (book, video, craft, etc.)
Wednesday – Second variation of first reading comprehension worksheet
Thursday – Supplemental activity (book, video, craft, etc.)
Friday – Third variation of first reading comprehension worksheet
Monday – Fourth variation of first reading comprehension worksheet
Tuesday – Supplemental activity (book, video, craft, etc.)
Wednesday - First variation of sentence-building exercise
Thursday – Supplemental activity (book, video, craft, etc.)
Friday - Supplemental activity (book, video, craft, etc.)

Monday – First variation of second reading comprehension worksheet
Tuesday – Supplemental activity (book, video, craft, etc.)
Wednesday – Second variation of second reading comprehension worksheet
Thursday – Supplemental activity (book, video, craft, etc.)
Friday – Third variation of second reading comprehension worksheet
Monday – Fourth variation of second reading comprehension worksheet
Tuesday – Supplemental activity (book, video, craft, etc.)
Wednesday – Second variation of sentence-building exercise
Thursday – Supplemental activity (book, video, craft, etc.)
Friday - Supplemental activity (book, video, craft, etc.)

The Process

In this section, I will walk you through "The Cat" lessons so you can have a clearer idea of how the lessons will play out in your classroom. After all, children with autism aren't the only ones who like to know what's ahead of them!

The worksheets you will need for the lessons are provided at http://fhautism.com/arc.html. You can print out the customizable worksheets if you prefer to write in the color words yourself, or you can print out ready-to-go worksheets for each variation.

The animals have been chosen because of the variety of colors they come in. The cat, for instance, can logically be black, gray, brown, or orange. It's also important that the cat and the table (or the two items that vary on the other worksheets) are two *different* colors, specifically, two highly contrasting colors. The more vivid the visual, the easier it will ultimately be for them to answer the questions. So for the first worksheet, the color combinations are:

Worksheet 1, Variation 1: brown cat, yellow table
Worksheet 1, Variation 2: orange cat, blue table
Worksheet 1, Variation 3: black cat, pink table
Worksheet 1, Variation 4: gray cat, red table

Let's say you have seven kids in your class and you have distributed Worksheet 1, Variation 1 to your students. Their desks should be clear of all writing utensils. Start by having a student volunteer to read the passage. If no one is able to read the passage, read it yourself, or have an aide read it aloud.

(An additional benefit to the lesson repetition—having the same sentence frame for several lessons—is that it allows children to memorize the simple sentences, ultimately enabling them to "read" them out loud to the class. So even though they're not actually reading the passage, they feel as if they are and, subsequently, feel successful. The more positive associations they have with reading and words, the better.)

Once the passage has been read aloud, say to the class, "Now we want to color the picture that goes with the story. What two crayons should we take out of our box?"

Having the kids stop and focus on the colors like this, right from the beginning, will help them to answer the questions later on. Once someone answers "brown and yellow," repeat the question and have another child answer. Some kids will still take out the wrong crayons, even if you repeat this question-and-answer round three or four times. Just be patient and get the information out there verbally, as often as you can. Once you do, help them physically take out the two correct crayons and a pencil. Check around the room and make sure that's all they have on their desks—their worksheet, their pencil, and (with this particular variation) their brown and yellow crayons.

Once they've successfully taken out the brown and yellow crayons, have them return the box of crayons to their pencil box or supply area, wherever the crayons are kept. You could even assign an aide to hang on to the boxes once the two correct crayons have been removed. Even something as simple as leaving a box of crayons out on the desk is distracting in an autism classroom. Children who have autism, through no fault of their own, can be so easily tempted that leaving the crayon box out can lead to disruptions. Trust me. I've seen it.

Have them pick up their pencils and write their name and the date first. You should write the date on the board. If there are students who don't know how to write their name, this is a good time to have them practice (daily) just the first letter or couple of letters of their first name. Baby steps.

Once the name and date are completed, remind them that they're going to be coloring the cat brown and the table yellow. Tell them that they will be starting with the cat. Say, "If we're starting with the cat, what color do we need?"

When the color brown is established, make sure that everyone has his or her brown crayon in hand and ready to go. Let them begin coloring ONLY the cat. Have aides dispersed around the room as best you can and be watchful. I can't tell you how many times I've watched the cat, the table, and the pizza all be colored brown in the blink of an eye. (This is another good reason for those back-up copies!) I've also tried to make the illustrations as simple as possible, with enough surface area for the students to color and, therefore, focus on the color they're using.

Check the room; make sure that all the cats have been colored brown. Repeat the words "brown cat" as often as possible. "Oh, that's a lovely brown cat," or "What a wonderful job you did coloring that brown cat." The more they hear the phrase "brown cat," the easier it will be for them to answer the upcoming question:

"Okay, now that we've colored the cat brown, what color should we color the table? Let's look back at our story if we need a reminder."

Proceed the same way with the table as you did with the cat, repeating the phrase "yellow table" as often as possible. Once the cat has been colored brown and the table has been colored yellow, have students put aside their two crayons and their pencils and refocus their attention on you. Again, if some students (as many of mine did) have trouble with writing utensils sitting idly on their desks, just have an aide temporarily remove temptation. It's important that they stay focused through this next section, because the next step is important.

This next section of the lesson is **spoken language**. Before any of the answers are going to be written down on the worksheet, the questions are going to be read aloud—by you, the teacher—and answered by the students. Start by playing to your students' strengths. If you know someone is going to have an easier time with a certain question, give him that question. Frustration is a huge problem for these kids, so allow them opportunities for success whenever and wherever you can. With that in mind, start with the first question, reading it aloud: "What color is the cat?"

Either ask a volunteer to answer or call on someone. If they can't get the answer right, coach them through it, guiding them back to the visual cues in front of them. The important thing is to get the right words out into the classroom. The answers are also written directly into the text. There's no need for conjecture here. Nothing even needs to be rephrased. The answer to the question "What color is the cat?" is directly embedded into the text, word for word, so those capable of reading can actually go back and read it. (This is true of all the questions on all the worksheets. They don't need to be challenged yet with inferences, so they're not. I've found that inferential and abstract thinking is tough for these kids.) Also, make sure they answer in complete sentences. This is crucial. So many times my students will just want to say, "brown" or "cat brown," but that's not enough. The answer must be "The cat is brown." They can begin building their communication skills on this foundation.

Remember, no one is writing anything during this phase. This phase is purely verbal.

Once the questions are asked (and answered) in order, then skip around, asking the questions again in random order. Many students will simply memorize the answers in order. Skipping around FORCES them to pay attention. That's the key to reading comprehension for students with autism. Forcing them to stop going by rote and to pay active attention to what's on the page and what's being asked of them. It also gives a student who may have struggled the first time around a chance to answer correctly, now that he's heard the correct answer.

When the questions have been asked in order and at random, and the students have all (hopefully) had a chance to answer a question (or at least have heard the correct answers being spoken by a classmate) have them pick up their pencils and get ready to write down the answers on their worksheets. So we're now moving from spoken language to written language, with the answers they've already processed. This transition is crucial—especially with simple-as-possible sentences—because it helps them to make the connection between spoken and written language, a connection they don't always make. To them, much of the time, the words on the page are meaningless. Bolstering the connection between those words on the page and the words we speak to communicate with one another is central to these lessons.

Start with the first question, reading it aloud as before.

At this point, the kids have practiced answering these questions, so they should be okay. However, there will probably still be some confusion, so go with a student you're certain can answer the question. It's now less about assessing individual students and more about giving everyone a clear example of spoken language transitioning into written language. As soon as the right answer is spoken aloud, you write it on the board, allowing them to copy it onto their worksheets. You could use one of the extra worksheets to do this modeling, but I find it more effective to write on the board, where I can use larger, easier-to-see handwriting. Even with this, some students still won't be able to copy the full sentence; that's okay. If they write only the first letter, praise them for trying, and then maybe have that be the focus of an individualized lesson later on. Conversely, some students will be able to write the whole sentence independently, without looking at the board. This is more unusual, but in my experience, it became less so as we progressed through these worksheets.

Don't forget—you're always going to be dealing with a huge range of skill sets. That's why these worksheets were so successful for me. Everyone was allowed to get SOMETHING from the experience. The kids in the middle of the pack (the majority) got the most.

The rest of the lesson is self-explanatory. You move through the remainder of the sentences in the same manner—read the question aloud, get the answer spoken aloud, and immediately transcribe that spoken answer into a written sentence, with the students following your model. When you get to the end of the sentences, you allow the kids to color the pizza (or whatever the food or extra item is on the worksheet you're on) as a reward. This, like so many things, falls under one of the basic teacher tenets: if you make it seem like a reward, it becomes a reward.

Then give lavish praise, pass out stickers, and display the children's work on the bulletin board.

You will do the whole thing again in two days. One worksheet, with its four variations, will take you a week and a day—Monday, Wednesday, Friday and the following Monday.

When you've finished the fourth variation of the first worksheet, you will do the first variation of the **sentence-building exercises**. This lesson will be implemented on the Wednesday after the fourth variation of the first worksheet. In other words, every fifth lesson will be a sentence-building exercise.

The sentence-building exercises concentrate on building your students' observation skills and corralling those observations into conversation. Not unlike the worksheet lessons, that conversation is then transformed into written language. However, this time, that written language will be plugged into a successive pair of graphic organizers and, ultimately, into actual sentences. Each sentence-building exercise will have two variations, one to follow each of the two animal worksheets. The first cat worksheet, with its four variations, will be followed by the first variation of the first sentence-building exercise, also about a cat. The second cat worksheet, with its four variations, will then be followed by the second variation of the first sentence-building exercise.

The goal of each sentence-building exercise is to build three sentences describing the animal in the picture and to illustrate those three sentences. Like the worksheets, it's about repeating the predictable lesson structure, so it's familiar and the kids get comfortable. When students are comfortable, they are open to learning, but they also stay alert because the details within that predictable structure are always changing. I will take you through each detail of the lesson's structure, with scripted suggestions for each lesson. The full-sized photographs of each animal and the two graphic organizers you'll need for each sentence-building exercise are found at http://fhautism.com/arc.html.

Before you start teaching this lesson, you're going to draw the two blank, graphic organizers on chart paper (I prefer chart paper to writing on the board because you can save the completed lesson charts for your records or for future IEP meetings). The first graphic organizer is a circle-in-circle chart, or a general-to-specific chart. It consists of one small circle inside a larger circle. This is what it should look like:

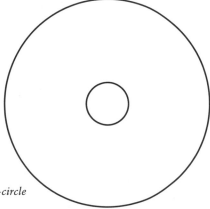

Get the free print PDF of circle-in-circle at http://fhautism.com/arc.html.

This second graphic organizer is a **branch organizer**, with three subtopics/categories. It should be drawn on the chart paper to the right of the circle-in-circle organizer. (Always emphasize a left-to-right progression when teaching reading and writing.)

The branch organizer is going to look like this:

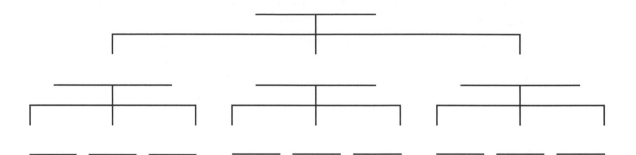

Get the free print PDF of the branch organizer at http://fhautism.com/arc.html.

After you've drawn both graphic organizers, the next step is to hold up the picture of that lesson's animal for the children to see. Since the lesson is going to start with a "conversation," it's best to gather the children in a less formal, circle-time-style arrangement. The first question you're going to ask your class is, "What animal is this?"

If no one is able to identify the animal, that's fine. You can cue an adult aide to answer the question, or you can even answer it yourself. Once the word "cat" has been spoken aloud, write the word "Cat" in the smaller, inner circle of the circle-in-circle chart, like this:

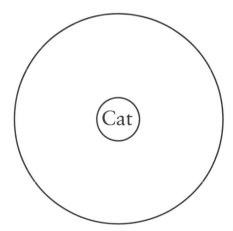

Your next goal is to write down **nine observations** about the cat in the bigger part of the circle, in the form of words or short phrases (usually no more than two words). The nine observations should fall into three different categories, with three observations in each category,

The three categories are **can**, **has**, and **likes**.

In the lesson plan, I provide three sample observations for each of the three categories:

<u>can</u>
jump
run
say meow

<u>has</u>
a tail
four legs
fur

<u>likes</u>
milk
fish
cat food

You will start the lesson with spoken language, trying to elicit these observations from the children. Start with the "can" category by asking, "What can the cat do?"

The first few times you attempt this, you're probably going to be met with stony silence and blank stares. Persevere! They'll get better at it. There's also no need to worry about that stony silence—you, as the teacher, know exactly how the conversation should go and which observations need to be made. Chances are it's going to be rough at the beginning. Yet, even if you (and your aides) have to do all the talking in the early stages, that's fine. The kids are still hearing the language and watching spoken language being transformed into written language and, ultimately, coherent sentences.

If students do not answer, prompt them. You can say something like, "Can the cat fly?" If still no one answers, have an aide answer or answer yourself: "Can the cat jump? Yes, the cat can jump."

Write this first observation in the larger circle, like this:

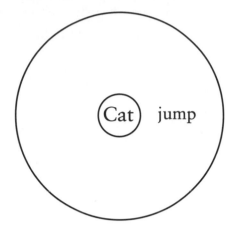

Throughout the exercise, continue to prompt with leading questions/conversations such as, "The cat likes to drink this white beverage. We like to pour it over cereal. Sometimes we like to put chocolate in it so we can have chocolate _____"

The lesson plans will provide the nine observations you need to make the lessons work. Those plans will serve as an instructional foundation you can rely on. The words I provide you with have been pre-selected to create manageable sentences—the ultimate goal. In the beginning, it's hard for children who have autism to generate their own conversation. As the kids get better at this activity, they might come up with observations and sentences even better and more creative than those provided by the script. That's great! The script is just there as a "back-up."

Once all nine observations have been spoken aloud and written down, the circle-in-circle graphic organizer should look like this:

Make sure the outer circle is large enough to contain all the words. Do your best to keep the handwriting legible. The kids will copy these words once they get back to their desks. Also, I advise against adding more than nine words or phrases. You need to keep the graphic organizer looking organized. If you have more than nine words (or short phrases) floating around in the larger circle, it could get messy, especially when the kids copy the words onto their own circle charts—which brings us to the next phase of the lesson.

The children (after much praise over their observation/conversation skills) now leave the conversation area and return to their desks. Have them take out a pencil (and only a pencil!), and distribute the students' graphic organizers, printed from http://fhautism.com/arc.html. Your students now have their own graphic organizers that match the ones on the chart paper.

Have them write their name on the top of the paper (or their initials, or just the first letter—whatever they can do). The first step of their seatwork is to copy the words from the circle-in-circle chart onto their own circle-in-circle chart. If they don't write all the words, it's okay. Especially in the beginning, it's more important that they become familiar with the process of using these graphic organizers to arrange words into sentences.

Once they've done their best to copy the words, move to the second graphic organizer, the branch chart.

Write "The Cat" on the top line and "can," "has," and "likes" on the three spaces on the second row. Have students do the same on their version of the branch chart.

Now it's time to fill in the rest of the branch chart. You will do this together. The time for free floating conversation is over. It's time for the first question: "What can the cat do?"

We stay on this topic until the first "can" column is filled with the appropriate three items. I found that this combination of graphic organizers worked particularly well together with my kids because the *information is right there in front of them*. When someone inevitably answers that first question with "milk," for example, you can form that question back for him or her to hear: "The cat can *milk*? Does that sentence sound right to us? Let's think again—what can he *do*? Let's look back in the circle and find something the cat can do."

Everything stays on a concrete, visual level, which works great for these kids. It's hard to veer very far off course.

Continue in this vein, first asking the students, "What else can the cat do?" until you've transferred all three answers to that question, found within the larger circle of the circle-in-circle chart, to the branch chart.

When all three blank spaces in the "can" column have been successfully filled in, move on to the next column. Say, "Okay class, what does the cat have?"

If someone answers, "jump," you can ask, "The cat has *jump*? Does that sound right to us? Why don't we look inside the big circle to see if we can find something that sounds better than that sentence? How about 'The cat has four legs.' Does that sound better to us?"

Every time you transfer a word from the circle-in-circle chart to the branch chart, take your students through the formation of the sentence. As you say each word of the sentence, point to the corresponding word on the branch chart. This way, they can become familiar with the way we use the chart to form the sentence.

Once the "has" column has been successfully filled in, move on to the "likes" column. I have experimented with erasing the words from the circle-in-circle chart as they were transferred to the branch chart, but I felt this robbed my students of some of the exercise's more important challenges. It's best if they think and observe throughout. If there's just one word left inside the circle at the end of the lesson, you've taken away a potential learning moment for them. However, this is an individual call. If your class is more challenged by this exercise, then make the lesson more manageable. It's more important for your students to succeed.

Once all three columns of the branch chart have been successfully filled in, you can choose to take a "reward-time" mini break. Go around and admire your students' work, giving them a sticker, a gold star, or whatever reward you've established in your classroom. You could even take a stretch break. I found this not to be a good idea with my kids, but if you have a group that can stay focused, this would be a logical place to take a *short* break. The connection still needs to be maintained between the graphic organizers and the sentences we're about to build, so really, no more than fifteen to twenty seconds. This is all up to you, though. You know your kids better than anyone.

Once you're all refocused, distribute the handouts that are lined on the bottom for sentences and blank on the top for illustrations (printed from http://fhautism.com/arc.html). They now have on their desks this new, blank sheet of paper, along with the filled-in graphic organizers. Some kids might become a little overwhelmed with all of this paper and information in front of them, but it's important that the graphic organizers stay on their desks for the sentence-building phase.

Tell the children it's time to make the first sentence. The first time, model it for them, using the branch chart as you do so. Point to the words on the branch chart as you slowly say them, forming your first sentence. Show the students the physical relationship between the words on the chart and how they go together to form a spoken sentence. This will help them read the chart and form the sentences using the chart themselves.

Say, "Let's make a sentence from the first column, using the word 'can.' 'The cat can jump.'"

After the sentence is spoken, write it on the chart paper.

Then, have students write the same sentence on the first line of their papers.

Ask the class if someone can now make a sentence from the second column, using the word "has." Making only one sentence from each column eventually will give the kids a feeling of authorial autonomy—they choose which sentence they want to form. They can choose any of the three words to make a sentence. Once a sentence is formed from the second column, write it on the chart paper, and have the students copy that sentence onto their papers.

Finally, have someone form a sentence from the third column.

You should now have written three sentences:

1. The cat can jump.
2. The cat has a tail.
3. The cat likes milk.

Now it's time for the final part of the sentence-building exercise—**the illustration**. This is a key component to further connecting the students to their writing. We want them to understand that these are not just jumbles of random words scribbled on a piece of paper. They have meaning, and the illustration helps engender a deeper understanding of this connection. Toward that end, the illustration must reflect the information in the sentence. It's okay to be a bit strict here, mostly because it's a drawing—not words—and the pressure decreases at this point. For example, if I see an illustration of a cat not drinking from a bowl of milk—or a cat missing a tail—it's easy for me to correct the students and guide them in the right direction.

Get the free PDF of the lined paper at at http://fhautism.com/arc.html.

You should now have three full sentences and beautiful drawings to illustrate the words. **This marks the halfway point of The Cat lessons.** The second half of The Cat lessons is structured the same way, except you'll begin a new worksheet and work with new sentences. Just like the ones I've described thus far, there will be four variations of the worksheet and then a sentence-building exercise, using the same graphic organizers and lined paper.

Don't forget about the off days; the supplemental activities are crucial for keeping the kids interested in the topics. It is also a much-needed break, and it helps students associate the topics—and reading in general—to good feelings. The lessons will be challenging and sometimes frustrating for them, but I hope they will become fun. The supplemental activities aren't anti-lessons; they are integral aspects of the curriculum that can make or break the program's effectiveness.

Having tried lots of different writing and sentence-building techniques and graphic organizers, I found this combination to be the most successful with my students. The concrete, visual transfer of the words from one graphic organizer to the next and then to sentences was a progression that my students could follow. It also provided many opportunities for conversation, which is always to be treasured in the autism classroom.

Best of all, it's a perfect group lesson! Any time you can employ a group lesson with these kids, you should. Not only is it good for building social skills, it cuts down enormously on the teacher's behavior management workload. Sure, it's more difficult to manage a group of children with autism, as opposed to teaching them one-on-one. I have found that a lesson plan like this, during which the students are almost unanimously engaged, helps with behavior management.

Still, the social and behavioral benefits are usually secondary to the lifelong benefits that reading comprehension skills will provide your students. The better they can process written language, the more they can learn. The more they can learn, the more choices they will have in their lives.

THE CAT

Get the free print PDF of the cat photo and this page at http://fhautism.com/arc.html.

Name_____ Date _____

The _____ cat is under the _____ table.

The cat is eating pizza.

1. What color is the cat?

_____

2. Where is the cat?

_____

THE CAT —Worksheet 1, Blank

3. What color is the table?

_____

4. What is the cat eating?

_____

THE CAT —Worksheet 1, Blank

THE CAT
Worksheet 1, Variation 1

Materials:

Worksheet 1 (Variation 1), pencils, and boxes of crayons for each child

Color Variation 1:

Brown Cat
Yellow Table

Before the Lesson:

At http://fhautism.com/arc.html, find Worksheet 1 (Variation 1). Print one for each student, plus a few extras. Write the date on the board.

Teaching the Lesson

1. Distribute the worksheets and pencils to your students. Say: "Write your name on your paper." Make sure everyone writes his or her name. Then say: "Write the date. It is on the board." Make sure everyone writes the date. Take the pencils from them.

2. Say: "(student's name), please read the sentences at the top of the paper." Ask several students to read. If no one can read the passage, read it yourself, or have an aide read it.

3. Say: "We want to color the picture. What two crayons do we need?" Ask the question several times, and allow different children to answer. Then help them find the brown and yellow crayons. Take the crayon boxes from them.

4. Say: "We will color the cat brown and the table yellow. What color do we color the cat?" Ask the question several times, and allow different children to answer.

5. Say: "Color the cat." Make sure they color only the cat. Repeat the words "brown cat" as often as possible. "Oh, that's a lovely brown cat," or "What a wonderful job you did coloring that brown cat." The more they hear the phrase "brown cat," the easier it will be for them to answer the upcoming question.

6. Say: "What color do we color the table? Let's look back at our story if we need a reminder." Ask the question several times, and allow different children to answer.

7. Say: "Color the table." Make sure they color only the table. Repeat the words "yellow table" as often as possible. Then take the crayons.

8. Ask comprehension questions. Lead students to answer orally, in a complete sentence. For each question, if the student answers incorrectly, guide him or her to read the text again. Questions: 1. What color is the cat? 2. Where is the cat? 3. What color is the table? 4. What is the cat eating? Answers: 1. The cat is brown. 2. The cat is under the table. 3. The cat is eating pizza. 4. The table is yellow.

9. Ask the questions again in random order. Give each student a chance to answer correctly, in complete sentences. This will encourage students to listen to the questions and not rely on rote memory.

10. Pass out pencils. This activity will help students make the connection between spoken and written language. Ask each comprehension question again. (See step 8 for questions and answers.) When a student answers correctly, write the sentence on the board. Say: "Copy the sentence onto your paper." Do this for each question and answer. Take pencils from them.

Some students will not be able to copy the full sentence. If they write only the first letter, praise them for trying. Teach individualized lessons later to practice copying sentences from the board.

11. Pass out boxes of crayons. Say: "Choose one crayon." Make sure they choose only one. Take boxes of crayons from them. Then say: "Color the pizza." Make sure they color only the pizza. Take papers from them.

12. Give out reinforcers.

THE CAT
Worksheet 1, Variation 2

Materials:

Worksheet 1 (Variation 2), pencils, and boxes of crayons for each child

Color Variation 2:

Orange Cat
Blue Table

Before the Lesson:

At http://fhautism.com/arc.html, find Worksheet 1 (Variation 2). Print one for each student, plus a few extras. Write the date on the board.

Teaching the Lesson

1. Distribute the worksheets and pencils to your students. Say: "Write your name on your paper." Make sure everyone writes his or her name. Then say: "Write the date. It is on the board." Make sure everyone writes the date. Take the pencils from them.

2. Say: "(student's name), please read the sentences at the top of the paper." Ask several students to read. If no one can read the passage, read it yourself, or have an aide read it.

3. Say: "We want to color the picture. What two crayons do we need?" Ask the question several times, and allow different children to answer. Then help them find the orange and blue crayons. Take the crayon boxes from them.

4. Say: "We will color the cat orange and the table blue. What color do we color the cat?" Ask the question several times, and allow different children to answer.

5. Say: "Color the cat." Make sure they color only the cat. Repeat the words "orange cat" as often as possible. "Oh, that's a lovely orange cat," or "What a wonderful job you did coloring that orange cat." The more they hear the phrase "orange cat," the easier it will be for them to answer the upcoming question.

6. Say: "What color do we color the table? Let's look back at our story if we need a reminder." Ask the question several times, and allow different children to answer.

7. Say: "Color the table." Make sure they color only the table. Repeat the words "blue table" as often as possible. Then take the crayons.

8. Ask comprehension questions. Lead students to answer orally, in a complete sentence. For each question, if the student answers incorrectly, guide him or her to read the text again. Questions: 1. What color is the cat? 2. Where is the cat? 3. What color is the table? 4. What is the cat eating? Answers: 1. The cat is orange. 2. The cat is under the table. 3. The cat is eating pizza. 4. The table is blue.

9. Ask the questions again in random order. Give each student a chance to answer correctly, in complete sentences. This will encourage students to listen to the questions and not rely on rote memory.

10. Pass out pencils. This activity will help students make the connection between spoken and written language. Ask each comprehension question again. (See step 8 for questions and answers.) When a student answers correctly, write the sentence on the board. Say: "Copy the sentence onto your paper." Do this for each question and answer. Take pencils from them.

Some students will not be able to copy the full sentence. If they write only the first letter, praise them for trying. Teach individualized lessons later to practice copying sentences from the board.

11. Pass out boxes of crayons. Say: "Choose one crayon." Make sure they choose only one. Take boxes of crayons from them. Then say: "Color the pizza." Make sure they color only the pizza. Take papers from them.

12. Give out reinforcers.

THE CAT
Worksheet 1, Variation 3

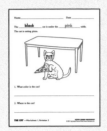

Materials:

Worksheet 1 (Variation 2), pencils, and boxes of crayons for each child

Color Variation 3:

Black Cat
Pink Table

Before the Lesson:

At http://fhautism.com/arc.html, find Worksheet 1 (Variation 3). Print one for each student, plus a few extras. Write the date on the board.

Teaching the Lesson

1. Distribute the worksheets and pencils to your students. Say: "Write your name on your paper." Make sure everyone writes his or her name. Then say: "Write the date. It is on the board." Make sure everyone writes the date. Take the pencils from them.

2. Say: "(student's name), please read the sentences at the top of the paper." Ask several students to read. If no one can read the passage, read it yourself, or have an aide read it.

3. Say: "We want to color the picture. What two crayons do we need?" Ask the question several times, and allow different children to answer. Then help them find the black and pink crayons. Take the crayon boxes from them.

4. Say: "We will color the cat black and the table pink. What color do we color the cat?" Ask the question several times, and allow different children to answer.

5. Say: "Color the cat." Make sure they color only the cat. Repeat the words "black cat" as often as possible. "Oh, that's a lovely black cat," or "What a wonderful job you did coloring that black cat." The more they hear the phrase "black cat," the easier it will be for them to answer the upcoming question.

6. Say: "What color do we color the table? Let's look back at our story if we need a reminder." Ask the question several times, and allow different children to answer.

7. Say: "Color the table." Make sure they color only the table. Repeat the words "pink table" as often as possible. Then take the crayons.

8. Ask comprehension questions. Lead students to answer orally, in a complete sentence. For each question, if the student answers incorrectly, guide him or her to read the text again. Questions: 1. What color is the cat? 2. Where is the cat? 3. What color is the table? 4. What is the cat eating? Answers: 1. The cat is black. 2. The cat is under the table. 3. The cat is eating pizza. 4. The table is pink.

9. Ask the questions again in random order. Give each student a chance to answer correctly, in complete sentences. This will encourage students to listen to the questions and not rely on rote memory.

10. Pass out pencils. This activity will help students make the connection between spoken and written language. Ask each comprehension question again. (See step 8 for questions and answers.) When a student answers correctly, write the sentence on the board. Say: "Copy the sentence onto your paper." Do this for each question and answer. Take pencils from them.

Some students will not be able to copy the full sentence. If they write only the first letter, praise them for trying. Teach individualized lessons later to practice copying sentences from the board.

11. Pass out boxes of crayons. Say: "Choose one crayon." Make sure they choose only one. Take boxes of crayons from them. Then say: "Color the pizza." Make sure they color only the pizza. Take papers from them.

12. Give out reinforcers.

THE CAT
Worksheet 1, Variation 4

Materials:

Worksheet 1 (Variation 4), pencils, and boxes of crayons for each child

Color Variation 4:

Gray Cat
Red Table

Before the Lesson:

At http://fhautism.com/arc.html, find Worksheet 1 (Variation 4). Print one for each student, plus a few extras. Write the date on the board.

Teaching the Lesson

1. Distribute the worksheets and pencils to your students. Say: "Write your name on your paper." Make sure everyone writes his or her name. Then say: "Write the date. It is on the board." Make sure everyone writes the date. Take the pencils from them.

2. Say: "(student's name), please read the sentences at the top of the paper." Ask several students to read. If no one can read the passage, read it yourself, or have an aide read it.

3. Say: "We want to color the picture. What two crayons do we need?" Ask the question several times, and allow different children to answer. Then help them find the gray and red crayons. Take the crayon boxes from them.

4. Say: "We will color the cat gray and the table red. What color do we color the cat?" Ask the question several times, and allow different children to answer.

5. Say: "Color the cat." Make sure they color only the cat. Repeat the words "gray cat" as often as possible. "Oh, that's a lovely gray cat," or "What a wonderful job you did coloring that gray cat." The more they hear the phrase "gray cat," the easier it will be for them to answer the upcoming question.

6. Say: "What color do we color the table? Let's look back at our story if we need a reminder." Ask the question several times, and allow different children to answer.

7. Say: "Color the table." Make sure they color only the table. Repeat the words "red table" as often as possible. Then take the crayons.

8. Ask comprehension questions. Lead students to answer orally, in a complete sentence. For each question, if the student answers incorrectly, guide him or her to read the text again. Questions: 1. What color is the cat? 2. Where is the cat? 3. What color is the table? 4. What is the cat eating? Answers: 1. The cat is gray. 2. The cat is under the table. 3. The cat is eating pizza. 4. The table is red.

9. Ask the questions again in random order. Give each student a chance to answer correctly, in complete sentences. This will encourage students to listen to the questions and not rely on rote memory.

10. Pass out pencils. This activity will help students make the connection between spoken and written language. Ask each comprehension question again. (See step 8 for questions and answers.) When a student answers correctly, write the sentence on the board. Say: "Copy the sentence onto your paper." Do this for each question and answer. Take pencils from them.

Some students will not be able to copy the full sentence. If they write only the first letter, praise them for trying. Teach individualized lessons later to practice copying sentences from the board.

11. Pass out boxes of crayons. Say: "Choose one crayon." Make sure they choose only one. Take boxes of crayons from them. Then say: "Color the pizza." Make sure they color only the pizza. Take papers from them.

12. Give out reinforcers.

THE CAT
Sentence-Building Exercise 1

Materials:

photograph of cat, students' circle-in-circle charts and branch organizers, lined paper, tape, three pieces of chart paper, dry-erase marker, watercolor marker

Before the Lesson:

1. At http://fhautism.com/arc.html, find the circle-in-circle chart, branch organizer, and lined paper. Print one of each for each student, plus a few extras. Then find the photograph of the cat and print one copy.

2. On the chart paper, draw a blank circle-in-circle chart, branch organizer, and lined paper.

3. On the board, hang a blank circle-in-circle chart on the left and a branch organizer on the right. Make them large enough to write all the words you will need.

4. Write the date on the board.

Teaching the Lesson

1. Gather the children in a circle. Hold up the photograph of the cat. Ask: "What animal is this?" If no one can identify the animal, ask an aide to answer, or answer the question yourself. Students are still hearing the oral language and watching it become written language.

2. When a student says, "cat," write "cat" in the smaller, inner circle of the circle-in-circle chart. Write very legibly. Students will be copying these words later.

3. Ask: "What can the cat do?" If no one answers, prompt the students. Ask: "Can the cat fly?" If no one answers, ask an aide to answer, or answer the question yourself. Possible answers include jump, run, say meow. Students may come up with different answers. Ask the question several times, and allow different children to answer. Write the answers in the large circle. Leave space between the words.

---

4. Ask: "What does the cat have? If no one answers, prompt the students. Ask: "Does a cat have wings?" If no one answers, ask an aide to answer, or answer the question yourself. Possible answers include four legs, two ears, a tail. Students may come up with different answers. Ask the question several times, and allow different children to answer. Write the answers in the large circle. Leave space between the words.

5. Ask: "What does the cat like? If no one answers, prompt the students with a guessing game. Say: "The cat likes to drink a white drink. We pour it over cereal. Sometimes we put chocolate syrup in it for chocolate _____." Do this for the other two answers. If no one answers, ask an aide to answer, or answer the question yourself. Possible answers include milk, fish, cat food. Students may come up with different answers. Ask the question several times, and allow different children to answer. Write the answers in the large circle. Leave space between the words. NOTE: Guessing games may be stressful for some children. If students appear to be getting agitated or panicky, just tell them the answer. The lesson is more important than the game.

Here is an example of what your circle-in-circle chart may look like (includes sample answers from paragraphs above):

6. Praise students and pass out reinforcers.

7. The children return to their desks. Pass out pencils and blank graphic organizers. On each desk, tape the circle-in-circle chart on the left and the branch organizer on

the right. (Always emphasize a left-to-right progression when teaching reading and writing.)

8. Say: "Write your name on your paper." Make sure everyone writes his or her name. Then say: "Write the date. It is on the board." Make sure everyone writes the date.

9. Say: "Copy the words from the circle-in-circle chart on the board onto your circle-in-circle chart." They do not have to copy all of the words at first.

10. Say: "Now we will do the branch organizer." On the branch organizer on the board, write "Cat" on the top line and "Can," "Has," and "Likes" on the three spaces under the top line. Say: "Copy the words onto your charts."

11. Ask: "What can the cat do?" Point to the words on the circle-in-circle chart. Encourage students to look at their own chart. If no one answers, ask an aide to answer, or answer the question yourself. Ask the question several times, and allow different children to answer.

    If someone uses a nonsensical word, e.g., "milk," say the whole sentence. Say: "The cat can milk? Does that make sense? Let's look back in the circle and find something the cat can do."

12. Write students' answers on the branch organizer on the board. For each answer, say: "Write (the answer) under the word 'Can' on your branch organizer."

    As you use words from the circle-in-circle chart, you may choose to cover up the words with a sticky note or leave them all showing.

13. For each word that students write, say the whole sentence, e.g., "The cat can jump." As you say each word of the sentence, point to the corresponding word on the branch chart. This way, they become familiar with the way we use the chart to form the sentences.

14. Ask: "What does the cat have?" Point to the words on the circle-in-circle chart. If no one answers, ask an aide to answer, or answer the question yourself. Ask the question several times, and allow different children to answer.

    If someone uses a nonsensical word, e.g., "run," say the whole sentence. Say: "The cat has run? Does that make sense? Let's look back in the circle and find something the cat has."

15. Write students' answers on the branch organizer on the board. For each answer, say: "Write (the answer) under the word 'Has' on your branch organizer."

16. For each word that students write, say the whole sentence, e.g., "The cat has a tail." As you say each word of the sentence, point to the corresponding word on the branch chart.

17. Ask: "What does the cat like?" Point to the words on the circle-in-circle chart. If no one answers, ask an aide to answer, or answer the question yourself. Ask the question several times, and allow different children to answer.

If someone uses a nonsensical word, e.g., "four legs," say the whole sentence. Say: "The cat likes four legs? Does that make sense? Let's look back in the circle and find something the cat likes."

18. Write students' answers on the branch organizer on the board. For each answer, say: "Write (the answer) under the word 'Likes' on your branch organizer."

19. For each word that students write, say the whole sentence, e.g., "The cat likes milk." As you say each word of the sentence, point to the corresponding word on the branch chart.

20. Praise students, pass out reinforcers, and take a short break.

21. Draw a large version of the lined paper on your chart paper, using the watercolor marker. Tape the chart paper to the board. Pass out the lined paper. Tape one to each desk, next to the branch organizer. It's important that all three graphic organizers stay in front of students for the sentence-building phase.

22. Say: "It's time to make a sentence. Let's make a sentence from the first column of the branch organizer, using the word 'Can.'" (Example sentence: The cat can jump.) Point to the words on the branch chart on the board as you slowly say them, forming the sentence. Show the students the relationship between the words on the chart and a spoken sentence. This will help them read the chart and form the sentences themselves.

23. Write the sentence on your "lined paper" on the board.

24. Say: "Copy the sentence on the first line of your paper."

25. Say: "Let's make a sentence from the second column of the branch organizer, using the word 'Has.'" (Example sentence: The cat has a tail.) Point to the words on the branch chart on the board as you slowly say them, forming the sentence.

26. Write the sentence on your "lined paper" on the board.

27. Say: "Copy the sentence on the second line of your paper." Make sure they write on the lines and not in the blank space above. This is for the illustration.

28. Say: "Let's make a sentence from the third column of the branch organizer, using the word 'Likes.'" (Example sentence: The cat likes milk.) Point to the words on the branch chart on the board as you slowly say them, forming the sentence.

29. Write the sentence on your "lined paper" on the board.

30. Say: "Copy the sentence on the third line of your paper."

When students become familiar with this process, they may choose any of the three words to make a sentence.

31. Say: "Now we will read our sentences aloud." Group students in pairs to read to each other, or let each child read aloud to you, an aide, or the whole class.

32. Praise students and pass out reinforcers.

33. Say: "Now we will draw a picture to go with our sentences." Lead students to read the first sentence and then draw a picture of it. Do this for each sentence, one sentence at a time at first. Monitor the drawings and try to limit them to drawing only one cat. If a higher-functioning child is drawing three cats, clearly intending one cat for each sentence, without exhibiting difficulties, then that is okay. Later in the program, they may be able to remember two or three details at once and incorporate them all into one cat picture.

The illustration must reflect the information in the sentence. If you see an illustration of a cat missing a tail or not drinking from a bowl of milk, ask the student to read the corresponding sentence again. Then show the student what's missing. ("Your sentence says, 'The cat has a tail.' Your picture of the cat does not have a tail. Draw a tail on the cat.")

34. Collect papers and pencils, praise students, and pass out reinforcers.

Name_____ Date _____

The _____ cat has a long tail. The cat can say meow.

The cat is drinking milk. The milk is in the bowl. The bowl is _____.

1. What color is the cat?

_____

2. What is the cat drinking?

_____

THE CAT —Worksheet 2, Blank

3. Where is the milk?

_____

4. What color is the bowl?

_____

THE CAT —Worksheet 2, Blank

THE CAT
Worksheet 2, Variation 1

Materials:

Worksheet 2 (Variation 1), pencils, and boxes of crayons for each child

Color Variation 1:

Orange Cat
Blue Bowl

Before the Lesson:

At http://fhautism.com/arc.html, find Worksheet 2 (Variation 1). Print one for each student, plus a few extras. Write the date on the board.

Teaching the Lesson

1. Distribute the worksheets and pencils to your students. Say: "Write your name on your paper." Make sure everyone writes his or her name. Then say: "Write the date. It is on the board." Make sure everyone writes the date. Take the pencils from them.

2. Say: "(student's name), please read the sentences at the top of the paper." Ask several students to read. If no one can read the passage, read it yourself, or have an aide read it.

3. Say: "We want to color the picture. What two crayons do we need?" Ask the question several times, and allow different children to answer. Then help them find the orange and blue crayons. Take the crayon boxes from them.

4. Say: "We will color the cat orange and the bowl blue. What color do we color the cat?" Ask the question several times, and allow different children to answer.

5. Say: "Color the cat." Make sure they color only the cat. Repeat the words "orange cat" as often as possible.

6. Say: "What color do we color the bowl? Let's look back at our story if we need a reminder." Ask the question several times, and allow different children to answer.

7. Say: "Color the bowl." Make sure they color only the bowl. Repeat the words "blue bowl" as often as possible. Then take the crayons.

---

8. Ask comprehension questions. Lead students to answer orally, in a complete sentence. For each question, if the student answers incorrectly, guide him or her to read the text again. Questions: 1. What color is the cat? 2. What is the cat drinking? 3. Where is the milk? 4. What color is the bowl? Answers: 1. The cat is orange. 2. The cat is drinking milk. 3. The milk is in the bowl. 4. The bowl is blue.

9. Ask the questions again in random order. Give each student a chance to answer correctly, in complete sentences.

10. Pass out pencils. This activity will help students make the connection between spoken and written language. Ask each comprehension question again. (See step 8 for questions and answers.) When a student answers correctly, write the sentence on the board. Say: "Copy the sentence onto your paper." Do this for each question and answer. Take pencils from them.

Some students will not be able to copy the full sentence. If they write only the first letter, praise them for trying. Teach individualized lessons later to practice copying sentences from the board.

11. Give out reinforcers.

THE CAT
Worksheet 2, Variation 2

Materials:

Worksheet 2 (Variation 2), pencils, and boxes of crayons for each child

Color Variation 2:

Brown Cat
Yellow Bowl

Before the Lesson:

At http://fhautism.com/arc.html, find Worksheet 2 (Variation 2). Print one for each student, plus a few extras. Write the date on the board.

Teaching the Lesson

1. Distribute the worksheets and pencils to your students. Say: "Write your name on your paper." Make sure everyone writes his or her name. Then say: "Write the date. It is on the board." Make sure everyone writes the date. Take the pencils from them.

2. Say: "(student's name), please read the sentences at the top of the paper." Ask several students to read. If no one can read the passage, read it yourself, or have an aide read it.

3. Say: "We want to color the picture. What two crayons do we need?" Ask the question several times, and allow different children to answer. Then help them find the brown and yellow crayons. Take the crayon boxes from them.

4. Say: "We will color the cat brown and the bowl yellow. What color do we color the cat?" Ask the question several times, and allow different children to answer.

5. Say: "Color the cat." Make sure they color only the cat. Repeat the words "brown cat" as often as possible.

6. Say: "What color do we color the bowl? Let's look back at our story if we need a reminder." Ask the question several times, and allow different children to answer.

7. Say: "Color the bowl." Make sure they color only the bowl. Repeat the words "yellow bowl" as often as possible. Then take the crayons.

8. Ask comprehension questions. Lead students to answer orally, in a complete sentence. For each question, if the student answers incorrectly, guide him or her to read the text again. Questions: 1. What color is the cat? 2. What is the cat drinking? 3. Where is the milk? 4. What color is the bowl? Answers: 1. The cat is brown. 2. The cat is drinking milk. 3. The milk is in the bowl. 4. The bowl is yellow.

9. Ask the questions again in random order. Give each student a chance to answer correctly, in complete sentences.

10. Pass out pencils. This activity will help students make the connection between spoken and written language. Ask each comprehension question again. (See step 8 for questions and answers.) When a student answers correctly, write the sentence on the board. Say: "Copy the sentence onto your paper." Do this for each question and answer. Take pencils from them.

Some students will not be able to copy the full sentence. If they write only the first letter, praise them for trying. Teach individualized lessons later to practice copying sentences from the board.

11. Give out reinforcers.

AUTISM & READING COMPREHENSION
© 2011 by Joseph Porter, M.Ed. Future Horizons, Inc.

THE CAT
Worksheet 2, Variation 3

Materials:
2 (Variation 3), pencils, and boxes of crayons for each child

Color Variation 3:

Black Cat
Pink Bowl

✔ ## Before the Lesson:
At http://fhautism.com/arc.html, find Worksheet 2 (Variation 3). Print one for each student, plus a few extras. Write the date on the board.

Teaching the Lesson

1. Distribute the worksheets and pencils to your students. Say: "Write your name on your paper." Make sure everyone writes his or her name. Then say: "Write the date. It is on the board." Make sure everyone writes the date. Take the pencils from them.

2. Say: "(student's name), please read the sentences at the top of the paper." Ask several students to read. If no one can read the passage, read it yourself, or have an aide read it.

3. Say: "We want to color the picture. What two crayons do we need?" Ask the question several times, and allow different children to answer. Then help them find the black and pink crayons. Take the crayon boxes from them.

4. Say: "We will color the cat black and the bowl pink. What color do we color the cat?" Ask the question several times, and allow different children to answer.

5. Say: "Color the cat." Make sure they color only the cat. Repeat the words "black cat" as often as possible.

6. Say: "What color do we color the bowl? Let's look back at our story if we need a reminder." Ask the question several times, and allow different children to answer.

7. Say: "Color the bowl." Make sure they color only the bowl. Repeat the words "pink bowl" as often as possible. Then take the crayons.

8. Ask comprehension questions. Lead students to answer orally, in a complete sentence. For each question, if the student answers incorrectly, guide him or her to read the text again. Questions: 1. What color is the cat? 2. What is the cat drinking? 3. Where is the milk? 4. What color is the bowl? Answers: 1. The cat is black. 2. The cat is drinking milk. 3. The milk is in the bowl. 4. The bowl is pink

9. Ask the questions again in random order. Give each student a chance to answer correctly, in complete sentences.

10. Pass out pencils. This activity will help students make the connection between spoken and written language. Ask each comprehension question again. (See step 8 for questions and answers.) When a student answers correctly, write the sentence on the board. Say: "Copy the sentence onto your paper." Do this for each question and answer. Take pencils from them.

Some students will not be able to copy the full sentence. If they write only the first letter, praise them for trying. Teach individualized lessons later to practice copying sentences from the board.

11. Give out reinforcers.

THE CAT
Worksheet 2, Variation 4

Materials:

Worksheet 2 (Variation 4), pencils, and boxes of crayons for each child

Color Variation 4:

Gray Cat
Red Bowl

Before the Lesson:

At http://fhautism.com/arc.html, find Worksheet 2 (Variation 4). Print one for each student, plus a few extras. Write the date on the board.

Teaching the Lesson

1. Distribute the worksheets and pencils to your students. Say: "Write your name on your paper." Make sure everyone writes his or her name. Then say: "Write the date. It is on the board." Make sure everyone writes the date. Take the pencils from them.

2. Say: "(student's name), please read the sentences at the top of the paper." Ask several students to read. If no one can read the passage, read it yourself, or have an aide read it.

3. Say: "We want to color the picture. What two crayons do we need?" Ask the question several times, and allow different children to answer. Then help them find the gray and red crayons. Take the crayon boxes from them.

4. Say: "We will color the cat gray and the bowl red. What color do we color the cat?" Ask the question several times, and allow different children to answer.

5. Say: "Color the cat." Make sure they color only the cat. Repeat the words "gray cat" as often as possible.

6. Say: "What color do we color the bowl? Let's look back at our story if we need a reminder." Ask the question several times, and allow different children to answer.

7. Say: "Color the bowl." Make sure they color only the bowl. Repeat the words "red bowl" as often as possible. Then take the crayons.

8. Ask comprehension questions. Lead students to answer orally, in a complete sentence. For each question, if the student answers incorrectly, guide him or her to read the text again. Questions: 1. What color is the cat? 2. What is the cat drinking? 3. Where is the milk? 4. What color is the bowl? Answers: 1. The cat is gray. 2. The cat is drinking milk. 3. The milk is in the bowl. 4. The bowl is red.

9. Ask the questions again in random order. Give each student a chance to answer correctly, in complete sentences.

10. Pass out pencils. This activity will help students make the connection between spoken and written language. Ask each comprehension question again. (See step 8 for questions and answers.) When a student answers correctly, write the sentence on the board. Say: "Copy the sentence onto your paper." Do this for each question and answer. Take pencils from them.

Some students will not be able to copy the full sentence. If they write only the first letter, praise them for trying. Teach individualized lessons later to practice copying sentences from the board.

11. Give out reinforcers.

THE CAT
Sentence-Building Exercise 2

Materials:

photograph of cat, students' circle-in-circle charts and branch organizers, lined paper, tape, completed circle-in-circle chart on chart paper (from Lesson 5 sentence-building exercise), two pieces of blank chart paper, dry-erase marker, watercolor marker

Before the Lesson:

1. At http://fhautism.com/arc.html, find the circle-in-circle chart, branch organizer, and lined paper. Print one of each for each student, plus a few extras.

2. On the blank chart paper, draw the lined paper and branch organizer.

3. On the board, hang the completed circle-in-circle chart on chart paper (from Lesson 5 sentence-building exercise) and blank branch organizer.

4. Write the date on the board.

Teaching the Lesson

1. Gather the children in a circle. Hold up the photograph of the cat. Ask: "What animal is this?" If no one can identify the animal, ask an aide to answer, or answer the question yourself.

2. Ask: "What can the cat do?" If no one answers, prompt the students to look at the circle-in-circle chart on the board. If no one answers, ask an aide to answer, or answer the question yourself. Possible answers include jump, run, say meow. Students may come up with different answers. Ask the question several times, and allow different children to answer.

3. Ask: "What does the cat have? If no one answers, prompt the students to look at the circle-in-circle chart on the board. If no one answers, ask an aide to answer, or answer the question yourself. Possible answers include four legs, two ears, a tail.

Students may come up with different answers. Ask the question several times, and allow different children to answer.

4. Ask: "What does the cat like? If no one answers, prompt the students to look at the circle-in-circle chart on the board. If no one answers, ask an aide to answer, or answer the question yourself. Possible answers include milk, fish, cat food. Students may come up with different answers. Ask the question several times, and allow different children to answer.

5. Praise students and pass out reinforcers.

6. The children return to their desks. Pass out pencils and blank graphic organizers. On each desk, tape a circle-in-circle chart on the left and the branch organizer on the right. (Always emphasize a left-to-right progression when teaching reading and writing.)

7. Say: "Write your name on your paper." Make sure everyone writes his or her name. Then say: "Write the date. It is on the board." Make sure everyone writes the date.

8. Say: "Copy the words from the circle-in-circle chart on the board onto your circle-in-circle chart." They do not have to copy all of the words at first.

9. Say: "Now we will do the branch organizer." On the branch organizer on the board, write "Cat" on the top line and "Can," "Has," and "Likes" on the three spaces under the top line. Say: "Copy the words onto your charts."

10. Ask: "What can the cat do?" Point to the words on the circle-in-circle chart. Encourage students to look at their own chart. If no one answers, ask an aide to answer, or answer the question yourself. Ask the question several times, and allow different children to answer.

    If someone uses a nonsensical word, e.g., "milk," say the whole sentence. Say: "The cat can milk? Does that make sense? Let's look back in the circle and find something the cat can do."

11. Write students' answers on the branch organizer on the board. For each answer, say: "Write (the answer) under the word 'Can' on your branch organizer."

    As you use words from the circle-in-circle chart, you may choose to cover up the words with a sticky note or leave them all showing.

12. For each word that students write, say the whole sentence, e.g., "The cat can jump." As you say each word of the sentence, point to the corresponding word on the branch chart. This way, they become familiar with the way we use the chart to form the sentences.

13. Ask: "What does the cat have?" Point to the words on the circle-in-circle chart. If no one answers, ask an aide to answer, or answer the question yourself. Ask the question several times, and allow different children to answer.

If someone uses a nonsensical word, e.g., "run," say the whole sentence. Say: "The cat has run? Does that make sense? Let's look back in the circle and find something the cat has."

14. Write students' answers on the branch chart. For each answer, say: "Write (the answer) under the word 'Has' on your branch organizer."

15. For each word that students write, say the whole sentence, e.g., "The cat has a tail." As you say each word of the sentence, point to the corresponding word on the branch chart.

16. Ask: "What does the cat like?" Point to the words on the circle-in-circle chart. If no one answers, ask an aide to answer, or answer the question yourself. Ask the question several times, and allow different children to answer.

If someone uses nonsensical words, e.g., "four legs," say the whole sentence. Say: "The cat likes four legs? Does that make sense? Let's look back in the circle and find something the cat likes."

17. Write students' answers on the branch organizer on the board. For each answer, say: "Write (the answer) under the word 'Likes' on your branch organizer."

18. For each word that students write, say the whole sentence, e.g., "The cat likes milk." As you say each word of the sentence, point to the corresponding word on the branch chart.

19. Praise students, pass out reinforcers, and take a short break.

20. Draw a large version of the lined paper on your chart paper, using the watercolor marker. Tape the chart paper to the board. Pass out the lined paper. Tape one to each desk, next to the branch organizer. It's important that all three graphic organizers stay in front of students for the sentence-building phase.

21. Say: "It's time to make a sentence. Let's make a sentence from the first column of the branch organizer, using the word 'Can.'" (Example sentence: The cat can say meow.) Point to the words on the branch chart on the board as you slowly say them, forming the sentence. Show the students the relationship between the words on the chart and a spoken sentence. This will help them read the chart and form the sentences themselves.

    Lead students to make different sentences than they did in the first sentence-building exercise.

22. Write the sentence on your "lined paper" on the board. Students could draw a speech bubble with "meow" in it, if they choose to write "The cat can say meow."

23. Say: "Copy the sentence on the first line of your paper."

24. Say: "Let's make a sentence from the second column of the branch organizer, using the word 'Has.'" (Example sentence: The cat has four legs.) Point to the words on the branch chart on the board as you slowly say them, forming the sentence.

25. Write the sentence on your "lined paper" on the board.

26. Say: "Copy the sentence on the second line of your paper." Make sure they write on the lines and not in the blank space above. This is for the illustration.

27. Say: "Let's make a sentence from the third column of the branch organizer, using the word 'Likes.'" (Example sentence: The cat likes fish.) Point to the words on the branch chart on the board as you slowly say them, forming the sentence.

28. Write the sentence on your "lined paper" on the board.

29. Say: "Copy the sentence on the third line of your paper."

    When students become familiar with this process, they may choose any of the three words to make a sentence.

30. Say: "Now we will read our sentences aloud." Group students in pairs to read to each other, or let each child read aloud to you, an aide, or the whole class.

31. Praise students and pass out reinforcers.

32. Say: "Now we will draw a picture to go with our sentences." Lead students to read the first sentence and then draw a picture of it. Do this for each sentence, one sentence at a time at first. Monitor the drawings and try to limit them to drawing only one cat. If a higher-functioning child is drawing three cats, clearly intending one cat for each sentence, without exhibiting difficulties, then that is okay. Later in the program, they may be able to remember two or three details at once and incorporate them all into one cat picture.

The illustration must reflect the information in the sentence. If you see an illustration of a cat missing legs or saying "Meow," ask the student to read the corresponding sentence again. Then show the student what's missing. ("Your sentence says, 'The cat has four legs.' Your picture of the cat does not have four legs. Draw four legs on the cat.")

33. Collect papers and pencils, praise students, and pass out reinforcers.

THE RABBIT

Get the free print PDF of the rabbit photo and this page at http://fhautism.com/arc.html.

Name_____ Date _____

The _____ rabbit is in the _____ basket.

The rabbit is eating a carrot.

1. What color is the rabbit?

_____

2. What color is the basket?

_____

THE RABBIT —Worksheet 3, Blank

AUTISM & READING COMPREHENSION
© 2011 by Joseph Porter, M.Ed. Future Horizons, Inc.

3. Where is the rabbit?

_____

4. What is the rabbit eating?

_____

THE RABBIT —Worksheet 3, Blank

AUTISM & READING COMPREHENSION
© 2011 by Joseph Porter, M.Ed. Future Horizons, Inc.

AUTISM & READING COMPREHENSION
© 2011 by Joseph Porter, M.Ed. Future Horizons, Inc.

THE RABBIT
Worksheet 3, Variation 1

Materials:

Worksheet 3 (Variation 1), pencils, and boxes of crayons for each child

Color Variation 1:

Brown Rabbit
Yellow Basket

Before the Lesson:

At http://fhautism.com/arc.html, find Worksheet 3 (Variation 1). Print one for each student, plus a few extras. Write the date on the board.

Teaching the Lesson

1. Distribute the worksheets and pencils to your students. Say: "Write your name on your paper." Make sure everyone writes his or her name. Then say: "Write the date. It is on the board." Make sure everyone writes the date. Take the pencils from them.

2. Say: "(student's name), please read the sentences at the top of the paper." Ask several students to read. If no one can read the passage, read it yourself, or have an aide read it.

3. Say: "We want to color the picture. What two crayons do we need?" Ask the question several times, and allow different children to answer. Then help them find the brown and yellow crayons. Take the crayon boxes from them.

4. Say: "We will color the rabbit brown and the basket yellow. What color do we color the rabbit?" Ask the question several times, and allow different children to answer.

5. Say: "Color the rabbit." Make sure they color only the rabbit. Repeat the words "brown rabbit" as often as possible.

6. Say: "What color do we color the basket? Let's look back at our story if we need a reminder." Ask the question several times, and allow different children to answer.

7. Say: "Color the basket." Make sure they color only the basket. Repeat the words "yellow basket" as often as possible. Then take the crayons.

8. Ask comprehension questions. Lead students to answer orally, in a complete sentence. For each question, if the student answers incorrectly, guide him or her to read the text again. Questions: 1. What color is the rabbit? 2. What color is the basket? 3. Where is the rabbit? 4. What is the rabbit eating? Answers: 1. The rabbit is brown. 2. The basket is yellow. 3. The rabbit is in the basket. 4. The rabbit is eating a carrot.

9. Ask the questions again in random order. Give each student a chance to answer correctly, in complete sentences.

10. Pass out pencils. Ask each comprehension question again. (See step 8 for questions and answers.) When a student answers correctly, write the sentence on the board. Say: "Copy the sentence onto your paper." Do this for each question and answer. Take pencils from them.

Some students will not be able to copy the full sentence. If they write only the first letter, praise them for trying. Teach individualized lessons later to practice copying sentences from the board.

11. Pass out boxes of crayons. Say: "Choose one crayon." Make sure they choose only one. Take boxes of crayons from them. Then say: "Color the carrot." Make sure they color only the carrot. Take papers from them.

12. Give out reinforcers.

AUTISM & READING COMPREHENSION
© 2011 by Joseph Porter, M.Ed. Future Horizons, Inc.

THE RABBIT
Worksheet 3, Variation 2

Materials:

Worksheet 3 (Variation 2), pencils, and boxes of crayons for each child

Color Variation 2:

Black Rabbit
Pink Basket

✔ ## Before the Lesson:

At http://fhautism.com/arc.html, find Worksheet 3 (Variation 2). Print one for each student, plus a few extras. Write the date on the board.

Teaching the Lesson

1. Distribute the worksheets and pencils to your students. Say: "Write your name on your paper." Make sure everyone writes his or her name. Then say: "Write the date. It is on the board." Make sure everyone writes the date. Take the pencils from them.

2. Say: "(student's name), please read the sentences at the top of the paper." Ask several students to read. If no one can read the passage, read it yourself, or have an aide read it.

3. Say: "We want to color the picture. What two crayons do we need?" Ask the question several times, and allow different children to answer. Then help them find the black and pink crayons. Take the crayon boxes from them.

4. Say: "We will color the rabbit black and the basket pink. What color do we color the rabbit?" Ask the question several times, and allow different children to answer.

5. Say: "Color the rabbit." Make sure they color only the rabbit. Repeat the words "black rabbit" as often as possible.

6. Say: "What color do we color the basket? Let's look back at our story if we need a reminder." Ask the question several times, and allow different children to answer.

7. Say: "Color the basket." Make sure they color only the basket. Repeat the words "pink basket" as often as possible. Then take the crayons.

8. Ask comprehension questions. Lead students to answer orally, in a complete sentence. For each question, if the student answers incorrectly, guide him or her to read the text again. Questions: 1. What color is the rabbit? 2. What color is the basket? 3. Where is the rabbit? 4. What is the rabbit eating? Answers: 1. The rabbit is black. 2. The basket is pink. 3. The rabbit is in the basket. 4. The rabbit is eating a carrot.

9. Ask the questions again in random order. Give each student a chance to answer correctly, in complete sentences.

10. Pass out pencils. Ask each comprehension question again. (See step 8 for questions and answers.) When a student answers correctly, write the sentence on the board. Say: "Copy the sentence onto your paper." Do this for each question and answer. Take pencils from them.

Some students will not be able to copy the full sentence. If they write only the first letter, praise them for trying. Teach individualized lessons later to practice copying sentences from the board.

11. Pass out boxes of crayons. Say: "Choose one crayon." Make sure they choose only one. Take boxes of crayons from them. Then say: "Color the carrot." Make sure they color only the carrot. Take papers from them.

12. Give out reinforcers.

AUTISM & READING COMPREHENSION
© 2011 by Joseph Porter, M.Ed. Future Horizons, Inc.

THE RABBIT
Worksheet 3, Variation 3

Materials:

Worksheet 3 (Variation 3), pencils, and boxes of crayons for each child

Color Variation 3:

Gray Rabbit
Orange Basket

Before the Lesson:

At http://fhautism.com/arc.html, find Worksheet 3 (Variation 3). Print one for each student, plus a few extras. Write the date on the board.

Teaching the Lesson

1. Distribute the worksheets and pencils to your students. Say: "Write your name on your paper." Make sure everyone writes his or her name. Then say: "Write the date. It is on the board." Make sure everyone writes the date. Take the pencils from them.

2. Say: "(student's name), please read the sentences at the top of the paper." Ask several students to read. If no one can read the passage, read it yourself, or have an aide read it.

3. Say: "We want to color the picture. What two crayons do we need?" Ask the question several times, and allow different children to answer. Then help them find the gray and orange crayons. Take the crayon boxes from them.

4. Say: "We will color the rabbit gray and the basket orange. What color do we color the rabbit?" Ask the question several times, and allow different children to answer.

5. Say: "Color the rabbit." Make sure they color only the rabbit. Repeat the words "gray rabbit" as often as possible.

6. Say: "What color do we color the basket? Let's look back at our story if we need a reminder." Ask the question several times, and allow different children to answer.

7. Say: "Color the basket." Make sure they color only the basket. Repeat the words "orange basket" as often as possible. Then take the crayons.

8. Ask comprehension questions. Lead students to answer orally, in a complete sentence. For each question, if the student answers incorrectly, guide him or her to read the text again. Questions: 1. What color is the rabbit? 2. What color is the basket? 3. Where is the rabbit? 4. What is the rabbit eating? Answers: 1. The rabbit is gray. 2. The basket is orange. 3. The rabbit is in the basket. 4. The rabbit is eating a carrot.

9. Ask the questions again in random order. Give each student a chance to answer correctly, in complete sentences.

10. Pass out pencils. Ask each comprehension question again. (See step 8 for questions and answers.) When a student answers correctly, write the sentence on the board. Say: "Copy the sentence onto your paper." Do this for each question and answer. Take pencils from them.

Some students will not be able to copy the full sentence. If they write only the first letter, praise them for trying. Teach individualized lessons later to practice copying sentences from the board.

11. Pass out boxes of crayons. Say: "Choose one crayon." Make sure they choose only one. Take boxes of crayons from them. Then say: "Color the carrot." Make sure they color only the carrot. Take papers from them.

12. Give out reinforcers.

AUTISM & READING COMPREHENSION
© 2011 by Joseph Porter, M.Ed. Future Horizons, Inc.

THE RABBIT
Worksheet 3, Variation 4

Materials:

Worksheet 3 (Variation 4), pencils, and boxes of crayons for each child

Color Variation 4:

Pink Rabbit
Blue Basket

Before the Lesson:

At http://fhautism.com/arc.html, find Worksheet 3 (Variation 4). Print one for each student, plus a few extras. Write the date on the board.

Teaching the Lesson

1. Distribute the worksheets and pencils to your students. Say: "Write your name on your paper." Make sure everyone writes his or her name. Then say: "Write the date. It is on the board." Make sure everyone writes the date. Take the pencils from them.

2. Say: "(student's name), please read the sentences at the top of the paper." Ask several students to read. If no one can read the passage, read it yourself, or have an aide read it.

3. Say: "We want to color the picture. What two crayons do we need?" Ask the question several times, and allow different children to answer. Then help them find the pink and blue crayons. Take the crayon boxes from them.

4. Say: "We will color the rabbit pink and the basket blue. What color do we color the rabbit?" Ask the question several times, and allow different children to answer.

5. Say: "Color the rabbit." Make sure they color only the rabbit. Repeat the words "pink rabbit" as often as possible.

6. Say: "What color do we color the basket? Let's look back at our story if we need a reminder." Ask the question several times, and allow different children to answer.

7. Say: "Color the basket." Make sure they color only the basket. Repeat the words "blue basket" as often as possible. Then take the crayons.

8. Ask comprehension questions. Lead students to answer orally, in a complete sentence. For each question, if the student answers incorrectly, guide him or her to read the text again. Questions: 1. What color is the rabbit? 2. What color is the basket? 3. Where is the rabbit? 4. What is the rabbit eating? Answers: 1. The rabbit is pink. 2. The basket is blue. 3. The rabbit is in the basket. 4. The rabbit is eating a carrot.

9. Ask the questions again in random order. Give each student a chance to answer correctly, in complete sentences.

10. Pass out pencils. Ask each comprehension question again. (See step 8 for questions and answers.) When a student answers correctly, write the sentence on the board. Say: "Copy the sentence onto your paper." Do this for each question and answer. Take pencils from them.

Some students will not be able to copy the full sentence. If they write only the first letter, praise them for trying. Teach individualized lessons later to practice copying sentences from the board.

11. Pass out boxes of crayons. Say: "Choose one crayon." Make sure they choose only one. Take boxes of crayons from them. Then say: "Color the carrot." Make sure they color only the carrot. Take papers from them.

12. Give out reinforcers.

THE RABBIT
Sentence-Building Exercise 1

Materials:

photograph of rabbit, students' circle-in-circle charts and branch organizers, lined paper, tape, three pieces of chart paper, dry-erase marker, watercolor marker

Before the Lesson:

1. At http://fhautism.com/arc.html, find the circle-in-circle chart, branch organizer, and lined paper. Print one of each for each student, plus a few extras.

2. On the chart paper, draw a blank circle-in-circle chart, branch organizer, and lined paper.

3. On the board, hang a blank circle-in-circle chart on the left and a branch organizer on the right. Make them large enough to write all the words you will need.

4. Write the date on the board.

Teaching the Lesson

1. Gather the children in a circle. Hold up the photograph of the rabbit. Ask: "What animal is this?" If no one can identify the animal, ask an aide to answer, or answer the question yourself.

2. When a student says, "rabbit," write "rabbit" in the smaller, inner circle of the circle-in-circle chart. Write very legibly. Students will be copying these words later.

3. Ask: "What can the rabbit do?" If no one answers, prompt the students. Ask: "Can the rabbit fly?" If no one answers, ask an aide to answer, or answer the question yourself. Possible answers include hop, run, dig. Students may come up with different answers. Ask the question several times, and allow different children to answer. Write the answers in the large circle. Leave space between the words.

4. Ask: "What does the rabbit have? If no one answers, prompt the students. Ask: "Does a rabbit have wings?" If no one answers, ask an aide to answer, or answer the question yourself. Possible answers include long ears, a nose, a tail. Students may come up with different answers. Ask the question several times, and allow different children to answer. Write the answers in the large circle. Leave space between the words.

5. Ask: "What does the rabbit like? If no one answers, prompt the students with a guessing game. Say: "The rabbit likes to eat a vegetable. It is long and orange. We put it in salad." Do this for the other two answers. If no one answers, ask an aide to answer, or answer the question yourself. Possible answers include carrots, leaves, lettuce. Students may come up with different answers. Ask the question several times, and allow different children to answer. Write the answers in the large circle. Leave space between the words. NOTE: Guessing games may be stressful for some children. If students appear to be getting agitated or panicky, just tell them the answer. The lesson is more important than the game.

6. Praise students and pass out reinforcers.

7. The children return to their desks. Pass out pencils and blank graphic organizers. On each desk, tape the circle-in-circle chart on the left and the branch organizer on the right. (Always emphasize a left-to-right progression when teaching reading and writing.)

8. Say: "Write your name on your paper." Make sure everyone writes his or her name. Then say: "Write the date. It is on the board." Make sure everyone writes the date.

9. Say: "Copy the words from the circle-in-circle chart on the board onto your circle-in-circle chart." They do not have to copy all of the words at first.

10. Say: "Now we will do the branch organizer." On the branch organizer on the board, write "Rabbit" on the top line and "Can," "Has," and "Likes" on the three spaces under the top line. Say: "Copy the words onto your charts."

11. Ask: "What can the rabbit do?" Point to the words on the circle-in-circle chart. Encourage students to look at their own chart. If no one answers, ask an aide to answer, or answer the question yourself. Ask the question several times, and allow different children to answer.

If someone uses a nonsensical word, e.g., "carrots," say the whole sentence. Say:

"The rabbit can carrots? Does that make sense? Let's look back in the circle and find something the rabbit can do."

12. Write students' answers on the branch organizer on the board. For each answer, say: "Write (the answer) under the word 'Can' on your branch organizer."

As you use words from the circle-in-circle chart, you may choose to cover up the words with a sticky note or leave them all showing.

13. For each word that students write, say the whole sentence, e.g., "The rabbit can hop." As you say each word of the sentence, point to the corresponding word on the branch chart.

14. Ask: "What does the rabbit have?" Point to the words on the circle-in-circle chart. If no one answers, ask an aide to answer, or answer the question yourself. Ask the question several times, and allow different children to answer.

If someone uses a nonsensical word, e.g., "hop," say the whole sentence. Say: "The rabbit has hop? Does that make sense? Let's look back in the circle and find something the rabbit has."

15. Write students' answers on the branch organizer on the board. For each answer, say: "Write (the answer) under the word 'Has' on your branch organizer."

16. For each word that students write, say the whole sentence, e.g., "The rabbit has a tail." As you say each word of the sentence, point to the corresponding word on the branch chart.

17. Ask: "What does the rabbit like?" Point to the words on the circle-in-circle chart. If no one answers, ask an aide to answer, or answer the question yourself. Ask the question several times, and allow different children to answer.

If someone uses a nonsensical word, e.g., "tail," say the whole sentence. Say: "The rabbit likes tail? Does that make sense? Let's look back in the circle and find something the rabbit likes."

18. Write students' answers on the branch organizer on the board. For each answer, say: "Write (the answer) under the word 'Likes' on your branch organizer."

19. For each word that students write, say the whole sentence, e.g., "The rabbit likes carrots." As you say each word of the sentence, point to the corresponding word on the branch chart.

20. Praise students, pass out reinforcers, and take a short break.

21. Draw a large version of the lined paper on your chart paper, using the watercolor marker. Tape the chart paper to the board. Pass out the lined paper. Tape one to each desk, next to the branch organizer. It's important that all three graphic organizers stay in front of students for the sentence-building phase.

22. Say: "It's time to make a sentence. Let's make a sentence from the first column of the branch organizer, using the word 'Can.'" (Example sentence: The rabbit can hop.) Point to the words on the branch chart on the board as you slowly say them, forming the sentence. Show the students the relationship between the words on the chart and a spoken sentence. This will help them read the chart and form the sentences themselves.

23. Write the sentence on your "lined paper" on the board.

24. Say: "Copy the sentence on the first line of your paper."

25. Say: "Let's make a sentence from the second column of the branch organizer, using the word 'Has.'" (Example sentence: The rabbit has a tail.) Point to the words on the branch chart on the board as you slowly say them, forming the sentence.

26. Write the sentence on your "lined paper" on the board.

27. Say: "Copy the sentence on the second line of your paper." Make sure they write on the lines and not in the blank space above. This is for the illustration.

28. Say: "Let's make a sentence from the third column of the branch organizer, using the word 'Likes.'" (Example sentence: The rabbit likes carrots.) Point to the words on the branch chart on the board as you slowly say them, forming the sentence.

29. Write the sentence on your "lined paper" on the board.

30. Say: "Copy the sentence on the third line of your paper."

When students become familiar with this process, they may choose any of the three words to make a sentence.

AUTISM & READING COMPREHENSION
© 2011 by Joseph Porter, M.Ed. Future Horizons, Inc.

31. Say: "Now we will read our sentences aloud." Group students in pairs to read to each other, or let each child read aloud to you, an aide, or the whole class.

32. Praise students and pass out reinforcers.

33. Say: "Now we will draw a picture to go with our sentences." Lead students to read the first sentence and then draw a picture of it. Do this for each sentence, one sentence at a time at first. Monitor the drawings and try to limit them to drawing only one rabbit. If a higher-functioning child is drawing three rabbits, clearly intending one rabbit for each sentence, without exhibiting difficulties, then that is okay. Later in the program, they may be able to remember two or three details at once and incorporate them all into one rabbit picture.

The illustration must reflect the information in the sentence. If you see an illustration of a rabbit missing a tail or not eating a carrot, ask the student to read the corresponding sentence again. Then show the student what's missing. ("Your sentence says, 'The rabbit has a tail.' Your picture of the rabbit does not have a tail. Draw a tail on the rabbit.")

34. Collect papers and pencils, praise students, and pass out reinforcers.

Name_____ Date _____

The _____ rabbit has two long ears. The _____ rabbit can hop. The rabbit is eating lettuce. The lettuce is in the bowl. The bowl is _____.

1. What color is the rabbit?

_____

2. What is the rabbit eating?

_____

THE RABBIT —Worksheet 4, Blank

3. Where is the lettuce?

_____

4. What color is the bowl?

_____

THE RABBIT —Worksheet 4, Blank

THE RABBIT
Worksheet 4, Variation 1

Materials:

Worksheet 4 (Variation 1), pencils, and boxes of crayons for each child

Color Variation 1:

Brown Rabbit
Yellow Bowl

Before the Lesson:

At http://fhautism.com/arc.html, find Worksheet 4 (Variation 1). Print one for each student, plus a few extras. Write the date on the board.

Teaching the Lesson

1. Distribute the worksheets and pencils to your students. Say: "Write your name on your paper." Make sure everyone writes his or her name. Then say: "Write the date. It is on the board." Make sure everyone writes the date. Take the pencils from them.

2. Say: "(student's name), please read the sentences at the top of the paper." Ask several students to read. If no one can read the passage, read it yourself, or have an aide read it.

3. Say: "We want to color the picture. What two crayons do we need?" Ask the question several times, and allow different children to answer. Then help them find the brown and yellow crayons. Take the crayon boxes from them.

4. Say: "We will color the rabbit brown and the bowl yellow. What color do we color the rabbit?" Ask the question several times, and allow different children to answer.

5. Say: "Color the rabbit." Make sure they color only the rabbit. Repeat the words "brown rabbit" as often as possible.

6. Say: "What color do we color the bowl? Let's look back at our story if we need a reminder." Ask the question several times, and allow different children to answer.

7. Say: "Color the bowl." Make sure they color only the bowl. Repeat the words "yellow bowl" as often as possible. Then take the crayons.

8. Ask comprehension questions. Lead students to answer orally, in a complete sentence. For each question, if the student answers incorrectly, guide him or her to read the text again. Questions: 1. What color is the rabbit? 2. What is the rabbit eating? 3. Where is the lettuce? 4. What color is the bowl? Answers: 1. The rabbit is brown. 2. The rabbit is eating lettuce. 3. The lettuce is in the bowl. 4. The bowl is yellow.

9. Ask the questions again in random order. Give each student a chance to answer correctly, in complete sentences.

10. Pass out pencils. Ask each comprehension question again. (See step 8 for questions and answers.) When a student answers correctly, write the sentence on the board. Say: "Copy the sentence onto your paper." Do this for each question and answer. Take pencils from them.

11. Pass out boxes of crayons. Say: "Choose one crayon." Make sure they choose only one. Take boxes of crayons from them. Then say: "Color the flowers." Make sure they color only the flowers. Take papers from them.

12. Give out reinforcers.

THE RABBIT
Worksheet 4, Variation 2

Materials:
Worksheet 4 (Variation 2), pencils, and boxes of crayons for each child

Color Variation 2:
Pink Rabbit
Blue Bowl

Before the Lesson:
At http://fhautism.com/arc.html, find Worksheet 4 (Variation 2). Print one for each student, plus a few extras. Write the date on the board.

Teaching the Lesson

1. Distribute the worksheets and pencils to your students. Say: "Write your name on your paper." Make sure everyone writes his or her name. Then say: "Write the date. It is on the board." Make sure everyone writes the date. Take the pencils from them.

2. Say: "(student's name), please read the sentences at the top of the paper." Ask several students to read. If no one can read the passage, read it yourself, or have an aide read it.

3. Say: "We want to color the picture. What two crayons do we need?" Ask the question several times, and allow different children to answer. Then help them find the pink and blue crayons. Take the crayon boxes from them.

4. Say: "We will color the rabbit pink and the bowl blue. What color do we color the rabbit?" Ask the question several times, and allow different children to answer.

5. Say: "Color the rabbit." Make sure they color only the rabbit. Repeat the words "pink rabbit" as often as possible.

6. Say: "What color do we color the bowl? Let's look back at our story if we need a reminder." Ask the question several times, and allow different children to answer.

7. Say: "Color the bowl." Make sure they color only the bowl. Repeat the words "blue bowl" as often as possible. Then take the crayons.

8. Ask comprehension questions. Lead students to answer orally, in a complete sentence. For each question, if the student answers incorrectly, guide him or her to read the text again. Questions: 1. What color is the rabbit? 2. What is the rabbit eating? 3. Where is the lettuce? 4. What color is the bowl? Answers: 1. The rabbit is pink. 2. The rabbit is eating lettuce. 3. The lettuce is in the bowl. 4. The bowl is blue.

9. Ask the questions again in random order. Give each student a chance to answer correctly, in complete sentences.

10. Pass out pencils. Ask each comprehension question again. (See step 8 for questions and answers.) When a student answers correctly, write the sentence on the board. Say: "Copy the sentence onto your paper." Do this for each question and answer. Take pencils from them.

11. Pass out boxes of crayons. Say: "Choose one crayon." Make sure they choose only one. Take boxes of crayons from them. Then say: "Color the lettuce." Make sure they color only the lettuce. Take papers from them.

12. Give out reinforcers.

THE RABBIT
Worksheet 4, Variation 3

Materials:

Worksheet 4 (Variation 3), pencils, and boxes of crayons for each child

Color Variation 3:

Black Rabbit
Pink Bowl

Before the Lesson:

At http://fhautism.com/arc.html, find Worksheet 4 (Variation 3). Print one for each student, plus a few extras. Write the date on the board.

Teaching the Lesson

1. Distribute the worksheets and pencils to your students. Say: "Write your name on your paper." Make sure everyone writes his or her name. Then say: "Write the date. It is on the board." Make sure everyone writes the date. Take the pencils from them.

2. Say: "(student's name), please read the sentences at the top of the paper." Ask several students to read. If no one can read the passage, read it yourself, or have an aide read it.

3. Say: "We want to color the picture. What two crayons do we need?" Ask the question several times, and allow different children to answer. Then help them find the black and pink crayons. Take the crayon boxes from them.

4. Say: "We will color the rabbit black and the bowl pink. What color do we color the rabbit?" Ask the question several times, and allow different children to answer.

5. Say: "Color the rabbit." Make sure they color only the rabbit. Repeat the words "black rabbit" as often as possible.

6. Say: "What color do we color the bowl? Let's look back at our story if we need a reminder." Ask the question several times, and allow different children to answer.

7. Say: "Color the bowl." Make sure they color only the bowl. Repeat the words "pink bowl" as often as possible. Then take the crayons.

8. Ask comprehension questions. Lead students to answer orally, in a complete sentence. For each question, if the student answers incorrectly, guide him or her to read the text again. Questions: 1. What color is the rabbit? 2. What is the rabbit eating? 3. Where is the lettuce? 4. What color is the bowl? Answers: 1. The rabbit is black. 2. The rabbit is eating lettuce. 3. The lettuce is in the bowl. 4. The bowl is pink.

9. Ask the questions again in random order. Give each student a chance to answer correctly, in complete sentences.

10. Pass out pencils. Ask each comprehension question again. (See step 8 for questions and answers.) When a student answers correctly, write the sentence on the board. Say: "Copy the sentence onto your paper." Do this for each question and answer. Take pencils from them.

11. Pass out boxes of crayons. Say: "Choose one crayon." Make sure they choose only one. Take boxes of crayons from them. Then say: "Color the lettuce." Make sure they color only the lettuce. Take papers from them.

12. Give out reinforcers.

AUTISM & READING COMPREHENSION
© 2011 by Joseph Porter, M.Ed. Future Horizons, Inc.

THE RABBIT
Worksheet 4, Variation 4

Materials:

Worksheet 4 (Variation 4), pencils, and boxes of crayons for each child

Color Variation 4:

Gray Rabbit
Orange Bowl

✔

Before the Lesson:

At http://fhautism.com/arc.html, find Worksheet 4 (Variation 4). Print one for each student, plus a few extras. Write the date on the board.

Teaching the Lesson

1. Distribute the worksheets and pencils to your students. Say: "Write your name on your paper." Make sure everyone writes his or her name. Then say: "Write the date. It is on the board." Make sure everyone writes the date. Take the pencils from them.

2. Say: "(student's name), please read the sentences at the top of the paper." Ask several students to read. If no one can read the passage, read it yourself, or have an aide read it.

3. Say: "We want to color the picture. What two crayons do we need?" Ask the question several times, and allow different children to answer. Then help them find the gray and orange crayons. Take the crayon boxes from them.

4. Say: "We will color the rabbit gray and the bowl orange. What color do we color the rabbit?" Ask the question several times, and allow different children to answer.

5. Say: "Color the rabbit." Make sure they color only the rabbit. Repeat the words "gray rabbit" as often as possible.

6. Say: "What color do we color the bowl? Let's look back at our story if we need a reminder." Ask the question several times, and allow different children to answer.

7. Say: "Color the bowl." Make sure they color only the bowl. Repeat the words "orange bowl" as often as possible. Then take the crayons.

8. Ask comprehension questions. Lead students to answer orally, in a complete sentence. For each question, if the student answers incorrectly, guide him or her to read the text again. Questions: 1. What color is the rabbit? 2. What is the rabbit eating? 3. Where is the lettuce? 4. What color is the bowl? Answers: 1. The rabbit is gray. 2. The rabbit is eating lettuce. 3. The lettuce is in the bowl. 4. The bowl is orange.

9. Ask the questions again in random order. Give each student a chance to answer correctly, in complete sentences.

10. Pass out pencils. Ask each comprehension question again. (See step 8 for questions and answers.) When a student answers correctly, write the sentence on the board. Say: "Copy the sentence onto your paper." Do this for each question and answer. Take pencils from them.

11. Pass out boxes of crayons. Say: "Choose one crayon." Make sure they choose only one. Take boxes of crayons from them. Then say: "Color the lettuce." Make sure they color only the lettuce. Take papers from them.

12. Give out reinforcers.

THE RABBIT
Sentence-Building Exercise 2

Materials:

photograph of rabbit, students' circle-in-circle charts and branch organizers, lined paper, tape, completed circle-in-circle chart on chart paper (from Lesson 15 sentence-building exercise), two pieces of blank chart paper, dry-erase marker, watercolor marker

Before the Lesson:

1. At http://fhautism.com/arc.html, find the circle-in-circle chart, branch organizer, and lined paper. Print one of each for each student, plus a few extras.

2. On the blank chart paper, draw the lined paper and branch organizer.

3. On the board, hang the completed circle-in-circle chart on chart paper (from Lesson 15 sentence-building exercise) and blank branch organizer.

4. Write the date on the board.

Teaching the Lesson

1. Gather the children in a circle. Hold up the photograph of the rabbit. Ask: "What animal is this?" If no one can identify the animal, ask an aide to answer, or answer the question yourself.

2. Ask: "What can the rabbit do?" If no one answers, prompt the students to look at the circle-in-circle chart on the board. If no one answers, ask an aide to answer, or answer the question yourself. Possible answers include hop, run, dig. Students may come up with different answers. Ask the question several times, and allow different children to answer.

3. Ask: "What does the rabbit have? If no one answers, prompt the students to look at the circle-in-circle chart on the board. If no one answers, ask an aide to answer, or answer the question yourself. Possible answers include long ears, a nose, a tail.

Students may come up with different answers. Ask the question several times, and allow different children to answer.

4. Ask: "What does the rabbit like? If no one answers, prompt the students to look at the circle-in-circle chart on the board. If no one answers, ask an aide to answer, or answer the question yourself. Possible answers include carrots, leaves, lettuce. Students may come up with different answers. Ask the question several times, and allow different children to answer.

5. Praise students and pass out reinforcers.

6. The children return to their desks. Pass out pencils and blank graphic organizers. On each desk, tape a circle-in-circle chart on the left and the branch organizer on the right. (Always emphasize a left-to-right progression when teaching reading and writing.)

7. Say: "Write your name on your paper." Make sure everyone writes his or her name. Then say: "Write the date. It is on the board." Make sure everyone writes the date.

8. Say: "Copy the words from the circle-in-circle chart on the board onto your circle-in-circle chart." They do not have to copy all of the words at first.

9. Say: "Now we will do the branch organizer." On the branch organizer on the board, write "Rabbit" on the top line and "Can," "Has," and "Likes" on the three spaces under the top line. Say: "Copy the words onto your charts."

10. Ask: "What can the rabbit do?" Point to the words on the circle-in-circle chart. Encourage students to look at their own chart. If no one answers, ask an aide to answer, or answer the question yourself. Ask the question several times, and allow different children to answer.

If someone uses a nonsensical word, e.g., "lettuce," say the whole sentence. Say: "The rabbit can lettuce? Does that make sense? Let's look back in the circle and find something the rabbit can do."

11. Write students' answers on the branch organizer on the board. For each answer, say: "Write (the answer) under the word 'Can' on your branch organizer."

As you use words from the circle-in-circle chart, you may choose to cover up the words with a sticky note or leave them all showing.

12. For each word that students write, say the whole sentence, e.g., "The rabbit can dig." As you say each word of the sentence, point to the corresponding word on the branch chart.

13. Ask: "What does the rabbit have?" Point to the words on the circle-in-circle chart. If no one answers, ask an aide to answer, or answer the question yourself. Ask the question several times, and allow different children to answer. Introduce adjectives. Ask: "Are the ears short? Are the ears long?"

    If someone uses a nonsensical word, e.g., "dig," say the whole sentence. Say: "The rabbit has dig? Does that make sense? Let's look back in the circle and find something the rabbit has."

14. Write students' answers on the branch chart. For each answer, say: "Write (the answer) under the word 'Has' on your branch organizer."

15. For each word that students write, say the whole sentence, e.g., "The rabbit has long ears." As you say each word of the sentence, point to the corresponding word on the branch chart.

16. Ask: "What does the rabbit like?" Point to the words on the circle-in-circle chart. If no one answers, ask an aide to answer, or answer the question yourself. Ask the question several times, and allow different children to answer.

    If someone uses nonsensical words, e.g., "long ears," say the whole sentence. Say: "The rabbit likes long ears? Does that make sense? Let's look back in the circle and find something the rabbit likes."

17. Write students' answers on the branch organizer on the board. For each answer, say: "Write (the answer) under the word 'Likes' on your branch organizer."

18. For each word that students write, say the whole sentence, e.g., "The rabbit likes lettuce." As you say each word of the sentence, point to the corresponding word on the branch chart.

19. Praise students, pass out reinforcers, and take a short break.

20. Draw a large version of the lined paper on your chart paper, using the watercolor marker. Tape the chart paper to the board. Pass out the lined paper. Tape one to each desk, next to the branch organizer. It's important that all three graphic organizers stay in front of students for the sentence-building phase.

21. Say: "It's time to make a sentence. Let's make a sentence from the first column of the branch organizer, using the word 'Can.'" (Example sentence: The rabbit can dig.) Point to the words on the branch chart on the board as you slowly say them, forming the sentence. Show the students the relationship between the words on the chart and a spoken sentence.

Lead students to make different sentences than they did in the first sentence-building exercise.

22. Write the sentence on your "lined paper" on the board.

23. Say: "Copy the sentence on the first line of your paper."

24. Say: "Let's make a sentence from the second column of the branch organizer, using the word 'Has.'" (Example sentence: The rabbit has long ears.) Point to the words on the branch chart on the board as you slowly say them, forming the sentence.

25. Write the sentence on your "lined paper" on the board.

26. Say: "Copy the sentence on the second line of your paper." Make sure they write on the lines and not in the blank space above. This is for the illustration.

27. Say: "Let's make a sentence from the third column of the branch organizer, using the word 'Likes.'" (Example sentence: The rabbit likes lettuce.) Point to the words on the branch chart on the board as you slowly say them, forming the sentence.

28. Write the sentence on your "lined paper" on the board.

29. Say: "Copy the sentence on the third line of your paper."

When students become familiar with this process, they may choose any of the three words to make a sentence.

30. Say: "Now we will read our sentences aloud." Group students in pairs to read to each other, or let each child read aloud to you, an aide, or the whole class.

31. Praise students and pass out reinforcers.

32. Say: "Now we will draw a picture to go with our sentences." Lead students to read the first sentence and then draw a picture of it. Do this for each sentence, one sentence at a time at first. Monitor the drawings and try to limit them to drawing only one rabbit. If a higher-functioning child is drawing three rabbits, clearly intending one rabbit for each sentence, without exhibiting difficulties, then that is okay. Later in the program, they may be able to remember two or three details at once and incorporate them all into one rabbit picture.

The illustration must reflect the information in the sentence. If you see an illustration of a rabbit missing long ears or not eating lettuce, ask the student to read the corresponding sentence again. Then show the student what's missing. ("Your sentence says, 'The rabbit has long ears.' Your picture of the rabbit does not have long ears. Draw long ears on the rabbit.")

33. Collect papers and pencils, praise students, and pass out reinforcers.

THE BEAR

Get the free print PDF of the bear photo and this page at http://fhautism.com/arc.html.

Name_____ Date _____

The _____ bear is behind the boy.

The boy is wearing _____ pants.

The bear is eating a hamburger.

The boy feels scared.

1. What color is the bear?

_____

2. Where is the bear?

_____

THE BEAR —Worksheet 5, Blank

AUTISM & READING COMPREHENSION
© 2011 by Joseph Porter, M.Ed. Future Horizons, Inc.

3. What color are the boy's pants?

_____

4. What is the bear eating?

_____

THE BEAR —Worksheet 5, Blank

THE BEAR
Worksheet 5, Variation 1

Materials:

Worksheet 5 (Variation 1), pencils, and boxes of crayons for each child

Color Variation 1:

Brown Bear
Yellow Pants

Before the Lesson:

At http://fhautism.com/arc.html, find Worksheet 5 (Variation 1). Print one for each student, plus a few extras. Write the date on the board.

Teaching the Lesson

1. Distribute the worksheets and pencils to your students. Say: "Write your name on your paper." Make sure everyone writes his or her name. Then say: "Write the date. It is on the board." Make sure everyone writes the date. Take the pencils from them.

2. Say: "(student's name), please read the sentences at the top of the paper." Ask several students to read. If no one can read the passage, read it yourself, or have an aide read it.

3. Say: "We want to color the picture. What two crayons do we need?" Ask the question several times, and allow different children to answer. Then help them find the brown and yellow crayons. Take the crayon boxes from them.

4. Say: "We will color the bear brown and the pants yellow. What color do we color the bear?" Ask the question several times, and allow different children to answer.

5. Say: "Color the bear." Make sure they color only the bear. Repeat the words "brown bear" as often as possible.

6. Say: "What color do we color the pants? Let's look back at our story if we need a reminder." Ask the question several times, and allow different children to answer.

7. Say: "Color the pants." Make sure they color only the pants. Repeat the words "yellow pants" as often as possible. Then take the crayons.

Get the free print PDF of this page at http://fhautism.com/arc.html. **91**

8. Ask comprehension questions. Lead students to answer orally, in a complete sentence. For each question, if the student answers incorrectly, guide him or her to read the text again. Questions: 1. What color is the bear? 2. Where is the bear? 3. What color are the boy's pants? 4. What is the bear eating? 5. How does the boy feel? Answers: 1. The bear is brown. 2. The bear is behind the boy. 3. The boy's pants are yellow. 4. The bear is eating a hamburger. 5. The boy feels scared.

9. Ask the questions again in random order. Give each student a chance to answer correctly, in complete sentences.

10. Pass out pencils. Ask each comprehension question again. (See step 8 for questions and answers.) When a student answers correctly, write the sentence on the board. Say: "Copy the sentence onto your paper." Do this for each question and answer. Take pencils from them.

11. Pass out boxes of crayons. Say: "Choose one crayon." Make sure they choose only one. Take boxes of crayons from them. Then say: "Color the hamburger." Make sure they color only the hamburger. Take papers from them.

12. Give out reinforcers.

THE BEAR
Worksheet 5, Variation 2

Materials:

Worksheet 5 (Variation 2), pencils, and boxes of crayons for each child

Color Variation 2:

Black Bear
Red Pants

Before the Lesson:

At http://fhautism.com/arc.html, find Worksheet 5 (Variation 2). Print one for each student, plus a few extras. Write the date on the board.

Teaching the Lesson

1. Distribute the worksheets and pencils to your students. Say: "Write your name on your paper." Make sure everyone writes his or her name. Then say: "Write the date. It is on the board." Make sure everyone writes the date. Take the pencils from them.

2. Say: "(student's name), please read the sentences at the top of the paper." Ask several students to read. If no one can read the passage, read it yourself, or have an aide read it.

3. Say: "We want to color the picture. What two crayons do we need?" Ask the question several times, and allow different children to answer. Then help them find the black and red crayons. Take the crayon boxes from them.

4. Say: "We will color the bear black and the pants red. What color do we color the bear?" Ask the question several times, and allow different children to answer.

5. Say: "Color the bear." Make sure they color only the bear. Repeat the words "black bear" as often as possible.

6. Say: "What color do we color the pants? Let's look back at our story if we need a reminder." Ask the question several times, and allow different children to answer.

7. Say: "Color the pants." Make sure they color only the pants. Repeat the words "red pants" as often as possible. Then take the crayons.

---

8. Ask comprehension questions. Lead students to answer orally, in a complete sentence. For each question, if the student answers incorrectly, guide him or her to read the text again. Questions: 1. What color is the bear? 2. Where is the bear? 3. What color are the boy's pants? 4. What is the bear eating? 5. How does the boy feel? Answers: 1. The bear is black. 2. The bear is behind the boy. 3. The boy's pants are red. 4. The bear is eating a hamburger. 5. The boy feels scared.

9. Ask the questions again in random order. Give each student a chance to answer correctly, in complete sentences.

10. Pass out pencils. Ask each comprehension question again. (See step 8 for questions and answers.) When a student answers correctly, write the sentence on the board. Say: "Copy the sentence onto your paper." Do this for each question and answer. Take pencils from them.

11. Pass out boxes of crayons. Say: "Choose one crayon." Make sure they choose only one. Take boxes of crayons from them. Then say: "Color the hamburger." Make sure they color only the hamburger. Take papers from them.

12. Give out reinforcers.

THE BEAR
Worksheet 5, Variation 3

Materials:

Worksheet 5 (Variation 3), pencils, and boxes of crayons for each child

Color Variation 3:

Orange Bear
Black Pants

Before the Lesson:

At http://fhautism.com/arc.html, find Worksheet 5 (Variation 3). Print one for each student, plus a few extras. Write the date on the board.

Teaching the Lesson

1. Distribute the worksheets and pencils to your students. Say: "Write your name on your paper." Make sure everyone writes his or her name. Then say: "Write the date. It is on the board." Make sure everyone writes the date. Take the pencils from them.

2. Say: "(student's name), please read the sentences at the top of the paper." Ask several students to read. If no one can read the passage, read it yourself, or have an aide read it.

3. Say: "We want to color the picture. What two crayons do we need?" Ask the question several times, and allow different children to answer. Then help them find the orange and black crayons. Take the crayon boxes from them.

4. Say: "We will color the bear orange and the pants black. What color do we color the bear?" Ask the question several times, and allow different children to answer.

5. Say: "Color the bear." Make sure they color only the bear. Repeat the words "orange bear" as often as possible.

6. Say: "What color do we color the pants? Let's look back at our story if we need a reminder." Ask the question several times, and allow different children to answer.

7. Say: "Color the pants." Make sure they color only the pants. Repeat the words "black pants" as often as possible. Then take the crayons.

8. Ask comprehension questions. Lead students to answer orally, in a complete sentence. For each question, if the student answers incorrectly, guide him or her to read the text again. Questions: 1. What color is the bear? 2. Where is the bear? 3. What color are the boy's pants? 4. What is the bear eating? 5. How does the boy feel? Answers: 1. The bear is orange. 2. The bear is behind the boy. 3. The boy's pants are black. 4. The bear is eating a hamburger. 5. The boy feels scared.

9. Ask the questions again in random order. Give each student a chance to answer correctly, in complete sentences.

10. Pass out pencils. Ask each comprehension question again. (See step 8 for questions and answers.) When a student answers correctly, write the sentence on the board. Say: "Copy the sentence onto your paper." Do this for each question and answer. Take pencils from them.

11. Pass out boxes of crayons. Say: "Choose one crayon." Make sure they choose only one. Take boxes of crayons from them. Then say: "Color the hamburger." Make sure they color only the hamburger. Take papers from them.

12. Give out reinforcers.

THE BEAR
Worksheet 5, Variation 4

Materials:

Worksheet 5 (Variation 4), pencils, and boxes of crayons for each child

Color Variation 4:

Gray Bear
Blue Pants

Before the Lesson:

At http://fhautism.com/arc.html, find Worksheet 5 (Variation 4). Print one for each student, plus a few extras. Write the date on the board.

Teaching the Lesson

1. Distribute the worksheets and pencils to your students. Say: "Write your name on your paper." Make sure everyone writes his or her name. Then say: "Write the date. It is on the board." Make sure everyone writes the date. Take the pencils from them.

2. Say: "(student's name), please read the sentences at the top of the paper." Ask several students to read. If no one can read the passage, read it yourself, or have an aide read it.

3. Say: "We want to color the picture. What two crayons do we need?" Ask the question several times, and allow different children to answer. Then help them find the gray and blue crayons. Take the crayon boxes from them.

4. Say: "We will color the bear gray and the pants blue. What color do we color the bear?" Ask the question several times, and allow different children to answer.

5. Say: "Color the bear." Make sure they color only the bear. Repeat the words "gray bear" as often as possible.

6. Say: "What color do we color the pants? Let's look back at our story if we need a reminder." Ask the question several times, and allow different children to answer.

7. Say: "Color the pants." Make sure they color only the pants. Repeat the words "blue pants" as often as possible. Then take the crayons.

8. Ask comprehension questions. Lead students to answer orally, in a complete sentence. For each question, if the student answers incorrectly, guide him or her to read the text again. Questions: 1. What color is the bear? 2. Where is the bear? 3. What color are the boy's pants? 4. What is the bear eating? 5. How does the boy feel? Answers: 1. The bear is gray. 2. The bear is behind the boy. 3. The boy's pants are blue. 4. The bear is eating a hamburger. 5. The boy feels scared.

9. Ask the questions again in random order. Give each student a chance to answer correctly, in complete sentences.

10. Pass out pencils. Ask each comprehension question again. (See step 8 for questions and answers.) When a student answers correctly, write the sentence on the board. Say: "Copy the sentence onto your paper." Do this for each question and answer. Take pencils from them.

11. Pass out boxes of crayons. Say: "Choose one crayon." Make sure they choose only one. Take boxes of crayons from them. Then say: "Color the hamburger." Make sure they color only the hamburger. Take papers from them.

12. Give out reinforcers.

THE BEAR
Sentence-Building Exercise 1

Materials:

photograph of bear, students' circle-in-circle charts and branch organizers, lined paper, tape, three pieces of chart paper, dry-erase marker, watercolor marker

Before the Lesson:

1. At http://fhautism.com/arc.html, find the circle-in-circle chart, branch organizer, and lined paper. Print one of each for each student, plus a few extras.

2. On the chart paper, draw a blank circle-in-circle chart, branch organizer, and lined paper.

3. On the board, hang a blank circle-in-circle chart on the left and a branch organizer on the right. Make them large enough to write all the words you will need.

4. Write the date on the board.

Teaching the Lesson

1. Gather the children in a circle. Hold up the photograph of the bear. Ask: "What animal is this?" If no one can identify the animal, ask an aide to answer, or answer the question yourself.

2. When a student says, "bear," write "bear" in the smaller, inner circle of the circle-in-circle chart. Write very legibly. Students will be copying these words later.

3. Ask: "What can the bear do?" If no one answers, prompt the students. Ask: "Can the bear fly?" Another good question: "Can the bear drive the bus?" If no one answers, ask an aide to answer, or answer the question yourself. Possible answers include walk, climb, roar. Students may come up with different answers. Ask the question several times, and allow different children to answer. Write the answers in the large circle. Leave space between the words.

---

4. Ask: "What does the bear have? If no one answers, prompt the students. Ask: "Does a bear have feathers?" This question should be repeated every time the animal in question has either fur or feathers. Other good questions: "Does the bear have four eyes?" "Does the bear have wings?" If no one answers, ask an aide to answer, or answer the question yourself. Possible answers include two eyes, claws, fur. Students may come up with different answers. Ask the question several times, and allow different children to answer. Write the answers in the large circle. Leave space between the words.

5. Ask: "What does the bear like? If no one answers, prompt the students with a guessing game. Say: "The bear likes to eat meat in a bun. We sometimes put ketchup on it. We get it from the drive-thru." Do this for the other two answers. If no one answers, ask an aide to answer, or answer the question yourself. Possible answers include honey, fish, hamburgers. Students may come up with different answers. Ask the question several times, and allow different children to answer. Write the answers in the large circle. Leave space between the words. NOTE: Guessing games may be stressful for some children. If students appear to be getting agitated or panicky, just tell them the answer. The lesson is more important than the game.

6. Praise students and pass out reinforcers.

7. The children return to their desks. Pass out pencils and blank graphic organizers. On each desk, tape the circle-in-circle chart on the left and the branch organizer on the right. (Always emphasize a left-to-right progression when teaching reading and writing.)

8. Say: "Write your name on your paper." Make sure everyone writes his or her name. Then say: "Write the date. It is on the board." Make sure everyone writes the date.

9. Say: "Copy the words from the circle-in-circle chart on the board onto your circle-in-circle chart." They do not have to copy all of the words at first.

10. Say: "Now we will do the branch organizer." On the branch organizer on the board, write "Bear" on the top line and "Can," "Has," and "Likes" on the three spaces under the top line. Say: "Copy the words onto your charts."

11. Ask: "What can the bear do?" Point to the words on the circle-in-circle chart. Encourage students to look at their own chart. If no one answers, ask an aide to answer, or answer the question yourself. Ask the question several times, and allow different children to answer.

If someone uses a nonsensical word, e.g., "hamburgers," say the whole sentence. Say: "The bear can hamburgers? Does that make sense? Let's look back in the circle and find something the bear can do."

12. Write students' answers on the branch organizer on the board. For each answer, say: "Write (the answer) under the word 'Can' on your branch organizer."

As you use words from the circle-in-circle chart, you may choose to cover up the words with a sticky note or leave them all showing.

13. For each word that students write, say the whole sentence, e.g., "The bear can roar." As you say each word of the sentence, point to the corresponding word on the branch chart.

14. Ask: "What does the bear have?" Point to the words on the circle-in-circle chart. If no one answers, ask an aide to answer, or answer the question yourself. Ask the question several times, and allow different children to answer.

If someone uses a nonsensical word, e.g., "roar," say the whole sentence. Say: "The bear has roar? Does that make sense? Let's look back in the circle and find something the bear has."

15. Write students' answers on the branch organizer on the board. For each answer, say: "Write (the answer) under the word 'Has' on your branch organizer."

16. For each word that students write, say the whole sentence, e.g., "The bear has claws." As you say each word of the sentence, point to the corresponding word on the branch chart.

17. Ask: "What does the bear like?" Point to the words on the circle-in-circle chart. If no one answers, ask an aide to answer, or answer the question yourself. Ask the question several times, and allow different children to answer.

If someone uses a nonsensical word, e.g., "claws," say the whole sentence. Say: "The bear likes claws? Does that make sense? Let's look back in the circle and find something the bear likes."

18. Write students' answers on the branch organizer on the board. For each answer, say: "Write (the answer) under the word 'Likes' on your branch organizer."

19. For each word that students write, say the whole sentence, e.g., "The bear likes hamburgers." As you say each word of the sentence, point to the corresponding word on the branch chart.

20. Praise students, pass out reinforcers, and take a short break.

21. Draw a large version of the lined paper on your chart paper, using the watercolor marker. Tape the chart paper to the board. Pass out the lined paper. Tape one to each desk, next to the branch organizer.

22. Say: "It's time to make a sentence. Let's make a sentence from the first column of the branch organizer, using the word 'Can.'" (Example sentence: The bear can roar.) Point to the words on the branch chart on the board as you slowly say them, forming the sentence. Show the students the relationship between the words on the chart and a spoken sentence. This will help them read the chart and form the sentences themselves.

23. Write the sentence on your "lined paper" on the board.

24. Say: "Copy the sentence on the first line of your paper."

25. Say: "Let's make a sentence from the second column of the branch organizer, using the word 'Has.'" (Example sentence: The bear has claws.) Point to the words on the branch chart on the board as you slowly say them, forming the sentence.

26. Write the sentence on your "lined paper" on the board.

27. Say: "Copy the sentence on the second line of your paper." Make sure they write on the lines and not in the blank space above.

28. Say: "Let's make a sentence from the third column of the branch organizer, using the word 'Likes.'" (Example sentence: The bear likes hamburgers.) Point to the words on the branch chart on the board as you slowly say them, forming the sentence.

29. Write the sentence on your "lined paper" on the board.

30. Say: "Copy the sentence on the third line of your paper."

When students become familiar with this process, they may choose any of the three words to make a sentence.

31. Say: "Now we will read our sentences aloud." Group students in pairs to read to each other, or let each child read aloud to you, an aide, or the whole class.

32. Praise students and pass out reinforcers.

33. Say: "Now we will draw a picture to go with our sentences." Lead students to read the first sentence and then draw a picture of it. Do this for each sentence, one sentence at a time at first. Monitor the drawings and try to limit them to drawing only one bear. If a higher-functioning child is drawing three bears, clearly intending one bear for each sentence, without exhibiting difficulties, then that is okay. Later in the program, they may be able to remember two or three details at once and incorporate them all into one bear picture.

The illustration must reflect the information in the sentence. If you see an illustration of a bear missing claws or not eating a hamburger, ask the student to read the corresponding sentence again. Then show the student what's missing. ("Your sentence says, 'The bear has claws.' Your picture of the bear does not have claws. Draw claws on the bear.")

34. Collect papers and pencils, praise students, and pass out reinforcers.

Name_____ Date _____

The _____ bear has fur.

The bear is eating a fish.

The fish is _____.

The fish is on a plate.

The plate is _____.

1. Does the bear have feathers or fur?

_____

2. What color is the bear?

_____

3. What is the bear eating?

_____

THE BEAR —Worksheet 6, Blank

4. What color is the fish?

_____

5. What color is the plate?

_____

THE BEAR —Worksheet 6, Blank

THE BEAR
Worksheet 6, Variation 1

Materials:

Worksheet 6 (Variation 1), pencils, and boxes of crayons for each child

Color Variation 1:

Brown Bear
Yellow Fish
Red Plate

Before the Lesson:

At http://fhautism.com/arc.html, find Worksheet 6 (Variation 1). Print one for each student, plus a few extras. Write the date on the board.

Teaching the Lesson

1. Distribute the worksheets and pencils to your students. Say: "Write your name on your paper." Make sure everyone writes his or her name. Then say: "Write the date. It is on the board." Make sure everyone writes the date. Take the pencils from them.

2. Say: "(student's name), please read the sentences at the top of the paper." Ask several students to read. If no one can read the passage, read it yourself, or have an aide read it.

3. Say: "We want to color the picture. What three crayons do we need?" Ask the question several times, and allow different children to answer. Then help them find the brown, yellow, and red crayons. Take the crayon boxes from them.

4. Say: "We will color the bear brown, the fish yellow, and the plate red. What color do we color the bear?" Ask the question several times, and allow different children to answer.

5. Say: "Color the bear." Make sure they color only the bear. Repeat the words "brown bear" as often as possible.

6. Say: "What color do we color the fish? Let's look back at our story if we need a reminder." Ask the question several times, and allow different children to answer.

7. Say: "Color the fish." Make sure they color only the fish. Repeat the words "yellow fish" as often as possible.

8. Say: "What color do we color the plate? Let's look back at our story if we need a reminder." Ask the question several times, and allow different children to answer.

9. Say: "Color the plate." Make sure they color only the plate. Repeat the words "red plate" as often as possible. Then take the crayons.

10. Ask comprehension questions. Lead students to answer orally, in a complete sentence. For each question, if the student answers incorrectly, guide him or her to read the text again. Questions: 1. Does the bear have feathers or fur? 2. What color is the bear? 3. What is the bear eating? 4. What color is the fish? 5. What color is the plate? Answers: 1. The bear has fur. 2. The bear is brown. 3. The bear is eating a fish. 4. The fish is yellow. 5. The plate is red.

11. Ask the questions again in random order. Give each student a chance to answer correctly, in complete sentences.

12. Pass out pencils. Ask each comprehension question again. (See step 10 for questions and answers.) When a student answers correctly, write the sentence on the board. Say: "Copy the sentence onto your paper." Do this for each question and answer. Take pencils from them.

13. Pass out boxes of crayons. Say: "Choose one crayon." Make sure they choose only one. Take boxes of crayons from them. Then say: "Color the flowers." Make sure they color only the flowers. Take papers from them.

14. Give out reinforcers.

THE BEAR
Worksheet 6, Variation 2

Materials:

Worksheet 6 (Variation 2), pencils, and boxes of crayons for each child

Color Variation 2:

Black Bear
Orange Fish
Purple Plate

Before the Lesson:

At http://fhautism.com/arc.html, find Worksheet 6 (Variation 2). Print one for each student, plus a few extras. Write the date on the board.

Teaching the Lesson

1. Distribute the worksheets and pencils to your students. Say: "Write your name on your paper." Make sure everyone writes his or her name. Then say: "Write the date. It is on the board." Make sure everyone writes the date. Take the pencils from them.

2. Say: "(student's name), please read the sentences at the top of the paper." Ask several students to read. If no one can read the passage, read it yourself, or have an aide read it.

3. Say: "We want to color the picture. What three crayons do we need?" Ask the question several times, and allow different children to answer. Then help them find the black, orange, and purple crayons. Take the crayon boxes from them.

4. Say: "We will color the bear black, the fish orange, and the plate purple. What color do we color the bear?" Ask the question several times, and allow different children to answer.

5. Say: "Color the bear." Make sure they color only the bear. Repeat the words "black bear" as often as possible.

6. Say: "What color do we color the fish? Let's look back at our story if we need a reminder." Ask the question several times, and allow different children to answer.

7. Say: "Color the fish." Make sure they color only the fish. Repeat the words "orange fish" as often as possible.

8. Say: "What color do we color the plate? Let's look back at our story if we need a reminder." Ask the question several times, and allow different children to answer.

9. Say: "Color the plate." Make sure they color only the plate. Repeat the words "purple plate" as often as possible. Then take the crayons.

10. Ask comprehension questions. Lead students to answer orally, in a complete sentence. For each question, if the student answers incorrectly, guide him or her to read the text again. Questions: 1. Does the bear have feathers or fur? 2. What color is the bear? 3. What is the bear eating? 4. What color is the fish? 5. What color is the plate? Answers: 1. The bear has fur. 2. The bear is brown. 3. The bear is eating a fish. 4. The fish is orange. 5. The plate is purple.

11. Ask the questions again in random order. Give each student a chance to answer correctly, in complete sentences.

12. Pass out pencils. Ask each comprehension question again. (See step 10 for questions and answers.) When a student answers correctly, write the sentence on the board. Say: "Copy the sentence onto your paper." Do this for each question and answer. Take pencils from them.

13. Pass out boxes of crayons. Say: "Choose one crayon." Make sure they choose only one. Take boxes of crayons from them. Then say: "Color the flowers." Make sure they color only the flowers. Take papers from them.

14. Give out reinforcers.

THE BEAR
Worksheet 6, Variation 3

Materials:

Worksheet 6 (Variation 3), pencils, and boxes of crayons for each child

Color Variation 3:

Orange Bear
Blue Fish
Yellow Plate

Before the Lesson:

At http://fhautism.com/arc.html, find Worksheet 6 (Variation 3). Print one for each student, plus a few extras. Write the date on the board.

Teaching the Lesson

1. Distribute the worksheets and pencils to your students. Say: "Write your name on your paper." Make sure everyone writes his or her name. Then say: "Write the date. It is on the board." Make sure everyone writes the date. Take the pencils from them.

2. Say: "(student's name), please read the sentences at the top of the paper." Ask several students to read. If no one can read the passage, read it yourself, or have an aide read it.

3. Say: "We want to color the picture. What three crayons do we need?" Ask the question several times, and allow different children to answer. Then help them find the orange, blue, and yellow crayons. Take the crayon boxes from them.

4. Say: "We will color the bear orange, the fish blue, and the plate yellow. What color do we color the bear?" Ask the question several times, and allow different children to answer.

5. Say: "Color the bear." Make sure they color only the bear. Repeat the words "orange bear" as often as possible.

6. Say: "What color do we color the fish? Let's look back at our story if we need a reminder." Ask the question several times, and allow different children to answer.

7. Say: "Color the fish." Make sure they color only the fish. Repeat the words "blue fish" as often as possible.

8. Say: "What color do we color the plate? Let's look back at our story if we need a reminder." Ask the question several times, and allow different children to answer.

9. Say: "Color the plate." Make sure they color only the plate. Repeat the words "yellow plate" as often as possible. Then take the crayons.

10. Ask comprehension questions. Lead students to answer orally, in a complete sentence. For each question, if the student answers incorrectly, guide him or her to read the text again. Questions: 1. Does the bear have feathers or fur? 2. What color is the bear? 3. What is the bear eating? 4. What color is the fish? 5. What color is the plate? Answers: 1. The bear has fur. 2. The bear is orange. 3. The bear is eating a fish. 4. The fish is blue. 5. The plate is yellow.

11. Ask the questions again in random order. Give each student a chance to answer correctly, in complete sentences.

12. Pass out pencils. Ask each comprehension question again. (See step 10 for questions and answers.) When a student answers correctly, write the sentence on the board. Say: "Copy the sentence onto your paper." Do this for each question and answer. Take pencils from them.

13. Pass out boxes of crayons. Say: "Choose one crayon." Make sure they choose only one. Take boxes of crayons from them. Then say: "Color the flowers." Make sure they color only the flowers. Take papers from them.

14. Give out reinforcers.

THE BEAR
Worksheet 6, Variation 4

Materials:

Worksheet 6 (Variation 4), pencils, and boxes of crayons for each child

Color Variation 3:

Gray Bear
Red Fish
Orange Plate

✔ ## Before the Lesson:

At http://fhautism.com/arc.html, find Worksheet 6 (Variation 4). Print one for each student, plus a few extras. Write the date on the board.

Teaching the Lesson

1. Distribute the worksheets and pencils to your students. Say: "Write your name on your paper." Make sure everyone writes his or her name. Then say: "Write the date. It is on the board." Make sure everyone writes the date. Take the pencils from them.

2. Say: "(student's name), please read the sentences at the top of the paper." Ask several students to read. If no one can read the passage, read it yourself, or have an aide read it.

3. Say: "We want to color the picture. What three crayons do we need?" Ask the question several times, and allow different children to answer. Then help them find the gray, red, and orange crayons. Take the crayon boxes from them.

4. Say: "We will color the bear gray, the fish red, and the plate orange. What color do we color the bear?" Ask the question several times, and allow different children to answer.

5. Say: "Color the bear." Make sure they color only the bear. Repeat the words "gray bear" as often as possible.

6. Say: "What color do we color the fish? Let's look back at our story if we need a reminder." Ask the question several times, and allow different children to answer.

7. Say: "Color the fish." Make sure they color only the fish. Repeat the words "red fish" as often as possible.

8. Say: "What color do we color the plate? Let's look back at our story if we need a reminder." Ask the question several times, and allow different children to answer.

9. Say: "Color the plate." Make sure they color only the plate. Repeat the words "orange plate" as often as possible. Then take the crayons.

10. Ask comprehension questions. Lead students to answer orally, in a complete sentence. For each question, if the student answers incorrectly, guide him or her to read the text again. Questions: 1. Does the bear have feathers or fur? 2. What color is the bear? 3. What is the bear eating? 4. What color is the fish? 5. What color is the plate? Answers: 1. The bear has fur. 2. The bear is gray. 3. The bear is eating a fish. 4. The fish is red. 5. The plate is orange.

11. Ask the questions again in random order. Give each student a chance to answer correctly, in complete sentences.

12. Pass out pencils. Ask each comprehension question again. (See step 10 for questions and answers.) When a student answers correctly, write the sentence on the board. Say: "Copy the sentence onto your paper." Do this for each question and answer. Take pencils from them.

13. Pass out boxes of crayons. Say: "Choose one crayon." Make sure they choose only one. Take boxes of crayons from them. Then say: "Color the flowers." Make sure they color only the flowers. Take papers from them.

14. Give out reinforcers.

AUTISM & READING COMPREHENSION
© 2011 by Joseph Porter, M.Ed. Future Horizons, Inc.

THE BEAR
Sentence-Building Exercise 2

Materials:

photograph of bear, students' circle-in-circle charts and branch organizers, lined paper, tape, completed circle-in-circle chart on chart paper (from Lesson 25 sentence-building exercise), two pieces of blank chart paper, dry-erase marker, watercolor marker

Before the Lesson:

1. At http://fhautism.com/arc.html, find the circle-in-circle chart, branch organizer, and lined paper. Print one of each for each student, plus a few extras.

2. On the blank chart paper, draw the lined paper and branch organizer.

3. On the board, hang the completed circle-in-circle chart on chart paper (from Lesson 25 sentence-building exercise) and blank branch organizer.

4. Write the date on the board.

Teaching the Lesson

1. Gather the children in a circle. Hold up the photograph of the bear. Ask: "What animal is this?" If no one can identify the animal, ask an aide to answer, or answer the question yourself.

2. Ask: "What can the bear do?" If no one answers, prompt the students to look at the circle-in-circle chart on the board. If no one answers, ask an aide to answer, or answer the question yourself. Possible answers include walk, climb, roar. Students may come up with different answers. Ask the question several times, and allow different children to answer.

3. Ask: "What does the bear have? If no one answers, prompt the students to look at the circle-in-circle chart on the board. If no one answers, ask an aide to answer, or answer the question yourself. Possible answers include two eyes, claws, fur. Students may come up with different answers. Ask the question several times, and allow different children to answer.

4. Ask: "What does the bear like? If no one answers, prompt the students to look at the circle-in-circle chart on the board. If no one answers, ask an aide to answer, or answer the question yourself. Possible answers include honey, fish, hamburgers. Students may come up with different answers. Ask the question several times, and allow different children to answer.

5. Praise students and pass out reinforcers.

6. The children return to their desks. Pass out pencils and blank graphic organizers. On each desk, tape a circle-in-circle chart on the left and the branch organizer on the right. (Always emphasize a left-to-right progression when teaching reading and writing.)

7. Say: "Write your name on your paper." Make sure everyone writes his or her name. Then say: "Write the date. It is on the board." Make sure everyone writes the date.

8. Say: "Copy the words from the circle-in-circle chart on the board onto your circle-in-circle chart." They do not have to copy all of the words at first.

9. Say: "Now we will do the branch organizer." On the branch organizer on the board, write "Bear" on the top line and "Can," "Has," and "Likes" on the three spaces under the top line. Say: "Copy the words onto your charts."

10. Ask: "What can the bear do?" Point to the words on the circle-in-circle chart. Encourage students to look at their own chart. If no one answers, ask an aide to answer, or answer the question yourself. Ask the question several times, and allow different children to answer.

If someone uses a nonsensical word, e.g., "honey," say the whole sentence. Say: "The bear can honey? Does that make sense? Let's look back in the circle and find something the bear can do."

11. Write students' answers on the branch organizer on the board. For each answer, say: "Write (the answer) under the word 'Can' on your branch organizer."

As you use words from the circle-in-circle chart, you may choose to cover up the words with a sticky note or leave them all showing.

12. For each word that students write, say the whole sentence, e.g., "The bear can climb." As you say each word of the sentence, point to the corresponding word on the branch chart.

13. Ask: "What does the bear have?" Point to the words on the circle-in-circle chart. If no one answers, ask an aide to answer, or answer the question yourself. Ask the question several times, and allow different children to answer.

If someone uses a nonsensical word, e.g., "climb," say the whole sentence. Say: "The bear has climb? Does that make sense? Let's look back in the circle and find something the bear has."

14. Write students' answers on the branch chart. For each answer, say: "Write (the answer) under the word 'Has' on your branch organizer."

15. For each word that students write, say the whole sentence, e.g., "The bear has fur." As you say each word of the sentence, point to the corresponding word on the branch chart.

16. Ask: "What does the bear like?" Point to the words on the circle-in-circle chart. If no one answers, ask an aide to answer, or answer the question yourself. Ask the question several times, and allow different children to answer.

If someone uses nonsensical words, e.g., "fur," say the whole sentence. Say: "The bear likes fur? Does that make sense? Let's look back in the circle and find something the bear likes."

17. Write students' answers on the branch organizer on the board. For each answer, say: "Write (the answer) under the word 'Likes' on your branch organizer."

18. For each word that students write, say the whole sentence, e.g., "The bear likes fish." As you say each word of the sentence, point to the corresponding word on the branch chart.

19. Praise students, pass out reinforcers, and take a short break.

20. Draw a large version of the lined paper on your chart paper, using the watercolor marker. Tape the chart paper to the board. Pass out the lined paper. Tape one to each desk, next to the branch organizer.

21. Say: "It's time to make a sentence. Let's make a sentence from the first column of the branch organizer, using the word 'Can.'" (Example sentence: The bear can climb.) Point to the words on the branch chart on the board as you slowly say them, forming the sentence. Show the students the relationship between the words on the chart and a spoken sentence.

    Lead students to make different sentences than they did in the first sentence-building exercise.

22. Write the sentence on your "lined paper" on the board.

23. Say: "Copy the sentence on the first line of your paper."

24. Say: "Let's make a sentence from the second column of the branch organizer, using the word 'Has.'" (Example sentence: The bear has fur.) Point to the words on the branch chart on the board as you slowly say them, forming the sentence.

25. Write the sentence on your "lined paper" on the board.

26. Say: "Copy the sentence on the second line of your paper." Make sure they write on the lines and not in the blank space above.

27. Say: "Let's make a sentence from the third column of the branch organizer, using the word 'Likes.'" (Example sentence: The bear likes fish.) Point to the words on the branch chart on the board as you slowly say them, forming the sentence.

28. Write the sentence on your "lined paper" on the board.

29. Say: "Copy the sentence on the third line of your paper."

    When students become familiar with this process, they may choose any of the three words to make a sentence.

30. Say: "Now we will read our sentences aloud." Group students in pairs to read to each other, or let each child read aloud to you, an aide, or the whole class.

31. Praise students and pass out reinforcers.

32. Say: "Now we will draw a picture to go with our sentences." Lead students to read the first sentence and then draw a picture of it. Do this for each sentence, one sentence at a time at first. Monitor the drawings and try to limit them to drawing

only one bear. If a higher-functioning child is drawing three bears, clearly intending one bear for each sentence, without exhibiting difficulties, then that is okay. Later in the program, they may be able to remember two or three details at once and incorporate them all into one bear picture.

The illustration must reflect the information in the sentence. If you see an illustration of a bear not eating fish, ask the student to read the corresponding sentence again. Then show the student what's missing. ("Your sentence says, 'The bear likes fish.' Your picture of the bear does not have a fish. Draw the bear eating a fish.")

33. Collect papers and pencils, praise students, and pass out reinforcers.

THE
MOUSE

Get the free print PDF of the mouse photo and this page at http://fhautism.com/arc.html.

Name_____ Date _____

The _____ mouse is on the _____ cat.

The mouse is eating cheese. The cat feels angry.

1. What color is the mouse?

_____

2. What color is the cat?

_____

THE MOUSE —Worksheet 7, Blank

3. Where is the mouse?

_____

4. What is the mouse eating?

_____

5. How does the cat feel?

_____

THE MOUSE —Worksheet 7, Blank

THE MOUSE
Worksheet 7, Variation 1

Materials:

Worksheet 7 (Variation 1), pencils, and boxes of crayons for each child

Color Variation 1:

Gray Mouse
Black Cat

Before the Lesson:

At http://fhautism.com/arc.html, find Worksheet 7 (Variation 1). Print one for each student, plus a few extras. Write the date on the board.

Teaching the Lesson

1. Distribute the worksheets and pencils to your students. Say: "Write your name on your paper." Make sure everyone writes his or her name. Then say: "Write the date. It is on the board." Make sure everyone writes the date. Take the pencils from them.

2. Say: "(student's name), please read the sentences at the top of the paper." Ask several students to read. If no one can read the passage, read it yourself, or have an aide read it.

3. Say: "We want to color the picture. What two crayons do we need?" Ask the question several times, and allow different children to answer. Then help them find the gray and black crayons. Take the crayon boxes from them.

4. Say: "We will color the mouse gray and the cat black. What color do we color the mouse?" Ask the question several times, and allow different children to answer.

5. Say: "Color the mouse." Make sure they color only the mouse. Repeat the words "gray mouse" as often as possible.

6. Say: "What color do we color the cat? Let's look back at our story if we need a reminder." Ask the question several times, and allow different children to answer.

7. Say: "Color the cat." Make sure they color only the cat. Repeat the words "black cat" as often as possible. Then take the crayons.

8. Ask comprehension questions. Lead students to answer orally, in a complete sentence. For each question, if the student answers incorrectly, guide him or her to read the text again. Questions: 1. What color is the mouse? 2. What color is the cat? 3. Where is the mouse? 4. What is the mouse eating? 5. How does the cat feel? Answers: 1. The mouse is gray. 2. The cat is black. 3. The mouse is on the cat. 4. The mouse is eating cheese. 5. The cat feels angry.

9. Ask the questions again in random order. Give each student a chance to answer correctly, in complete sentences.

10. Pass out pencils. Ask each comprehension question again. (See step 8 for questions and answers.) When a student answers correctly, write the sentence on the board. Say: "Copy the sentence onto your paper." Do this for each question and answer. Take pencils from them.

11. Pass out boxes of crayons. Say: "Choose one crayon." Make sure they choose only one. Take boxes of crayons from them. Then say: "Color the cheese." Make sure they color only the cheese. Take papers from them.

12. Give out reinforcers.

THE MOUSE
Worksheet 7, Variation 2

Materials:

Worksheet 7 (Variation 2), pencils, and boxes of crayons for each child

Color Variation 2:

Pink Mouse
Brown Cat

✔ ## Before the Lesson:

At http://fhautism.com/arc.html, find Worksheet 7 (Variation 2). Print one for each student, plus a few extras. Write the date on the board.

Teaching the Lesson

1. Distribute the worksheets and pencils to your students. Say: "Write your name on your paper." Make sure everyone writes his or her name. Then say: "Write the date. It is on the board." Make sure everyone writes the date. Take the pencils from them.

2. Say: "(student's name), please read the sentences at the top of the paper." Ask several students to read. If no one can read the passage, read it yourself, or have an aide read it.

3. Say: "We want to color the picture. What two crayons do we need?" Ask the question several times, and allow different children to answer. Then help them find the pink and brown crayons. Take the crayon boxes from them.

4. Say: "We will color the mouse pink and the cat brown. What color do we color the mouse?" Ask the question several times, and allow different children to answer.

5. Say: "Color the mouse." Make sure they color only the mouse. Repeat the words "pink mouse" as often as possible.

6. Say: "What color do we color the cat? Let's look back at our story if we need a reminder." Ask the question several times, and allow different children to answer.

7. Say: "Color the cat." Make sure they color only the cat. Repeat the words "brown cat" as often as possible. Then take the crayons.

8. Ask comprehension questions. Lead students to answer orally, in a complete sentence. For each question, if the student answers incorrectly, guide him or her to read the text again. Questions: 1. What color is the mouse? 2. What color is the cat? 3. Where is the mouse? 4. What is the mouse eating? 5. How does the cat feel? Answers: 1. The mouse is pink. 2. The cat is brown. 3. The mouse is on the cat. 4. The mouse is eating cheese. 5. The cat feels angry.

9. Ask the questions again in random order. Give each student a chance to answer correctly, in complete sentences.

10. Pass out pencils. Ask each comprehension question again. (See step 8 for questions and answers.) When a student answers correctly, write the sentence on the board. Say: "Copy the sentence onto your paper." Do this for each question and answer. Take pencils from them.

11. Pass out boxes of crayons. Say: "Choose one crayon." Make sure they choose only one. Take boxes of crayons from them. Then say: "Color the cheese." Make sure they color only the cheese. Take papers from them.

12. Give out reinforcers.

THE MOUSE
Worksheet 7, Variation 3

Materials:

Worksheet 7 (Variation 3), pencils, and boxes of crayons for each child

Color Variation 3:

Black Mouse
Orange Cat

Before the Lesson:

At http://fhautism.com/arc.html, find Worksheet 7 (Variation 3). Print one for each student, plus a few extras. Write the date on the board.

Teaching the Lesson

1. Distribute the worksheets and pencils to your students. Say: "Write your name on your paper." Make sure everyone writes his or her name. Then say: "Write the date. It is on the board." Make sure everyone writes the date. Take the pencils from them.

2. Say: "(student's name), please read the sentences at the top of the paper." Ask several students to read. If no one can read the passage, read it yourself, or have an aide read it.

3. Say: "We want to color the picture. What two crayons do we need?" Ask the question several times, and allow different children to answer. Then help them find the black and orange crayons. Take the crayon boxes from them.

4. Say: "We will color the mouse black and the cat orange. What color do we color the mouse?" Ask the question several times, and allow different children to answer.

5. Say: "Color the mouse." Make sure they color only the mouse. Repeat the words "black mouse" as often as possible.

6. Say: "What color do we color the cat? Let's look back at our story if we need a reminder." Ask the question several times, and allow different children to answer.

7. Say: "Color the cat." Make sure they color only the cat. Repeat the words "orange cat" as often as possible. Then take the crayons.

8. Ask comprehension questions. Lead students to answer orally, in a complete sentence. For each question, if the student answers incorrectly, guide him or her to read the text again. Questions: 1. What color is the mouse? 2. What color is the cat? 3. Where is the mouse? 4. What is the mouse eating? 5. How does the cat feel? Answers: 1. The mouse is black. 2. The cat is orange. 3. The mouse is on the cat. 4. The mouse is eating cheese. 5. The cat feels angry.

9. Ask the questions again in random order. Give each student a chance to answer correctly, in complete sentences.

10. Pass out pencils. Ask each comprehension question again. (See step 8 for questions and answers.) When a student answers correctly, write the sentence on the board. Say: "Copy the sentence onto your paper." Do this for each question and answer. Take pencils from them.

11. Pass out boxes of crayons. Say: "Choose one crayon." Make sure they choose only one. Take boxes of crayons from them. Then say: "Color the cheese." Make sure they color only the cheese. Take papers from them.

12. Give out reinforcers.

THE MOUSE
Worksheet 7, Variation 4

Materials:

Worksheet 7 (Variation 4), pencils, and boxes of crayons for each child

Color Variation 4:

Brown Mouse
Yellow Cat

Before the Lesson:

At http://fhautism.com/arc.html, find Worksheet 7 (Variation 4). Print one for each student, plus a few extras. Write the date on the board.

Teaching the Lesson

1. Distribute the worksheets and pencils to your students. Say: "Write your name on your paper." Make sure everyone writes his or her name. Then say: "Write the date. It is on the board." Make sure everyone writes the date. Take the pencils from them.

2. Say: "(student's name), please read the sentences at the top of the paper." Ask several students to read. If no one can read the passage, read it yourself, or have an aide read it.

3. Say: "We want to color the picture. What two crayons do we need?" Ask the question several times, and allow different children to answer. Then help them find the brown and yellow crayons. Take the crayon boxes from them.

4. Say: "We will color the mouse brown and the cat yellow. What color do we color the mouse?" Ask the question several times, and allow different children to answer.

5. Say: "Color the mouse." Make sure they color only the mouse. Repeat the words "brown mouse" as often as possible.

6. Say: "What color do we color the cat? Let's look back at our story if we need a reminder." Ask the question several times, and allow different children to answer.

7. Say: "Color the cat." Make sure they color only the cat. Repeat the words "yellow cat" as often as possible. Then take the crayons.

8. Ask comprehension questions. Lead students to answer orally, in a complete sentence. For each question, if the student answers incorrectly, guide him or her to read the text again. Questions: 1. What color is the mouse? 2. What color is the cat? 3. Where is the mouse? 4. What is the mouse eating? 5. How does the cat feel? Answers: 1. The mouse is brown. 2. The cat is yellow. 3. The mouse is on the cat. 4. The mouse is eating cheese. 5. The cat feels angry.

9. Ask the questions again in random order. Give each student a chance to answer correctly, in complete sentences.

10. Pass out pencils. Ask each comprehension question again. (See step 8 for questions and answers.) When a student answers correctly, write the sentence on the board. Say: "Copy the sentence onto your paper." Do this for each question and answer. Take pencils from them.

11. Pass out boxes of crayons. Say: "Choose one crayon." Make sure they choose only one. Take boxes of crayons from them. Then say: "Color the cheese." Make sure they color only the cheese. Take papers from them.

12. Give out reinforcers.

THE MOUSE
Sentence-Building Exercise 1

Materials:

photograph of mouse, students' circle-in-circle charts and branch organizers, lined paper, tape, three pieces of chart paper, dry-erase marker, watercolor marker

Before the Lesson:

1. At http://fhautism.com/arc.html, find the circle-in-circle chart, branch organizer, and lined paper. Print one of each for each student, plus a few extras.

2. On the chart paper, draw a blank circle-in-circle chart, branch organizer, and lined paper.

3. On the board, hang a blank circle-in-circle chart on the left and a branch organizer on the right. Make them large enough to write all the words you will need.

4. Write the date on the board.

Teaching the Lesson

1. Gather the children in a circle. Hold up the photograph of the mouse. Ask: "What animal is this?" If no one can identify the animal, ask an aide to answer, or answer the question yourself.

2. When a student says, "mouse," write "mouse" in the smaller, inner circle of the circle-in-circle chart.

   If you wish, you can allow the students to start the conversation. They've had plenty of practice now, and they might give creative responses if given time to think.

3. If no one spontaneously offers any observations, ask: "What can the mouse do?" If no one answers, prompt the students. Ask: "Can the mouse fly?" If no one answers, ask an aide to answer, or answer the question yourself. Possible answers include run, jump, chew. Students may come up with different answers. Ask the question several

times, and allow different children to answer. Write the answers in the large circle. Leave space between the words.

4. Ask: "What does the mouse have? If no one answers, prompt the students. Ask: "Does a mouse have feathers?" This question should be repeated every time the animal in question has either fur or feathers. Other good questions: "Does the mouse have four eyes?" "Does the mouse have wings?" If no one answers, ask an aide to answer, or answer the question yourself. Possible answers include a long tail, two ears, teeth. Students may come up with different answers. Ask the question several times, and allow different children to answer. Write the answers in the large circle.

5. Ask: "What does the mouse like? If no one answers, prompt the students with a guessing game. Say: "The mouse likes to eat this yellow food. We like to put it on sandwiches or crackers. Different types of this food are cheddar and Swiss. I like to eat a sandwich made of ham and ... ." Do this for the other two answers. If no one answers, ask an aide to answer, or answer the question yourself. Possible answers include cheese, fruit, seeds. Students may come up with different answers. Ask the question several times, and allow different children to answer. Write the answers in the large circle. NOTE: Guessing games may be stressful for some children. If students appear to be getting agitated or panicky, just tell them the answer. The lesson is more important than the game.

6. Praise students and pass out reinforcers.

7. The children return to their desks. Pass out pencils and blank graphic organizers. On each desk, tape the circle-in-circle chart on the left and the branch organizer on the right. (Always emphasize a left-to-right progression when teaching reading and writing.)

8. Say: "Write your name on your paper." Make sure everyone writes his or her name. Then say: "Write the date. It is on the board." Make sure everyone writes the date.

9. Say: "Copy the words from the circle-in-circle chart on the board onto your circle-in-circle chart." They do not have to copy all of the words at first.

10. Say: "Now we will do the branch organizer." On the branch organizer on the board, write "Mouse" on the top line and "Can," "Has," and "Likes" on the three spaces under the top line. Say: "Copy the words onto your charts."

11. Ask: "What can the mouse do?" Point to the words on the circle-in-circle chart. Encourage students to look at their own chart. If no one answers, ask an aide to answer, or answer the question yourself. Ask the question several times, and allow different children to answer.

If someone uses a nonsensical word, e.g., "cheese," say the whole sentence. Say: "The mouse can cheese? Does that make sense? Let's look back in the circle and find something the mouse can do."

12. Write students' answers on the branch organizer on the board. For each answer, say: "Write (the answer) under the word 'Can' on your branch organizer."

As you use words from the circle-in-circle chart, you may choose to cover up the words with a sticky note or leave them all showing.

13. For each word that students write, say the whole sentence, e.g., "The mouse can jump." As you say each word of the sentence, point to the corresponding word on the branch chart.

14. Ask: "What does the mouse have?" Point to the words on the circle-in-circle chart. If no one answers, ask an aide to answer, or answer the question yourself. Ask the question several times, and allow different children to answer.

If someone uses a nonsensical word, e.g., "jump," say the whole sentence. Say: "The mouse has jump? Does that make sense? Let's look back in the circle and find something the mouse has."

15. Write students' answers on the branch organizer on the board. For each answer, say: "Write (the answer) under the word 'Has' on your branch organizer."

16. For each word that students write, say the whole sentence, e.g., "The mouse has teeth." As you say each word of the sentence, point to the corresponding word on the branch chart.

17. Ask: "What does the mouse like?" Point to the words on the circle-in-circle chart. If no one answers, ask an aide to answer, or answer the question yourself. Ask the question several times, and allow different children to answer.

If someone uses a nonsensical word, e.g., "teeth," say the whole sentence. Say:

"The mouse likes teeth? Does that make sense? Let's look back in the circle and find something the mouse likes."

18. Write students' answers on the branch organizer on the board. For each answer, say: "Write (the answer) under the word 'Likes' on your branch organizer."

19. For each word that students write, say the whole sentence, e.g., "The mouse likes cheese." As you say each word of the sentence, point to the corresponding word on the branch chart.

20. Praise students, pass out reinforcers, and take a short break.

21. Draw a large version of the lined paper on your chart paper, using the watercolor marker. Tape the chart paper to the board. Pass out the lined paper. Tape one to each desk, next to the branch organizer.

22. Say: "It's time to make a sentence. Let's make a sentence from the first column of the branch organizer, using the word 'Can.'" (Example sentence: The mouse can jump.) Point to the words on the branch chart on the board as you slowly say them, forming the sentence.

23. Write the sentence on your "lined paper" on the board.

24. Say: "Copy the sentence on the first line of your paper."

25. Say: "Let's make a sentence from the second column of the branch organizer, using the word 'Has.'" (Example sentence: The mouse has teeth.) Point to the words on the branch chart on the board as you slowly say them, forming the sentence.

26. Write the sentence on your "lined paper" on the board.

27. Say: "Copy the sentence on the second line of your paper." Make sure they write on the lines and not in the blank space above.

28. Say: "Let's make a sentence from the third column of the branch organizer, using the word 'Likes.'" (Example sentence: The mouse likes cheese.) Point to the words on the branch chart on the board as you slowly say them, forming the sentence.

29. Write the sentence on your "lined paper" on the board.

30. Say: "Copy the sentence on the third line of your paper."

When students become familiar with this process, they may choose any of the three words to make a sentence.

31. Say: "Now we will read our sentences aloud." Group students in pairs to read to each other, or let each child read aloud to you, an aide, or the whole class.

32. Praise students and pass out reinforcers.

33. Say: "Now we will draw a picture to go with our sentences." Lead students to read the first sentence and then draw a picture of it. Do this for each sentence, one sentence at a time at first. Monitor the drawings and try to limit them to drawing only one mouse. If a higher-functioning child is drawing three mice, clearly intending one mouse for each sentence, without exhibiting difficulties, then that is okay. Later in the program, they may be able to remember two or three details at once and incorporate them all into one mouse picture.

The illustration must reflect the information in the sentence. If you see an illustration of a mouse missing teeth or not eating cheese, ask the student to read the corresponding sentence again. Then show the student what's missing. ("Your sentence says, 'The mouse has teeth.' Your picture of the mouse does not have teeth. Draw teeth on the mouse.")

34. Collect papers and pencils, praise students, and pass out reinforcers.

Name_____   Date _____

The _____ mouse is running away from the cat. The mouse has

four legs and a long tail. The cat is _____. The mouse is jumping

over the ball. The ball is _____.

1. What color is the mouse?

_____

2. Does the mouse have a short tail or long tail?

_____

THE MOUSE —Worksheet 8, Blank

AUTISM & READING COMPREHENSION
© 2011 by Joseph Porter, M.Ed. Future Horizons, Inc.

3. What color is the cat?

_____

4. What is the mouse jumping over?

_____

5. What color is the ball?

_____

THE MOUSE —Worksheet 8, Blank

THE MOUSE
Worksheet 8, Variation 1

Materials:

Worksheet 8 (Variation 1), pencils, and boxes of crayons for each child

Color Variation 1:

Brown Mouse
Orange Cat
Yellow Ball

Before the Lesson:

At http://fhautism.com/arc.html, find Worksheet 8 (Variation 1). Print one for each student, plus a few extras. Write the date on the board.

Teaching the Lesson

1. Distribute the worksheets and pencils to your students. Say: "Write your name on your paper." Make sure everyone writes his or her name. Then say: "Write the date. It is on the board." Make sure everyone writes the date. Take the pencils from them.

2. Say: "(student's name), please read the sentences at the top of the paper." Ask several students to read. If no one can read the passage, read it yourself, or have an aide read it.

3. Say: "We want to color the picture. What three crayons do we need?" Ask the question several times, and allow different children to answer. Then help them find the brown, orange, and yellow crayons. Take the crayon boxes from them.

4. Say: "We will color the mouse brown, the cat orange, and the ball yellow. What color do we color the mouse?" Ask the question several times, and allow different children to answer.

5. Say: "Color the mouse." Make sure they color only the mouse. Repeat the words "brown mouse" as often as possible.

6. Say: "What color do we color the cat? Let's look back at our story if we need a reminder." Ask the question several times, and allow different children to answer.

7. Say: "Color the cat." Make sure they color only the cat. Repeat the words "orange cat" as often as possible.

8. Say: "What color do we color the ball? Let's look back at our story if we need a reminder." Ask the question several times, and allow different children to answer.

9. Say: "Color the ball." Make sure they color only the ball. Repeat the words "yellow ball" as often as possible. Then take the crayons.

10. Ask comprehension questions. Lead students to answer orally, in a complete sentence. For each question, if the student answers incorrectly, guide him or her to read the text again. Questions: 1. What color is the mouse? 2. Does the mouse have a short tail or a long tail? 3. What color is the cat? 4. What is the mouse jumping over? 5. What color is the ball? Answers: 1. The mouse is brown. 2. The mouse has a long tail. 3. The cat is orange. 4. The mouse is jumping over the ball. 5. The ball is yellow.

11. Ask the questions again in random order. Give each student a chance to answer correctly, in complete sentences.

12. Pass out pencils. Ask each comprehension question again. (See step 10 for questions and answers.) When a student answers correctly, write the sentence on the board. Say: "Copy the sentence onto your paper." Do this for each question and answer. Take pencils from them.

13. Give out reinforcers.

THE MOUSE
Worksheet 8, Variation 2

Materials:

Worksheet 8 (Variation 2), pencils, and boxes of crayons for each child

Color
Variation 2:

Black Mouse
Yellow Cat
Orange Ball

Before the Lesson:

At http://fhautism.com/arc.html, find Worksheet 8 (Variation 2). Print one for each student, plus a few extras. Write the date on the board.

Teaching the Lesson

1. Distribute the worksheets and pencils to your students. Say: "Write your name on your paper." Make sure everyone writes his or her name. Then say: "Write the date. It is on the board." Make sure everyone writes the date. Take the pencils from them.

2. Say: "(student's name), please read the sentences at the top of the paper." Ask several students to read. If no one can read the passage, read it yourself, or have an aide read it.

3. Say: "We want to color the picture. What three crayons do we need?" Ask the question several times, and allow different children to answer. Then help them find the black, yellow, and orange crayons. Take the crayon boxes from them.

4. Say: "We will color the mouse black, the cat yellow, and the ball orange. What color do we color the mouse?" Ask the question several times, and allow different children to answer.

5. Say: "Color the mouse." Make sure they color only the mouse. Repeat the words "black mouse" as often as possible.

6. Say: "What color do we color the cat? Let's look back at our story if we need a reminder." Ask the question several times, and allow different children to answer.

7. Say: "Color the cat." Make sure they color only the cat. Repeat the words "yellow cat" as often as possible.

8. Say: "What color do we color the ball? Let's look back at our story if we need a reminder." Ask the question several times, and allow different children to answer.

9. Say: "Color the ball." Make sure they color only the ball. Repeat the words "orange ball" as often as possible. Then take the crayons.

10. Ask comprehension questions. Lead students to answer orally, in a complete sentence. For each question, if the student answers incorrectly, guide him or her to read the text again. Questions: 1. What color is the mouse? 2. Does the mouse have a short tail or a long tail? 3. What color is the cat? 4. What is the mouse jumping over? 5. What color is the ball? Answers: 1. The mouse is black. 2. The mouse has a long tail. 3. The cat is yellow. 4. The mouse is jumping over the ball. 5. The ball is orange.

11. Ask the questions again in random order. Give each student a chance to answer correctly, in complete sentences.

12. Pass out pencils. Ask each comprehension question again. (See step 10 for questions and answers.) When a student answers correctly, write the sentence on the board. Say: "Copy the sentence onto your paper." Do this for each question and answer. Take pencils from them.

13. Give out reinforcers.

AUTISM & READING COMPREHENSION
© 2011 by Joseph Porter, M.Ed. Future Horizons, Inc.

THE MOUSE
Worksheet 8, Variation 3

Materials:
Worksheet 8 (Variation 3), pencils, and boxes of crayons for each child

Color Variation 3:

Gray Mouse
Black Cat
Purple Ball

Before the Lesson:
At http://fhautism.com/arc.html, find Worksheet 8 (Variation 3). Print one for each student, plus a few extras. Write the date on the board.

Teaching the Lesson

1. Distribute the worksheets and pencils to your students. Say: "Write your name on your paper." Make sure everyone writes his or her name. Then say: "Write the date. It is on the board." Make sure everyone writes the date. Take the pencils from them.

2. Say: "(student's name), please read the sentences at the top of the paper." Ask several students to read. If no one can read the passage, read it yourself, or have an aide read it.

3. Say: "We want to color the picture. What three crayons do we need?" Ask the question several times, and allow different children to answer. Then help them find the gray, black, and purple crayons. Take the crayon boxes from them.

4. Say: "We will color the mouse gray, the cat black, and the ball purple. What color do we color the mouse?" Ask the question several times, and allow different children to answer.

5. Say: "Color the mouse." Make sure they color only the mouse. Repeat the words "gray mouse" as often as possible.

6. Say: "What color do we color the cat? Let's look back at our story if we need a reminder." Ask the question several times, and allow different children to answer.

7. Say: "Color the cat." Make sure they color only the cat. Repeat the words "black cat" as often as possible.

8. Say: "What color do we color the ball? Let's look back at our story if we need a reminder." Ask the question several times, and allow different children to answer.

9. Say: "Color the ball." Make sure they color only the ball. Repeat the words "purple ball" as often as possible. Then take the crayons.

10. Ask comprehension questions. Lead students to answer orally, in a complete sentence. For each question, if the student answers incorrectly, guide him or her to read the text again. Questions: 1. What color is the mouse? 2. Does the mouse have a short tail or a long tail? 3. What color is the cat? 4. What is the mouse jumping over? 5. What color is the ball? Answers: 1. The mouse is gray. 2. The mouse has a long tail. 3. The cat is black. 4. The mouse is jumping over the ball. 5. The ball is purple.

11. Ask the questions again in random order. Give each student a chance to answer correctly, in complete sentences.

12. Pass out pencils. Ask each comprehension question again. (See step 10 for questions and answers.) When a student answers correctly, write the sentence on the board. Say: "Copy the sentence onto your paper." Do this for each question and answer. Take pencils from them.

13. Give out reinforcers.

THE MOUSE
Worksheet 8, Variation 4

Materials:

Worksheet 8 (Variation 4), pencils, and boxes of crayons for each child

Color Variation 4:

Pink Mouse
Brown Cat
Green Ball

Before the Lesson:

At http://fhautism.com/arc.html, find Worksheet 8 (Variation 4). Print one for each student, plus a few extras. Write the date on the board.

Teaching the Lesson

1. Distribute the worksheets and pencils to your students. Say: "Write your name on your paper." Make sure everyone writes his or her name. Then say: "Write the date. It is on the board." Make sure everyone writes the date. Take the pencils from them.

2. Say: "(student's name), please read the sentences at the top of the paper." Ask several students to read. If no one can read the passage, read it yourself, or have an aide read it.

3. Say: "We want to color the picture. What three crayons do we need?" Ask the question several times, and allow different children to answer. Then help them find the pink, brown, and green crayons. Take the crayon boxes from them.

4. Say: "We will color the mouse pink, the cat brown, and the ball green. What color do we color the mouse?" Ask the question several times, and allow different children to answer.

5. Say: "Color the mouse." Make sure they color only the mouse. Repeat the words "pink mouse" as often as possible.

6. Say: "What color do we color the cat? Let's look back at our story if we need a reminder." Ask the question several times, and allow different children to answer.

7. Say: "Color the cat." Make sure they color only the cat. Repeat the words "brown cat" as often as possible.

8. Say: "What color do we color the ball? Let's look back at our story if we need a reminder." Ask the question several times, and allow different children to answer.

9. Say: "Color the ball." Make sure they color only the ball. Repeat the words "green ball" as often as possible. Then take the crayons.

10. Ask comprehension questions. Lead students to answer orally, in a complete sentence. For each question, if the student answers incorrectly, guide him or her to read the text again. Questions: 1. What color is the mouse? 2. Does the mouse have a short tail or a long tail? 3. What color is the cat? 4. What is the mouse jumping over? 5. What color is the ball? Answers: 1. The mouse is pink. 2. The mouse has a long tail. 3. The cat is brown. 4. The mouse is jumping over the ball. 5. The ball is green.

11. Ask the questions again in random order. Give each student a chance to answer correctly, in complete sentences.

12. Pass out pencils. Ask each comprehension question again. (See step 10 for questions and answers.) When a student answers correctly, write the sentence on the board. Say: "Copy the sentence onto your paper." Do this for each question and answer. Take pencils from them.

13. Give out reinforcers.

THE MOUSE
Sentence-Building Exercise 2

Materials:

photograph of mouse, students' circle-in-circle charts and branch organizers, lined paper, tape, completed circle-in-circle chart on chart paper (from Lesson 35 sentence-building exercise), two pieces of blank chart paper, dry-erase marker, watercolor marker

Before the Lesson:

1. At http://fhautism.com/arc.html, find the circle-in-circle chart, branch organizer, and lined paper. Print one of each for each student, plus a few extras.

2. On the blank chart paper, draw the lined paper and branch organizer.

3. On the board, hang the completed circle-in-circle chart on chart paper (from Lesson 35 sentence-building exercise) and blank branch organizer.

4. Write the date on the board.

Teaching the Lesson

1. Gather the children in a circle. Hold up the photograph of the mouse. Ask: "What animal is this?" If no one can identify the animal, ask an aide to answer, or answer the question yourself.

2. Ask: "What can the mouse do?" If no one answers, prompt the students to look at the circle-in-circle chart on the board. If no one answers, ask an aide to answer, or answer the question yourself. Possible answers include run, jump, chew. Students may come up with different answers. Ask the question several times, and allow different children to answer.

3. Ask: "What does the mouse have? If no one answers, prompt the students to look at the circle-in-circle chart on the board. If no one answers, ask an aide to answer, or answer the question yourself. Possible answers include a long tail, two ears, teeth.

Students may come up with different answers. Ask the question several times, and allow different children to answer.

4. Ask: "What does the mouse like? If no one answers, prompt the students to look at the circle-in-circle chart on the board. If no one answers, ask an aide to answer, or answer the question yourself. Possible answers include cheese, fruit, seeds. Students may come up with different answers. Ask the question several times, and allow different children to answer.

5. Praise students and pass out reinforcers.

6. The children return to their desks. Pass out pencils and blank graphic organizers. On each desk, tape a circle-in-circle chart on the left and the branch organizer on the right.

7. Say: "Write your name on your paper." Make sure everyone writes his or her name. Then say: "Write the date. It is on the board." Make sure everyone writes the date.

8. Say: "Copy the words from the circle-in-circle chart on the board onto your circle-in-circle chart." They do not have to copy all of the words at first.

9. Say: "Now we will do the branch organizer." On the branch organizer on the board, write "Mouse" on the top line and "Can," "Has," and "Likes" on the three spaces under the top line. Say: "Copy the words onto your charts."

10. Ask: "What can the mouse do?" Point to the words on the circle-in-circle chart. Encourage students to look at their own chart. If no one answers, ask an aide to answer, or answer the question yourself. Ask the question several times, and allow different children to answer.

    If someone uses a nonsensical word, e.g., "seeds," say the whole sentence. Say: "The mouse can seeds? Does that make sense? Let's look back in the circle and find something the mouse can do."

11. Write students' answers on the branch organizer on the board. For each answer, say: "Write (the answer) under the word 'Can' on your branch organizer."

    As you use words from the circle-in-circle chart, you may choose to cover up the words with a sticky note or leave them all showing.

AUTISM & READING COMPREHENSION
© 2011 by Joseph Porter, M.Ed. Future Horizons, Inc.

12. For each word that students write, say the whole sentence, e.g., "The mouse can chew." As you say each word of the sentence, point to the corresponding word on the branch chart.

13. Ask: "What does the mouse have?" Point to the words on the circle-in-circle chart. If no one answers, ask an aide to answer, or answer the question yourself. Ask the question several times, and allow different children to answer.

If someone uses a nonsensical word, e.g., "chew," say the whole sentence. Say: "The mouse has chew? Does that make sense? Let's look back in the circle and find something the mouse has."

14. Write students' answers on the branch chart. For each answer, say: "Write (the answer) under the word 'Has' on your branch organizer."

15. For each word that students write, say the whole sentence, e.g., "The mouse has a long tail." As you say each word of the sentence, point to the corresponding word on the branch chart.

16. Ask: "What does the mouse like?" Point to the words on the circle-in-circle chart. If no one answers, ask an aide to answer, or answer the question yourself. Ask the question several times, and allow different children to answer.

If someone uses nonsensical words, e.g., "a long tail," say the whole sentence. Say: "The mouse likes a long tail? Does that make sense? Let's look back in the circle and find something the mouse likes."

17. Write students' answers on the branch organizer on the board. For each answer, say: "Write (the answer) under the word 'Likes' on your branch organizer."

18. For each word that students write, say the whole sentence, e.g., "The mouse likes seeds." As you say each word of the sentence, point to the corresponding word on the branch chart.

19. Praise students, pass out reinforcers, and take a short break.

20. Draw a large version of the lined paper on your chart paper, using the watercolor marker. Tape the chart paper to the board. Pass out the lined paper. Tape one to each desk, next to the branch organizer.

21. Say: "It's time to make a sentence. Let's make a sentence from the first column of the branch organizer, using the word 'Can.'" (Example sentence: The mouse can chew.) Point to the words on the branch chart on the board as you slowly say them, forming the sentence.

    Lead students to make different sentences than they did in the first sentence-building exercise.

22. Write the sentence on your "lined paper" on the board.

23. Say: "Copy the sentence on the first line of your paper."

24. Say: "Let's make a sentence from the second column of the branch organizer, using the word 'Has.'" (Example sentence: The mouse has a long tail.) Point to the words on the branch chart on the board as you slowly say them, forming the sentence.

25. Write the sentence on your "lined paper" on the board.

26. Say: "Copy the sentence on the second line of your paper." Make sure they write on the lines and not in the blank space above.

27. Say: "Let's make a sentence from the third column of the branch organizer, using the word 'Likes.'" (Example sentence: The mouse likes seeds.) Point to the words on the branch chart on the board as you slowly say them, forming the sentence.

28. Write the sentence on your "lined paper" on the board.

29. Say: "Copy the sentence on the third line of your paper."

    When students become familiar with this process, they may choose any of the three words to make a sentence.

30. Say: "Now we will read our sentences aloud." Group students in pairs to read to each other, or let each child read aloud to you, an aide, or the whole class.

31. Praise students and pass out reinforcers.

32. Say: "Now we will draw a picture to go with our sentences." Lead students to read the first sentence and then draw a picture of it. Do this for each sentence, one sentence at a time at first. Monitor the drawings and try to limit them to drawing only one mouse. If a higher-functioning child is drawing three mice, clearly intending

one mouse for each sentence, without exhibiting difficulties, then that is okay. Later in the program, they may be able to remember two or three details at once and incorporate them all into one mouse picture.

Students might be tempted to draw the same picture as in the first sentence-building exercise. Keep students connected to the meaning of the words. If you see an illustration of a mouse not eating seeds, ask the student to read the corresponding sentence again. Then show the student what's missing. ("Your sentence says, 'The mouse likes seeds.' Your picture of the mouse does not have seeds. Draw the mouse eating seeds.")

33. Collect papers and pencils, praise students, and pass out reinforcers.

THE MONKEY

Get the free print PDF of the monkey photo and this page at http://fhautism.com/arc.html.

Name_____ Date _____

The _____ monkey is outside the cage. He is eating a banana.

The zookeeper is inside the cage. He is wearing a _____ jacket.

The zookeeper feels angry.

1. Where is the monkey?

_____

2. What color is the monkey?

_____

THE MONKEY —Worksheet 9, Blank

AUTISM & READING COMPREHENSION
© 2011 by Joseph Porter, M.Ed. Future Horizons, Inc.

3. What is the monkey eating?

_____

4. Where is the zookeeper?

_____

5. What color is the zookeeper's jacket?

_____

6. How does the zookeeper feel?

_____

THE MONKEY —Worksheet 9, Blank

THE MONKEY
Worksheet 9, Variation 1

Materials:
Worksheet 9 (Variation 1), pencils, and boxes of crayons for each child

Color Variation 1:

Black Monkey
Orange Jacket

✓ ## Before the Lesson:
At http://fhautism.com/arc.html, find Worksheet 9 (Variation 1). Print one for each student, plus a few extras. Write the date on the board.

Teaching the Lesson

1. Distribute the worksheets and pencils to your students. Say: "Write your name on your paper." Make sure everyone writes his or her name. Then say: "Write the date. It is on the board." Make sure everyone writes the date. Take the pencils from them.

2. Say: "(student's name), please read the sentences at the top of the paper." Ask several students to read. If no one can read the passage, read it yourself, or have an aide read it.

3. Say: "We want to color the picture. What two crayons do we need?" Ask the question several times, and allow different children to answer. Then help them find the black and orange crayons. Take the crayon boxes from them.

4. Say: "We will color the monkey black and the jacket orange. What color do we color the monkey?" Ask the question several times, and allow different children to answer.

5. Say: "Color the monkey." Make sure they color only the monkey. Repeat the words "black monkey" as often as possible.

6. Say: "What color do we color the jacket? Let's look back at our story if we need a reminder." Ask the question several times, and allow different children to answer.

7. Say: "Color the jacket." Make sure they color only the jacket. Repeat the words "orange jacket" as often as possible. Then take the crayons.

8. Ask comprehension questions. Lead students to answer orally, in a complete sentence. For each question, if the student answers incorrectly, guide him or her to read the text again. Questions: 1. Where is the monkey? 2. What color is the monkey? 3. What is the monkey eating? 4. Where is the zookeeper? 5. What color is the zookeeper's jacket? 6. How does the zookeeper feel? Answers: 1. The monkey is outside the cage. 2. The monkey is black. 3. The monkey is eating a banana. 4. The zookeeper is inside the cage. 5. The zookeeper is wearing an orange jacket. 6. The zookeeper feels angry.

9. Ask the questions again in random order. Give each student a chance to answer correctly, in complete sentences.

10. Pass out pencils. Ask each comprehension question again. (See step 8 for questions and answers.) When a student answers correctly, write the sentence on the board. Say: "Copy the sentence onto your paper." Do this for each question and answer. Take pencils from them.

11. Pass out boxes of crayons. Say: "Choose one crayon." Make sure they choose only one. Take boxes of crayons from them. Then say: "Color the zookeeper." Make sure they color only the zookeeper. Take papers from them.

12. Give out reinforcers.

THE MONKEY
Worksheet 9, Variation 2

Materials:

Worksheet 9 (Variation 2), pencils, and boxes of crayons for each child

Color Variation 2:

Brown Monkey
Red Jacket

Before the Lesson:

At http://fhautism.com/arc.html, find Worksheet 9 (Variation 2). Print one for each student, plus a few extras. Write the date on the board.

Teaching the Lesson

1. Distribute the worksheets and pencils to your students. Say: "Write your name on your paper." Make sure everyone writes his or her name. Then say: "Write the date. It is on the board." Make sure everyone writes the date. Take the pencils from them.

2. Say: "(student's name), please read the sentences at the top of the paper." Ask several students to read. If no one can read the passage, read it yourself, or have an aide read it.

3. Say: "We want to color the picture. What two crayons do we need?" Ask the question several times, and allow different children to answer. Then help them find the brown and red crayons. Take the crayon boxes from them.

4. Say: "We will color the monkey brown and the jacket red. What color do we color the monkey?" Ask the question several times, and allow different children to answer.

5. Say: "Color the monkey." Make sure they color only the monkey. Repeat the words "brown monkey" as often as possible.

6. Say: "What color do we color the jacket? Let's look back at our story if we need a reminder." Ask the question several times, and allow different children to answer.

7. Say: "Color the jacket." Make sure they color only the jacket. Repeat the words "red jacket" as often as possible. Then take the crayons.

8. Ask comprehension questions. Lead students to answer orally, in a complete sentence. For each question, if the student answers incorrectly, guide him or her to read the text again. Questions: 1. Where is the monkey? 2. What color is the monkey? 3. What is the monkey eating? 4. Where is the zookeeper? 5. What color is the zookeeper's jacket? 6. How does the zookeeper feel? Answers: 1. The monkey is outside the cage. 2. The monkey is brown. 3. The monkey is eating a banana. 4. The zookeeper is inside the cage. 5. The zookeeper is wearing a red jacket. 6. The zookeeper feels angry.

9. Ask the questions again in random order. Give each student a chance to answer correctly, in complete sentences.

10. Pass out pencils. Ask each comprehension question again. (See step 8 for questions and answers.) When a student answers correctly, write the sentence on the board. Say: "Copy the sentence onto your paper." Do this for each question and answer. Take pencils from them.

11. Pass out boxes of crayons. Say: "Choose one crayon." Make sure they choose only one. Take boxes of crayons from them. Then say: "Color the zookeeper." Make sure they color only the zookeeper. Take papers from them.

12. Give out reinforcers.

THE MONKEY
Worksheet 9, Variation 3

Materials:

Worksheet 9 (Variation 3), pencils, and boxes of crayons for each child

Color Variation 3:

Orange Monkey
Green Jacket

✔ Before the Lesson:

At http://fhautism.com/arc.html, find Worksheet 9 (Variation 3). Print one for each student, plus a few extras. Write the date on the board.

Teaching the Lesson

1. Distribute the worksheets and pencils to your students. Say: "Write your name on your paper." Make sure everyone writes his or her name. Then say: "Write the date. It is on the board." Make sure everyone writes the date. Take the pencils from them.

2. Say: "(student's name), please read the sentences at the top of the paper." Ask several students to read. If no one can read the passage, read it yourself, or have an aide read it.

3. Say: "We want to color the picture. What two crayons do we need?" Ask the question several times, and allow different children to answer. Then help them find the orange and green crayons. Take the crayon boxes from them.

4. Say: "We will color the monkey orange and the jacket green. What color do we color the monkey?" Ask the question several times, and allow different children to answer.

5. Say: "Color the monkey." Make sure they color only the monkey. Repeat the words "orange monkey" as often as possible.

6. Say: "What color do we color the jacket? Let's look back at our story if we need a reminder." Ask the question several times, and allow different children to answer.

7. Say: "Color the jacket." Make sure they color only the jacket. Repeat the words "green jacket" as often as possible. Then take the crayons.

8. Ask comprehension questions. Lead students to answer orally, in a complete sentence. For each question, if the student answers incorrectly, guide him or her to read the text again. Questions: 1. Where is the monkey? 2. What color is the monkey? 3. What is the monkey eating? 4. Where is the zookeeper? 5. What color is the zookeeper's jacket? 6. How does the zookeeper feel? Answers: 1. The monkey is outside the cage. 2. The monkey is orange. 3. The monkey is eating a banana. 4. The zookeeper is inside the cage. 5. The zookeeper is wearing a green jacket. 6. The zookeeper feels angry.

9. Ask the questions again in random order. Give each student a chance to answer correctly, in complete sentences.

10. Pass out pencils. Ask each comprehension question again. (See step 8 for questions and answers.) When a student answers correctly, write the sentence on the board. Say: "Copy the sentence onto your paper." Do this for each question and answer. Take pencils from them.

11. Pass out boxes of crayons. Say: "Choose one crayon." Make sure they choose only one. Take boxes of crayons from them. Then say: "Color the zookeeper." Make sure they color only the zookeeper. Take papers from them.

12. Give out reinforcers.

THE MONKEY
Worksheet 9, Variation 4

Materials:

Worksheet 9 (Variation 4), pencils, and boxes of crayons for each child

Color Variation 4:

Yellow Monkey
Blue Jacket

Before the Lesson:

At http://fhautism.com/arc.html, find Worksheet 9 (Variation 4). Print one for each student, plus a few extras. Write the date on the board.

Teaching the Lesson

1. Distribute the worksheets and pencils to your students. Say: "Write your name on your paper." Make sure everyone writes his or her name. Then say: "Write the date. It is on the board." Make sure everyone writes the date. Take the pencils from them.

2. Say: "(student's name), please read the sentences at the top of the paper." Ask several students to read. If no one can read the passage, read it yourself, or have an aide read it.

3. Say: "We want to color the picture. What two crayons do we need?" Ask the question several times, and allow different children to answer. Then help them find the yellow and blue crayons. Take the crayon boxes from them.

4. Say: "We will color the monkey yellow and the jacket blue. What color do we color the monkey?" Ask the question several times, and allow different children to answer.

5. Say: "Color the monkey." Make sure they color only the monkey. Repeat the words "yellow monkey" as often as possible.

6. Say: "What color do we color the jacket? Let's look back at our story if we need a reminder." Ask the question several times, and allow different children to answer.

7. Say: "Color the jacket." Make sure they color only the jacket. Repeat the words "blue jacket" as often as possible. Then take the crayons.

8. Ask comprehension questions. Lead students to answer orally, in a complete sentence. For each question, if the student answers incorrectly, guide him or her to read the text again. Questions: 1. Where is the monkey? 2. What color is the monkey? 3. What is the monkey eating? 4. Where is the zookeeper? 5. What color is the zookeeper's jacket? 6. How does the zookeeper feel? Answers: 1. The monkey is outside the cage. 2. The monkey is yellow. 3. The monkey is eating a banana. 4. The zookeeper is inside the cage. 5. The zookeeper is wearing a blue jacket. 6. The zookeeper feels angry.

9. Ask the questions again in random order. Give each student a chance to answer correctly, in complete sentences.

10. Pass out pencils. Ask each comprehension question again. (See step 8 for questions and answers.) When a student answers correctly, write the sentence on the board. Say: "Copy the sentence onto your paper." Do this for each question and answer. Take pencils from them.

11. Pass out boxes of crayons. Say: "Choose one crayon." Make sure they choose only one. Take boxes of crayons from them. Then say: "Color the zookeeper." Make sure they color only the zookeeper. Take papers from them.

12. Give out reinforcers.

THE MONKEY
Sentence-Building Exercise 1

Materials:

photograph of monkey, students' circle-in-circle charts and branch organizers, lined paper, tape, three pieces of chart paper, dry-erase marker, watercolor marker

Before the Lesson:

1. At http://fhautism.com/arc.html, find the circle-in-circle chart, branch organizer, and lined paper. Print one of each for each student, plus a few extras.

2. On the chart paper, draw a blank circle-in-circle chart, branch organizer, and lined paper.

3. On the board, hang a blank circle-in-circle chart on the left and a branch organizer on the right. Make them large enough to write all the words you will need.

4. Write the date on the board.

Teaching the Lesson

1. Gather the children in a circle. Hold up the photograph of the monkey. Ask: "What animal is this?" If no one can identify the animal, ask an aide to answer, or answer the question yourself.

2. When a student says, "monkey," write "monkey" in the smaller, inner circle of the circle-in-circle chart.

   If you wish, you can allow the students to start the conversation. They've had plenty of practice now, and they might give creative responses if given time to think.

3. Ask: "Who can tell me something about the monkey?" If no one answers, ask: "What can the monkey do?" If no one answers, prompt the students. Ask: "Can the monkey fly?" If no one answers, ask an aide to answer, or answer the question yourself. Possible answers include climb, swing, jump. Students may come up with

different answers. Ask the question several times, and allow different children to answer. Write the answers in the large circle.

4. Ask: "What does the monkey have? If no one answers, prompt the students. Ask: "Does a monkey have feathers?" This question should be repeated every time the animal in question has either fur or feathers. Other good questions: "Does the monkey have four eyes?" "Does the monkey have wings?" If no one answers, ask an aide to answer, or answer the question yourself. Possible answers include a tail, fur, two ears. Students may come up with different answers. Ask the question several times, and allow different children to answer. Write the answers in the large circle.

5. Ask: "What does the monkey like? If no one answers, prompt the students with a guessing game. Say: "The monkey likes to eat this yellow fruit. This fruit grows on trees. You peel the skin off this fruit and take a bite." Do this for the other two answers. If no one answers, ask an aide to answer, or answer the question yourself. Possible answers include bananas, apples, coconuts. Students may come up with different answers. Ask the question several times, and allow different children to answer. Write the answers in the large circle. NOTE: Guessing games may be stressful for some children. If students appear to be getting agitated or panicky, just tell them the answer. The lesson is more important than the game.

6. Praise students and pass out reinforcers.

7. The children return to their desks. Pass out pencils and blank graphic organizers. On each desk, tape the circle-in-circle chart on the left and the branch organizer on the right.

8. Say: "Write your name on your paper." Make sure everyone writes his or her name. Then say: "Write the date. It is on the board." Make sure everyone writes the date.

9. Say: "Copy the words from the circle-in-circle chart on the board onto your circle-in-circle chart." They do not have to copy all of the words at first.

10. Say: "Now we will do the branch organizer." On the branch organizer on the board, write "Monkey" on the top line and "Can," "Has," and "Likes" on the three spaces under the top line. Say: "Copy the words onto your charts."

11. Ask: "What can the monkey do?" Point to the words on the circle-in-circle chart. Encourage students to look at their own chart. If no one answers, ask an aide to answer, or answer the question yourself. Ask the question several times, and allow different children to answer.

If someone uses a nonsensical word, e.g., "bananas," say the whole sentence. Say: "The monkey can bananas? Does that make sense? Let's look back in the circle and find something the monkey can do."

12. Write students' answers on the branch organizer on the board. For each answer, say: "Write (the answer) under the word 'Can' on your branch organizer."

13. For each word that students write, say the whole sentence, e.g., "The monkey can swing." As you say each word of the sentence, point to the corresponding word on the branch chart.

14. Ask: "What does the monkey have?" Point to the words on the circle-in-circle chart. If no one answers, ask an aide to answer, or answer the question yourself. Ask the question several times, and allow different children to answer.

If someone uses a nonsensical word, e.g., "swing," say the whole sentence. Say: "The monkey has swing? Does that make sense? Let's look back in the circle and find something the monkey has."

15. Write students' answers on the branch organizer on the board. For each answer, say: "Write (the answer) under the word 'Has' on your branch organizer."

16. For each word that students write, say the whole sentence, e.g., "The monkey has fur." As you say each word of the sentence, point to the corresponding word on the branch chart.

17. Ask: "What does the monkey like?" Point to the words on the circle-in-circle chart. If no one answers, ask an aide to answer, or answer the question yourself. Ask the question several times, and allow different children to answer.

If someone uses a nonsensical word, e.g., "fur," say the whole sentence. Say: "The monkey likes fur? Does that make sense? Let's look back in the circle and find something the monkey likes."

18. Write students' answers on the branch organizer on the board. For each answer, say: "Write (the answer) under the word 'Likes' on your branch organizer."

19. For each word that students write, say the whole sentence, e.g., "The monkey likes bananas." As you say each word of the sentence, point to the corresponding word on the branch chart.

20. Praise students, pass out reinforcers, and take a short break.

21. Draw a large version of the lined paper on your chart paper, using the watercolor marker. Tape the chart paper to the board. Pass out the lined paper. Tape one to each desk, next to the branch organizer.

22. Say: "Today we are going to try making a longer sentence. We are going to use two words from the 'Can' column of the branch organizer. Let me show you how." Point to the words on the branch chart on the board as you slowly say them, forming the sentence. (Example sentence: The monkey can swing and jump.) Show the students the relationship between the words on the chart and a spoken sentence. This will help them read the chart and form the sentences themselves.

Use only one compound phrase per exercise.

23. Write the sentence on your "lined paper" on the board.

24. Say: "Copy the sentence on the first line of your paper."

25. Say: "Let's make a sentence from the second column of the branch organizer, using the word 'Has.'" (Example sentence: The monkey has fur.) Point to the words on the branch chart on the board as you slowly say them, forming the sentence.

26. Write the sentence on your "lined paper" on the board.

27. Say: "Copy the sentence on the second line of your paper." Make sure they write on the lines and not in the blank space above. This is for the illustration.

28. Say: "Let's make a sentence from the third column of the branch organizer, using the word 'Likes.'" (Example sentence: The monkey likes bananas.) Point to the words on the branch chart on the board as you slowly say them, forming the sentence.

29. Write the sentence on your "lined paper" on the board.

30. Say: "Copy the sentence on the third line of your paper."

When students become familiar with this process, they may choose any of the three words to make a sentence.

31. Say: "Now we will read our sentences aloud." Group students in pairs to read to each other, or let each child read aloud to you, an aide, or the whole class.

32. Praise students and pass out reinforcers.

33. Say: "Now we will draw a picture to go with our sentences." Lead students to read the first sentence and then draw a picture of it. Do this for each sentence, one sentence at a time at first. Monitor the drawings and try to limit them to drawing only one monkey. If a higher-functioning child is drawing three monkeys, clearly intending one monkey for each sentence, without exhibiting difficulties, then that is okay. Later in the program, they may be able to remember two or three details at once and incorporate them all into one monkey picture.

If you see an illustration of a monkey missing fur or not eating bananas, ask the student to read the corresponding sentence again. Then show the student what's missing. ("Your sentence says, 'The monkey likes bananas.' Your picture of the monkey does not have a banana. Draw the monkey eating a banana.")

34. Collect papers and pencils, praise students, and pass out reinforcers.

Name_____ Date _____

The _____ monkey has fur.

The _____ monkey is swinging from a vine.

The vine is _____.

The monkey is eating an apple.

The apple is _____.

1. Does the monkey have feathers or fur?

_____

2. What color is the monkey?

_____

THE MONKEY —Worksheet 10, Blank

3. What is the monkey doing?

_____

4. What color is the vine?

_____

5. What is the monkey eating?

_____

6. What color is the apple?

_____

THE MONKEY —Worksheet 10, Blank

THE MONKEY
Worksheet 10, Variation 1

Materials:

Worksheet 10 (Variation 1), pencils, and boxes of crayons for each child

Color Variation 1:

Brown Monkey
Yellow Vine
Red Apple

Before the Lesson:

At http://fhautism.com/arc.html, find Worksheet 10 (Variation 1). Print one for each student, plus a few extras. Write the date on the board.

Teaching the Lesson

1. Distribute the worksheets and pencils to your students. Say: "Write your name on your paper." Make sure everyone writes his or her name. Then say: "Write the date. It is on the board." Make sure everyone writes the date. Take the pencils from them.

2. Say: "(student's name), please read the sentences at the top of the paper." Ask several students to read. If no one can read the passage, read it yourself, or have an aide read it.

3. Say: "We want to color the picture. What three crayons do we need?" Ask the question several times, and allow different children to answer. Then help them find the brown, yellow, and red crayons. Take the crayon boxes from them.

4. Say: "We will color the monkey brown, the vine yellow, and the apple red. What color do we color the monkey?" Ask the question several times, and allow different children to answer.

5. Say: "Color the monkey." Make sure they color only the monkey. Repeat the words "brown monkey" as often as possible.

6. Say: "What color do we color the vine? Let's look back at our story if we need a reminder." Ask the question several times, and allow different children to answer.

7. Say: "Color the vine." Make sure they color only the vine. Repeat the words "yellow vine" as often as possible.

8. Say: "What color do we color the apple? Let's look back at our story if we need a reminder." Ask the question several times, and allow different children to answer.

9. Say: "Color the apple." Make sure they color only the apple. Repeat the words "red apple" as often as possible. Then take the crayons.

10. Ask comprehension questions. Lead students to answer orally, in a complete sentence. For each question, if the student answers incorrectly, guide him or her to read the text again. Questions: 1. Does the monkey have feathers or fur? 2. What color is the monkey? 3. What is the monkey doing? 4. What color is the vine? 5. What is the monkey eating? 6. What color is the apple? Answers: 1. The monkey has fur. 2. The monkey is brown. 3. The monkey is swinging from a vine. 4. The vine is yellow. 5. The monkey is eating an apple. 6. The apple is red.

11. Ask the questions again in random order. Give each student a chance to answer correctly, in complete sentences.

12. Pass out pencils. Ask each comprehension question again. (See step 10 for questions and answers.) When a student answers correctly, write the sentence on the board. Say: "Copy the sentence onto your paper." Do this for each question and answer. Take pencils from them.

13. Give out reinforcers.

THE MONKEY
Worksheet 10, Variation 2

Materials:

Worksheet 10 (Variation 2), pencils, and boxes of crayons for each child

Color Variation 2:

Black Monkey
Orange Vine
Green Apple

✔ Before the Lesson:

At http://fhautism.com/arc.html, find Worksheet 10 (Variation 2). Print one for each student, plus a few extras. Write the date on the board.

Teaching the Lesson

1. Distribute the worksheets and pencils to your students. Say: "Write your name on your paper." Make sure everyone writes his or her name. Then say: "Write the date. It is on the board." Make sure everyone writes the date. Take the pencils from them.

2. Say: "(student's name), please read the sentences at the top of the paper." Ask several students to read. If no one can read the passage, read it yourself, or have an aide read it.

3. Say: "We want to color the picture. What three crayons do we need?" Ask the question several times, and allow different children to answer. Then help them find the black, orange, and green crayons. Take the crayon boxes from them.

4. Say: "We will color the monkey black, the vine orange, and the apple green. What color do we color the monkey?" Ask the question several times, and allow different children to answer.

5. Say: "Color the monkey." Make sure they color only the monkey. Repeat the words "black monkey" as often as possible.

6. Say: "What color do we color the vine? Let's look back at our story if we need a reminder." Ask the question several times, and allow different children to answer.

7. Say: "Color the vine." Make sure they color only the vine. Repeat the words "orange vine" as often as possible.

8. Say: "What color do we color the apple? Let's look back at our story if we need a reminder." Ask the question several times, and allow different children to answer.

9. Say: "Color the apple." Make sure they color only the apple. Repeat the words "green apple" as often as possible. Then take the crayons.

10. Ask comprehension questions. Lead students to answer orally, in a complete sentence. For each question, if the student answers incorrectly, guide him or her to read the text again. Questions: 1. Does the monkey have feathers or fur? 2. What color is the monkey? 3. What is the monkey doing? 4. What color is the vine? 5. What is the monkey eating? 6. What color is the apple? Answers: 1. The monkey has fur. 2. The monkey is black. 3. The monkey is swinging from a vine. 4. The vine is orange. 5. The monkey is eating an apple. 6. The apple is green.

11. Ask the questions again in random order. Give each student a chance to answer correctly, in complete sentences.

12. Pass out pencils. Ask each comprehension question again. (See step 10 for questions and answers.) When a student answers correctly, write the sentence on the board. Say: "Copy the sentence onto your paper." Do this for each question and answer. Take pencils from them.

13. Give out reinforcers.

THE MONKEY
Worksheet 10, Variation 3

Materials:

Worksheet 10 (Variation 3), pencils, and boxes of crayons for each child

Color Variation 3:

Orange Monkey
Green Vine
Yellow Apple

Before the Lesson:

At http://fhautism.com/arc.html, find Worksheet 10 (Variation 3). Print one for each student, plus a few extras. Write the date on the board.

Teaching the Lesson

1. Distribute the worksheets and pencils to your students. Say: "Write your name on your paper." Make sure everyone writes his or her name. Then say: "Write the date. It is on the board." Make sure everyone writes the date. Take the pencils from them.

2. Say: "(student's name), please read the sentences at the top of the paper." Ask several students to read. If no one can read the passage, read it yourself, or have an aide read it.

3. Say: "We want to color the picture. What three crayons do we need?" Ask the question several times, and allow different children to answer. Then help them find the orange, green, and yellow crayons. Take the crayon boxes from them.

4. Say: "We will color the monkey orange, the vine green, and the apple yellow. What color do we color the monkey?" Ask the question several times, and allow different children to answer.

5. Say: "Color the monkey." Make sure they color only the monkey. Repeat the words "orange monkey" as often as possible.

6. Say: "What color do we color the vine? Let's look back at our story if we need a reminder." Ask the question several times, and allow different children to answer.

7. Say: "Color the vine." Make sure they color only the vine. Repeat the words "green vine" as often as possible.

8. Say: "What color do we color the apple? Let's look back at our story if we need a reminder." Ask the question several times, and allow different children to answer.

9. Say: "Color the apple." Make sure they color only the apple. Repeat the words "yellow apple" as often as possible. Then take the crayons.

10. Ask comprehension questions. Lead students to answer orally, in a complete sentence. For each question, if the student answers incorrectly, guide him or her to read the text again. Questions: 1. Does the monkey have feathers or fur? 2. What color is the monkey? 3. What is the monkey doing? 4. What color is the vine? 5. What is the monkey eating? 6. What color is the apple? Answers: 1. The monkey has fur. 2. The monkey is orange. 3. The monkey is swinging from a vine. 4. The vine is green. 5. The monkey is eating an apple. 6. The apple is yellow.

11. Ask the questions again in random order. Give each student a chance to answer correctly, in complete sentences.

12. Pass out pencils. Ask each comprehension question again. (See step 10 for questions and answers.) When a student answers correctly, write the sentence on the board. Say: "Copy the sentence onto your paper." Do this for each question and answer. Take pencils from them.

13. Give out reinforcers.

THE MONKEY
Worksheet 10, Variation 4

Materials:

Worksheet 10 (Variation 4), pencils, and boxes of crayons for each child

Color Variation 4:

Yellow Monkey
Red Vine
Pink Apple

✓ ### Before the Lesson:

At http://fhautism.com/arc.html, find Worksheet 10 (Variation 4). Print one for each student, plus a few extras. Write the date on the board.

Teaching the Lesson

1. Distribute the worksheets and pencils to your students. Say: "Write your name on your paper." Make sure everyone writes his or her name. Then say: "Write the date. It is on the board." Make sure everyone writes the date. Take the pencils from them.

2. Say: "(student's name), please read the sentences at the top of the paper." Ask several students to read. If no one can read the passage, read it yourself, or have an aide read it.

3. Say: "We want to color the picture. What three crayons do we need?" Ask the question several times, and allow different children to answer. Then help them find the yellow, red, and pink crayons. Take the crayon boxes from them.

4. Say: "We will color the monkey yellow, the vine red, and the apple pink. What color do we color the monkey?" Ask the question several times, and allow different children to answer.

5. Say: "Color the monkey." Make sure they color only the monkey. Repeat the words "yellow monkey" as often as possible.

6. Say: "What color do we color the vine? Let's look back at our story if we need a reminder." Ask the question several times, and allow different children to answer.

7. Say: "Color the vine." Make sure they color only the vine. Repeat the words "red vine" as often as possible.

8. Say: "What color do we color the apple? Let's look back at our story if we need a reminder." Ask the question several times, and allow different children to answer.

9. Say: "Color the apple." Make sure they color only the apple. Repeat the words "pink apple" as often as possible. Then take the crayons.

10. Ask comprehension questions. Lead students to answer orally, in a complete sentence. For each question, if the student answers incorrectly, guide him or her to read the text again. Questions: 1. Does the monkey have feathers or fur? 2. What color is the monkey? 3. What is the monkey doing? 4. What color is the vine? 5. What is the monkey eating? 6. What color is the apple? Answers: 1. The monkey has fur. 2. The monkey is yellow. 3. The monkey is swinging from a vine. 4. The vine is red. 5. The monkey is eating an apple. 6. The apple is pink.

11. Ask the questions again in random order. Give each student a chance to answer correctly, in complete sentences.

12. Pass out pencils. Ask each comprehension question again. (See step 10 for questions and answers.) When a student answers correctly, write the sentence on the board. Say: "Copy the sentence onto your paper." Do this for each question and answer. Take pencils from them.

13. Give out reinforcers.

THE MONKEY
Sentence-Building Exercise 2

Materials:

photograph of monkey, students' circle-in-circle charts and branch organizers, lined paper, tape, completed circle-in-circle chart on chart paper (from Lesson 45 sentence-building exercise), two pieces of blank chart paper, dry-erase marker, watercolor marker

Before the Lesson:

1. At http://fhautism.com/arc.html, find the circle-in-circle chart, branch organizer, and lined paper. Print one of each for each student, plus a few extras.

2. On the blank chart paper, draw the lined paper and branch organizer.

3. On the board, hang the completed circle-in-circle chart on chart paper (from Lesson 45 sentence-building exercise) and blank branch organizer.

4. Write the date on the board.

Teaching the Lesson

1. Gather the children in a circle. Hold up the photograph of the monkey. Ask: "What animal is this?" If no one can identify the animal, ask an aide to answer, or answer the question yourself.

2. Ask: "Who can tell me something about the monkey?" If no one answers, ask: "What can the monkey do?" If no one answers, prompt the students to look at the circle-in-circle chart on the board. If no one answers, ask an aide to answer, or answer the question yourself. Possible answers include climb, swing, jump. Students may come up with different answers. Ask the question several times, and allow different children to answer.

3. Ask: "What does the monkey have? If no one answers, prompt the students to look at the circle-in-circle chart on the board. If no one answers, ask an aide to answer, or answer the question yourself. Possible answers include a tail, fur, two ears. Students

may come up with different answers. Ask the question several times, and allow different children to answer.

4. Ask: "What does the monkey like? If no one answers, prompt the students to look at the circle-in-circle chart on the board. If no one answers, ask an aide to answer, or answer the question yourself. Possible answers include bananas, apples, coconuts. Students may come up with different answers. Ask the question several times, and allow different children to answer.

5. Praise students and pass out reinforcers.

6. The children return to their desks. Pass out pencils and blank graphic organizers. On each desk, tape a circle-in-circle chart on the left and the branch organizer on the right.

7. Say: "Write your name on your paper." Make sure everyone writes his or her name. Then say: "Write the date. It is on the board." Make sure everyone writes the date.

8. Say: "Copy the words from the circle-in-circle chart on the board onto your circle-in-circle chart."

9. Say: "Now we will do the branch organizer." On the branch organizer on the board, write "Monkey" on the top line and "Can," "Has," and "Likes" on the three spaces under the top line. Say: "Copy the words onto your charts."

10. Ask: "What can the monkey do?" Point to the words on the circle-in-circle chart. Encourage students to look at their own chart. If no one answers, ask an aide to answer, or answer the question yourself. Ask the question several times, and allow different children to answer.

If someone uses a nonsensical word, e.g., "coconuts," say the whole sentence. Say: "The monkey can coconuts? Does that make sense? Let's look back in the circle and find something the monkey can do."

11. Write students' answers on the branch organizer on the board. For each answer, say: "Write (the answer) under the word 'Can' on your branch organizer."

12. For each word that students write, say the whole sentence, e.g., "The monkey can climb." As you say each word of the sentence, point to the corresponding word on the branch chart.

13. Ask: "What does the monkey have?" Point to the words on the circle-in-circle chart. If no one answers, ask an aide to answer, or answer the question yourself. Ask the question several times, and allow different children to answer.

If someone uses a nonsensical word, e.g., "climb," say the whole sentence. Say: "The monkey has climb? Does that make sense? Let's look back in the circle and find something the monkey has."

14. Write students' answers on the branch chart. For each answer, say: "Write (the answer) under the word 'Has' on your branch organizer."

15. For each word that students write, say the whole sentence, e.g., "The monkey has a tail." As you say each word of the sentence, point to the corresponding word on the branch chart.

16. Ask: "What does the monkey like?" Point to the words on the circle-in-circle chart. If no one answers, ask an aide to answer, or answer the question yourself. Ask the question several times, and allow different children to answer.

If someone uses nonsensical words, e.g., "two ears," say the whole sentence. Say: "The monkey likes two ears? Does that make sense? Let's look back in the circle and find something the monkey likes."

17. Write students' answers on the branch organizer on the board. For each answer, say: "Write (the answer) under the word 'Likes' on your branch organizer."

18. For each word that students write, say the whole sentence, e.g., "The monkey likes coconuts." As you say each word of the sentence, point to the corresponding word on the branch chart.

19. Praise students, pass out reinforcers, and take a short break.

20. Draw a large version of the lined paper on your chart paper, using the watercolor marker. Tape the chart paper to the board. Pass out the lined paper. Tape one to each desk, next to the branch organizer.

21. Say: "It's time to make a sentence. Let's make a sentence from the first column of the branch organizer, using the word 'Can.'" (Example sentence: The monkey can climb.) Point to the words on the branch chart on the board as you slowly say them, forming the sentence.

Lead students to make different sentences than they did in the first sentence-building exercise.

22. Write the sentence on your "lined paper" on the board.

23. Say: "Copy the sentence on the first line of your paper."

24. Say: "Today we are going to try making a longer sentence. We are going to use two words from the 'Has' column of the branch organizer. Let me show you how." Point to the words on the branch chart on the board as you slowly say them, forming the sentence. (Example sentence: The monkey has a tail and two ears.) Show the students the relationship between the words on the chart and a spoken sentence. This will help them read the chart and form the sentences themselves.

Use only one compound phrase per exercise.

25. Write the sentence on your "lined paper" on the board.

26. Say: "Copy the sentence on the second line of your paper." Make sure they write on the lines and not in the blank space above. This is for the illustration.

27. Say: "Let's make a sentence from the third column of the branch organizer, using the word 'Likes.'" (Example sentence: The monkey likes coconuts.) Point to the words on the branch chart on the board as you slowly say them, forming the sentence.

28. Write the sentence on your "lined paper" on the board.

29. Say: "Copy the sentence on the third line of your paper."

When students become familiar with this process, they may choose any of the three words to make a sentence.

30. Say: "Now we will read our sentences aloud." Group students in pairs to read to each other, or let each child read aloud to you, an aide, or the whole class.

31. Praise students and pass out reinforcers.

32. Say: "Now we will draw a picture to go with our sentences." Lead students to read the first sentence and then draw a picture of it. Do this for each sentence, one sentence at a time at first. Monitor the drawings and try to limit them to drawing only one monkey. If a higher-functioning child is drawing three monkeys, clearly intending one monkey for each sentence, without exhibiting difficulties, then that is okay. Later in the program, they may be able to remember two or three details at once and incorporate them all into one monkey picture.

Students might be tempted to draw the same picture as in the first sentence-building exercise. Keep students connected to the meaning of the words. If you see an illustration of a monkey not eating coconuts, ask the student to read the corresponding sentence again. Then show the student what's missing. ("Your sentence says, 'The monkey likes coconuts.' Your picture of the monkey does not have coconuts. Draw the monkey eating coconuts.")

33. Collect papers and pencils, praise students, and pass out reinforcers.

THE
DOG

*Get the free print PDF of the dog photo and
this page at http://fhautism.com/arc.html.*

Name_____ Date _____

The _____ dog is on the _____ couch. The dog is eating
a bone. Mother is next to the couch. She is wearing a _____ dress.
Mother feels angry.

1. Where is the dog?

_____

2. What color is the dog?

_____

THE DOG —Worksheet 11, Blank

3. What color is the couch?

_____

4. What is the dog eating?

_____

5. Where is Mother?

_____

6. What color is Mother's dress?

_____

7. How does Mother feel?

_____

THE DOG —Worksheet 11, Blank

THE DOG
Worksheet 11, Variation 1

Materials:

Worksheet 11 (Variation 1), pencils, and boxes of crayons for each child

Color Variation 1:

Orange Dog
Blue Couch
Pink Dress

Before the Lesson:

At http://fhautism.com/arc.html, find Worksheet 11 (Variation 1). Print one for each student, plus a few extras. Write the date on the board.

Teaching the Lesson

1. Distribute the worksheets and pencils to your students. Say: "Write your name on your paper." Make sure everyone writes his or her name. Then say: "Write the date. It is on the board." Make sure everyone writes the date. Take the pencils from them.

2. Say: "(student's name), please read the sentences at the top of the paper." Ask several students to read. If no one can read the passage, read it yourself, or have an aide read it.

3. Say: "We want to color the picture. What three crayons do we need?" Ask the question several times, and allow different children to answer. Then help them find the orange, blue, and pink crayons. Take the crayon boxes from them.

4. Say: "We will color the dog orange, the couch blue, and the dress pink. What color do we color the dog?" Ask the question several times, and allow different children to answer.

5. Say: "Color the dog." Make sure they color only the dog. Repeat the words "orange dog" as often as possible.

6. Say: "What color do we color the couch? Let's look back at our story if we need a reminder." Ask the question several times, and allow different children to answer.

7. Say: "Color the couch." Make sure they color only the couch. Repeat the words "blue couch" as often as possible.

8. Say: "What color do we color the dress? Let's look back at our story if we need a reminder." Ask the question several times, and allow different children to answer.

9. Say: "Color the dress." Make sure they color only the dress. Repeat the words "pink dress" as often as possible. Then take the crayons.

10. Ask comprehension questions. Lead students to answer orally, in a complete sentence. For each question, if the student answers incorrectly, guide him or her to read the text again. Questions: 1. Where is the dog? 2. What color is the dog? 3. What color is the couch? 4. What is the dog eating? 5. Where is Mother? 6. What color is Mother's dress? 7. How does Mother feel? Answers: 1. The dog is on the couch 2. The dog is orange. 3. The couch is blue. 4. The dog is eating a bone. 5. Mother is next to the couch. 6. Mother is wearing a pink dress. 7. Mother feels angry.

11. Ask the questions again in random order. Give each student a chance to answer correctly, in complete sentences.

12. Pass out pencils. Ask each comprehension question again. (See step 10 for questions and answers.) When a student answers correctly, write the sentence on the board. Say: "Copy the sentence onto your paper." Do this for each question and answer. Take pencils from them.

13. Pass out boxes of crayons. Say: "Choose one crayon." Make sure they choose only one. Take boxes of crayons from them. Then say: "Color the bone." Make sure they color only the bone. Take papers from them.

14. Give out reinforcers.

THE DOG
Worksheet 11, Variation 2

Materials:

Worksheet 11 (Variation 2), pencils, and boxes of crayons for each child

Color Variation 2:

Black Dog
Yellow Couch
Green Dress

Before the Lesson:

At http://fhautism.com/arc.html, find Worksheet 11 (Variation 2). Print one for each student, plus a few extras. Write the date on the board.

Teaching the Lesson

1. Distribute the worksheets and pencils to your students. Say: "Write your name on your paper." Make sure everyone writes his or her name. Then say: "Write the date. It is on the board." Make sure everyone writes the date. Take the pencils from them.

2. Say: "(student's name), please read the sentences at the top of the paper." Ask several students to read. If no one can read the passage, read it yourself, or have an aide read it.

3. Say: "We want to color the picture. What three crayons do we need?" Ask the question several times, and allow different children to answer. Then help them find the black, yellow, and green crayons. Take the crayon boxes from them.

4. Say: "We will color the dog black, the couch yellow, and the dress green. What color do we color the dog?" Ask the question several times, and allow different children to answer.

5. Say: "Color the dog." Make sure they color only the dog. Repeat the words "black dog" as often as possible.

6. Say: "What color do we color the couch? Let's look back at our story if we need a reminder." Ask the question several times, and allow different children to answer.

7. Say: "Color the couch." Make sure they color only the couch. Repeat the words "yellow couch" as often as possible.

8. Say: "What color do we color the dress? Let's look back at our story if we need a reminder." Ask the question several times, and allow different children to answer.

9. Say: "Color the dress." Make sure they color only the dress. Repeat the words "green dress" as often as possible. Then take the crayons.

10. Ask comprehension questions. Lead students to answer orally, in a complete sentence. For each question, if the student answers incorrectly, guide him or her to read the text again. Questions: 1. Where is the dog? 2. What color is the dog? 3. What color is the couch? 4. What is the dog eating? 5. Where is Mother? 6. What color is Mother's dress? 7. How does Mother feel? Answers: 1. The dog is on the couch 2. The dog is black. 3. The couch is yellow. 4. The dog is eating a bone. 5. Mother is next to the couch. 6. Mother is wearing a green dress. 7. Mother feels angry.

11. Ask the questions again in random order. Give each student a chance to answer correctly, in complete sentences.

12. Pass out pencils. Ask each comprehension question again. (See step 10 for questions and answers.) When a student answers correctly, write the sentence on the board. Say: "Copy the sentence onto your paper." Do this for each question and answer. Take pencils from them.

13. Pass out boxes of crayons. Say: "Choose one crayon." Make sure they choose only one. Take boxes of crayons from them. Then say: "Color the bone." Make sure they color only the bone. Take papers from them.

14. Give out reinforcers.

THE DOG
Worksheet 11, Variation 3

Materials:

Worksheet 11 (Variation 3), pencils, and boxes of crayons for each child

Color Variation 3:

Brown Dog
Pink Couch
Blue Dress

Before the Lesson:

At http://fhautism.com/arc.html, find Worksheet 11 (Variation 3). Print one for each student, plus a few extras. Write the date on the board.

Teaching the Lesson

1. Distribute the worksheets and pencils to your students. Say: "Write your name on your paper." Make sure everyone writes his or her name. Then say: "Write the date. It is on the board." Make sure everyone writes the date. Take the pencils from them.

2. Say: "(student's name), please read the sentences at the top of the paper." Ask several students to read. If no one can read the passage, read it yourself, or have an aide read it.

3. Say: "We want to color the picture. What three crayons do we need?" Ask the question several times, and allow different children to answer. Then help them find the brown, pink, and blue crayons. Take the crayon boxes from them.

4. Say: "We will color the dog brown, the couch pink, and the dress blue. What color do we color the dog?" Ask the question several times, and allow different children to answer.

5. Say: "Color the dog." Make sure they color only the dog. Repeat the words "brown dog" as often as possible.

6. Say: "What color do we color the couch? Let's look back at our story if we need a reminder." Ask the question several times, and allow different children to answer.

7. Say: "Color the couch." Make sure they color only the couch. Repeat the words "pink couch" as often as possible.

8. Say: "What color do we color the dress? Let's look back at our story if we need a reminder." Ask the question several times, and allow different children to answer.

9. Say: "Color the dress." Make sure they color only the dress. Repeat the words "blue dress" as often as possible. Then take the crayons.

10. Ask comprehension questions. Lead students to answer orally, in a complete sentence. For each question, if the student answers incorrectly, guide him or her to read the text again. Questions: 1. Where is the dog? 2. What color is the dog? 3. What color is the couch? 4. What is the dog eating? 5. Where is Mother? 6. What color is Mother's dress? 7. How does Mother feel? Answers: 1. The dog is on the couch 2. The dog is brown. 3. The couch is pink. 4. The dog is eating a bone. 5. Mother is next to the couch. 6. Mother is wearing a blue dress. 7. Mother feels angry.

11. Ask the questions again in random order. Give each student a chance to answer correctly, in complete sentences.

12. Pass out pencils. Ask each comprehension question again. (See step 10 for questions and answers.) When a student answers correctly, write the sentence on the board. Say: "Copy the sentence onto your paper." Do this for each question and answer. Take pencils from them.

13. Pass out boxes of crayons. Say: "Choose one crayon." Make sure they choose only one. Take boxes of crayons from them. Then say: "Color the bone." Make sure they color only the bone. Take papers from them.

14. Give out reinforcers.

THE DOG
Worksheet 11, Variation 4

Materials:

Worksheet 11 (Variation 4), pencils, and boxes of crayons for each child

Color Variation 4:

Yellow Dog
Red Couch
Orange Dress

✔ ### Before the Lesson:

At http://fhautism.com/arc.html, find Worksheet 11 (Variation 4). Print one for each student, plus a few extras. Write the date on the board.

Teaching the Lesson

1. Distribute the worksheets and pencils to your students. Say: "Write your name on your paper." Make sure everyone writes his or her name. Then say: "Write the date. It is on the board." Make sure everyone writes the date. Take the pencils from them.

2. Say: "(student's name), please read the sentences at the top of the paper." Ask several students to read. If no one can read the passage, read it yourself, or have an aide read it.

3. Say: "We want to color the picture. What three crayons do we need?" Ask the question several times, and allow different children to answer. Then help them find the yellow, red, and orange crayons. Take the crayon boxes from them.

4. Say: "We will color the dog yellow, the couch red, and the dress orange. What color do we color the dog?" Ask the question several times, and allow different children to answer.

5. Say: "Color the dog." Make sure they color only the dog. Repeat the words "yellow dog" as often as possible.

6. Say: "What color do we color the couch? Let's look back at our story if we need a reminder." Ask the question several times, and allow different children to answer.

7. Say: "Color the couch." Make sure they color only the couch. Repeat the words "red couch" as often as possible.

8. Say: "What color do we color the dress? Let's look back at our story if we need a reminder." Ask the question several times, and allow different children to answer.

9. Say: "Color the dress." Make sure they color only the dress. Repeat the words "orange dress" as often as possible. Then take the crayons.

10. Ask comprehension questions. Lead students to answer orally, in a complete sentence. For each question, if the student answers incorrectly, guide him or her to read the text again. Questions: 1. Where is the dog? 2. What color is the dog? 3. What color is the couch? 4. What is the dog eating? 5. Where is Mother? 6. What color is Mother's dress? 7. How does Mother feel? Answers: 1. The dog is on the couch 2. The dog is yellow. 3. The couch is red. 4. The dog is eating a bone. 5. Mother is next to the couch. 6. Mother is wearing an orange dress. 7. Mother feels angry.

11. Ask the questions again in random order. Give each student a chance to answer correctly, in complete sentences.

12. Pass out pencils. Ask each comprehension question again. (See step 10 for questions and answers.) When a student answers correctly, write the sentence on the board. Say: "Copy the sentence onto your paper." Do this for each question and answer. Take pencils from them.

13. Pass out boxes of crayons. Say: "Choose one crayon." Make sure they choose only one. Take boxes of crayons from them. Then say: "Color the bone." Make sure they color only the bone. Take papers from them.

14. Give out reinforcers.

THE DOG
Sentence-Building Exercise 1

55

Materials:

photograph of dog, students' circle-in-circle charts and branch organizers, lined paper, tape, three pieces of chart paper, dry-erase marker, watercolor marker

Before the Lesson:

1. At http://fhautism.com/arc.html, find the circle-in-circle chart, branch organizer, and lined paper. Print one of each for each student, plus a few extras.

2. On the chart paper, draw a blank circle-in-circle chart, branch organizer, and lined paper.

3. On the board, hang a blank circle-in-circle chart on the left and a branch organizer on the right. Make them large enough to write all the words you will need.

4. Write the date on the board.

Teaching the Lesson

1. Gather the children in a circle. Hold up the photograph of the dog. Ask: "What animal is this?" If no one can identify the animal, ask an aide to answer, or answer the question yourself.

2. When a student says, "dog," write "dog" in the smaller, inner circle of the circle-in-circle chart.

3. Ask: "Who can tell me something about the dog?" If no one answers, ask: "What can the dog do?" If no one answers, prompt the students. Ask: "Can the dog ride a bike?" If no one answers, ask an aide to answer, or answer the question yourself. Possible answers include bark, wag his tail, dig. Students may come up with different answers. Ask the question several times, and allow different children to answer. Write the answers in the large circle.

4. Ask: "What does the dog have? If no one answers, prompt the students. Ask: "Does the dog have fur or feathers?" Other good questions: "Does the dog have four eyes?" "Does the dog have wings?" If no one answers, ask an aide to answer, or answer the question yourself. Possible answers include four legs, a tail, teeth. Students may come up with different answers. Ask the question several times, and allow different children to answer. Write the answers in the large circle.

5. Ask: "What does the dog like? If no one answers, prompt the students with a guessing game. Say: "The dog likes to eat something hard and white. It sometimes has meat on it. The dog chews it. Sometimes the dog buries it. " Do this for the other two answers. If no one answers, ask an aide to answer, or answer the question yourself. Possible answers include dog food, bones, hamburger. Students may come up with different answers. Ask the question several times, and allow different children to answer. Write the answers in the large circle. NOTE: If students appear to be getting agitated or panicky, just tell them the answer.

6. Praise students and pass out reinforcers.

7. The children return to their desks. Pass out pencils and blank graphic organizers. On each desk, tape the circle-in-circle chart on the left and the branch organizer on the right.

8. Say: "Write your name on your paper." Make sure everyone writes his or her name. Then say: "Write the date. It is on the board." Make sure everyone writes the date.

9. Say: "Copy the words from the circle-in-circle chart on the board onto your circle-in-circle chart." They do not have to copy all of the words at first.

10. Say: "Now we will do the branch organizer." On the branch organizer on the board, write "Dog" on the top line and "Can," "Has," and "Likes" on the three spaces under the top line. Say: "Copy the words onto your charts."

11. Ask: "What can the dog do?" Point to the words on the circle-in-circle chart. Encourage students to look at their own chart. If no one answers, ask an aide to answer, or answer the question yourself. Ask the question several times, and allow different children to answer.

If someone uses a nonsensical word, e.g., "bones," say the whole sentence. Say: "The dog can bones? Does that make sense? Let's look back in the circle and find something the dog can do."

12. Write students' answers on the branch organizer on the board. For each answer, say: "Write (the answer) under the word 'Can' on your branch organizer."

13. For each word that students write, say the whole sentence, e.g., "The dog can bark." As you say each word of the sentence, point to the corresponding word on the branch chart.

14. Ask: "What does the dog have?" Point to the words on the circle-in-circle chart. If no one answers, ask an aide to answer, or answer the question yourself. Ask the question several times, and allow different children to answer.

If someone uses a nonsensical word, e.g., "bark," say the whole sentence. Say: "The dog has bark? Does that make sense? Let's look back in the circle and find something the dog has."

15. Write students' answers on the branch organizer on the board. For each answer, say: "Write (the answer) under the word 'Has' on your branch organizer."

16. For each word that students write, say the whole sentence, e.g., "The dog has a tail." As you say each word of the sentence, point to the corresponding word on the branch chart.

17. Ask: "What does the dog like?" Point to the words on the circle-in-circle chart. If no one answers, ask an aide to answer, or answer the question yourself. Ask the question several times, and allow different children to answer.

If someone uses a nonsensical word, e.g., "teeth," say the whole sentence. Say: "The dog likes teeth? Does that make sense? Let's look back in the circle and find something the dog likes."

18. Write students' answers on the branch organizer on the board. For each answer, say: "Write (the answer) under the word 'Likes' on your branch organizer."

19. For each word that students write, say the whole sentence, e.g., "The dog likes bones." As you say each word of the sentence, point to the corresponding word on the branch chart.

20. Praise students, pass out reinforcers, and take a short break.

21. Draw a large version of the lined paper on your chart paper, using the watercolor marker. Tape the chart paper to the board. Pass out the lined paper. Tape one to each desk, next to the branch organizer.

22. Say: "Today we are going to try making a longer sentence. We are going to use two words from the 'Can' column of the branch organizer. Let me show you how." Point to the words on the branch chart on the board as you slowly say them, forming the sentence. (Example sentence: The dog can bark and wag his tail.)

Use only one compound phrase per exercise.

23. Write the sentence on your "lined paper" on the board.

24. Say: "Copy the sentence on the first line of your paper."

25. Say: "Let's make a sentence from the second column of the branch organizer, using the word 'Has.'" (Example sentence: The dog has a tail.) Point to the words on the branch chart on the board as you slowly say them, forming the sentence.

26. Write the sentence on your "lined paper" on the board.

27. Say: "Copy the sentence on the second line of your paper." Make sure they write on the lines and not in the blank space above.

28. Say: "Let's make a sentence from the third column of the branch organizer, using the word 'Likes.'" (Example sentence: The dog likes bones.) Point to the words on the branch chart on the board as you slowly say them, forming the sentence.

29. Write the sentence on your "lined paper" on the board.

30. Say: "Copy the sentence on the third line of your paper."

When students become familiar with this process, they may choose any of the three words to make a sentence.

31. Say: "Now we will read our sentences aloud." Group students in pairs to read to each other, or let each child read aloud to you, an aide, or the whole class.

32. Praise students and pass out reinforcers.

33. Say: "Now we will draw a picture to go with our sentences." Lead students to read the first sentence and then draw a picture of it. Do this for each sentence, one sentence at a time at first. Monitor the drawings and try to limit them to drawing only one dog. If a higher-functioning child is drawing three dogs, clearly intending one dog for each sentence, without exhibiting difficulties, then that is okay. Later in the program, they may be able to remember two or three details at once and incorporate them all into one dog picture. Remember, the illustration must reflect the information in the sentence.

34. Collect papers and pencils, praise students, and pass out reinforcers.

Name_____ Date _____

The dog is _____. The dog has fur. The dog is next to his doghouse.

The doghouse is _____. The ball is inside the doghouse. The ball

is _____. The dog is holding a bone.

1. Does the dog have feathers or fur?

_____

2. What color is the dog?

_____

THE DOG —Worksheet 12, Blank

3. Where is the dog?

_____

4. What color is the doghouse?

_____

5. Where is the ball?

_____

6. What color is the ball?

_____

7. What is the dog holding?

_____

THE DOG —Worksheet 12, Blank

THE DOG
Worksheet 12, Variation 1

Materials:

Worksheet 12 (Variation 1), pencils, and boxes of crayons for each child

Color Variation 1:

Brown Dog
Yellow Doghouse
Blue Ball

✔ Before the Lesson:

At http://fhautism.com/arc.html, find Worksheet 12 (Variation 1). Print one for each student, plus a few extras. Write the date on the board.

Teaching the Lesson

1. Distribute the worksheets and pencils to your students. Say: "Write your name on your paper." Make sure everyone writes his or her name. Then say: "Write the date. It is on the board." Make sure everyone writes the date. Take the pencils from them.

2. Say: "(student's name), please read the sentences at the top of the paper." Ask several students to read. If no one can read the passage, read it yourself, or have an aide read it.

3. Say: "We want to color the picture. What three crayons do we need?" Ask the question several times, and allow different children to answer. Then help them find the brown, yellow, and blue crayons. Take the crayon boxes from them.

4. Say: "We will color the dog brown, the doghouse yellow, and the ball blue. What color do we color the dog?" Ask the question several times, and allow different children to answer.

5. Say: "Color the dog." Make sure they color only the dog. Repeat the words "brown dog" as often as possible.

6. Say: "What color do we color the doghouse? Let's look back at our story if we need a reminder." Ask the question several times, and allow different children to answer.

7. Say: "Color the doghouse." Make sure they color only the doghouse. Repeat the words "yellow doghouse" as often as possible.

8. Say: "What color do we color the ball? Let's look back at our story if we need a reminder." Ask the question several times, and allow different children to answer.

9. Say: "Color the ball." Make sure they color only the ball. Repeat the words "blue ball" as often as possible. Then take the crayons.

10. Ask comprehension questions. Lead students to answer orally, in a complete sentence. For each question, if the student answers incorrectly, guide him or her to read the text again. Questions: 1. Does the dog have feathers or fur? 2. What color is the dog? 3. Where is the dog? 4. What color is the doghouse? 5. Where is the ball? 6. What color is the ball? 7. What is the dog holding? Answers: 1. The dog has fur. 2. The dog is brown. 3. The dog is next to his doghouse. 4. The doghouse is yellow. 5. The ball is inside the doghouse. 6. The ball is blue. 7. The dog is holding a bone.

11. Ask the questions again in random order. Give each student a chance to answer correctly, in complete sentences.

12. Pass out pencils. Ask each comprehension question again. (See step 10 for questions and answers.) When a student answers correctly, write the sentence on the board. Say: "Copy the sentence onto your paper." Do this for each question and answer. Take pencils from them.

13. Pass out boxes of crayons. Say: "Choose one crayon." Make sure they choose only one. Take boxes of crayons from them. Then say: "Color the flowers." Make sure they color only the flowers. Take papers from them.

14. Give out reinforcers.

THE DOG
Worksheet 12, Variation 2

Materials:

Worksheet 12 (Variation 2), pencils, and boxes of crayons for each child

Color Variation 2:

Black Dog
Red Doghouse
Yellow Ball

✔ ## Before the Lesson:

At http://fhautism.com/arc.html, find Worksheet 12 (Variation 2). Print one for each student, plus a few extras. Write the date on the board.

Teaching the Lesson

1. Distribute the worksheets and pencils to your students. Say: "Write your name on your paper." Make sure everyone writes his or her name. Then say: "Write the date. It is on the board." Make sure everyone writes the date. Take the pencils from them.

2. Say: "(student's name), please read the sentences at the top of the paper." Ask several students to read. If no one can read the passage, read it yourself, or have an aide read it.

3. Say: "We want to color the picture. What three crayons do we need?" Ask the question several times, and allow different children to answer. Then help them find the black, red, and yellow crayons. Take the crayon boxes from them.

4. Say: "We will color the dog black, the doghouse red, and the ball yellow. What color do we color the dog?" Ask the question several times, and allow different children to answer.

5. Say: "Color the dog." Make sure they color only the dog. Repeat the words "black dog" as often as possible.

6. Say: "What color do we color the doghouse? Let's look back at our story if we need a reminder." Ask the question several times, and allow different children to answer.

7. Say: "Color the doghouse." Make sure they color only the doghouse. Repeat the words "red doghouse" as often as possible.

8. Say: "What color do we color the ball? Let's look back at our story if we need a reminder." Ask the question several times, and allow different children to answer.

9. Say: "Color the ball." Make sure they color only the ball. Repeat the words "yellow ball" as often as possible. Then take the crayons.

10. Ask comprehension questions. Lead students to answer orally, in a complete sentence. For each question, if the student answers incorrectly, guide him or her to read the text again. Questions: 1. Does the dog have feathers or fur? 2. What color is the dog? 3. Where is the dog? 4. What color is the doghouse? 5. Where is the ball? 6. What color is the ball? 7. What is the dog holding? Answers: 1. The dog has fur. 2. The dog is black. 3. The dog is next to his doghouse. 4. The doghouse is red. 5. The ball is inside the doghouse. 6. The ball is yellow. 7. The dog is holding a bone.

11. Ask the questions again in random order. Give each student a chance to answer correctly, in complete sentences.

12. Pass out pencils. Ask each comprehension question again. (See step 10 for questions and answers.) When a student answers correctly, write the sentence on the board. Say: "Copy the sentence onto your paper." Do this for each question and answer. Take pencils from them.

13. Pass out boxes of crayons. Say: "Choose one crayon." Make sure they choose only one. Take boxes of crayons from them. Then say: "Color the flowers." Make sure they color only the flowers. Take papers from them.

14. Give out reinforcers.

THE DOG
Worksheet 12, Variation 3

Materials:

Worksheet 12 (Variation 3), pencils, and boxes of crayons for each child

Color Variation 3:

Orange Dog
Blue Doghouse
Pink Ball

Before the Lesson:

At http://fhautism.com/arc.html, find Worksheet 12 (Variation 3). Print one for each student, plus a few extras. Write the date on the board.

Teaching the Lesson

1. Distribute the worksheets and pencils to your students. Say: "Write your name on your paper." Make sure everyone writes his or her name. Then say: "Write the date. It is on the board." Make sure everyone writes the date. Take the pencils from them.

2. Say: "(student's name), please read the sentences at the top of the paper." Ask several students to read. If no one can read the passage, read it yourself, or have an aide read it.

3. Say: "We want to color the picture. What three crayons do we need?" Ask the question several times, and allow different children to answer. Then help them find the orange, blue, and pink crayons. Take the crayon boxes from them.

4. Say: "We will color the dog orange, the doghouse blue, and the ball pink. What color do we color the dog?" Ask the question several times, and allow different children to answer.

5. Say: "Color the dog." Make sure they color only the dog. Repeat the words "orange dog" as often as possible.

6. Say: "What color do we color the doghouse? Let's look back at our story if we need a reminder." Ask the question several times, and allow different children to answer.

7. Say: "Color the doghouse." Make sure they color only the doghouse. Repeat the words "blue doghouse" as often as possible.

8. Say: "What color do we color the ball? Let's look back at our story if we need a reminder." Ask the question several times, and allow different children to answer.

9. Say: "Color the ball." Make sure they color only the ball. Repeat the words "pink ball" as often as possible. Then take the crayons.

10. Ask comprehension questions. Lead students to answer orally, in a complete sentence. For each question, if the student answers incorrectly, guide him or her to read the text again. Questions: 1. Does the dog have feathers or fur? 2. What color is the dog? 3. Where is the dog? 4. What color is the doghouse? 5. Where is the ball? 6. What color is the ball? 7. What is the dog holding? Answers: 1. The dog has fur. 2. The dog is orange. 3. The dog is next to his doghouse. 4. The doghouse is blue. 5. The ball is inside the doghouse. 6. The ball is pink. 7. The dog is holding a bone.

11. Ask the questions again in random order. Give each student a chance to answer correctly, in complete sentences.

12. Pass out pencils. Ask each comprehension question again. (See step 10 for questions and answers.) When a student answers correctly, write the sentence on the board. Say: "Copy the sentence onto your paper." Do this for each question and answer. Take pencils from them.

13. Pass out boxes of crayons. Say: "Choose one crayon." Make sure they choose only one. Take boxes of crayons from them. Then say: "Color the flowers." Make sure they color only the flowers. Take papers from them.

14. Give out reinforcers.

AUTISM & READING COMPREHENSION
© 2011 by Joseph Porter, M.Ed. Future Horizons, Inc.

THE DOG
Worksheet 12, Variation 4

Materials:

Worksheet 12 (Variation 4), pencils, and boxes of crayons for each child

Color Variation 4:

Yellow Dog
Purple Doghouse
Orange Ball

✔ Before the Lesson:

At http://fhautism.com/arc.html, find Worksheet 12 (Variation 4). Print one for each student, plus a few extras. Write the date on the board.

Teaching the Lesson

1. Distribute the worksheets and pencils to your students. Say: "Write your name on your paper." Make sure everyone writes his or her name. Then say: "Write the date. It is on the board." Make sure everyone writes the date. Take the pencils from them.

2. Say: "(student's name), please read the sentences at the top of the paper." Ask several students to read. If no one can read the passage, read it yourself, or have an aide read it.

3. Say: "We want to color the picture. What three crayons do we need?" Ask the question several times, and allow different children to answer. Then help them find the yellow, purple, and orange crayons. Take the crayon boxes from them.

4. Say: "We will color the dog yellow, the doghouse purple, and the ball orange. What color do we color the dog?" Ask the question several times, and allow different children to answer.

5. Say: "Color the dog." Make sure they color only the dog. Repeat the words "yellow dog" as often as possible.

6. Say: "What color do we color the doghouse? Let's look back at our story if we need a reminder." Ask the question several times, and allow different children to answer.

7. Say: "Color the doghouse." Make sure they color only the doghouse. Repeat the words "purple doghouse" as often as possible.

8. Say: "What color do we color the ball? Let's look back at our story if we need a reminder." Ask the question several times, and allow different children to answer.

9. Say: "Color the ball." Make sure they color only the ball. Repeat the words "orange ball" as often as possible. Then take the crayons.

10. Ask comprehension questions. Lead students to answer orally, in a complete sentence. For each question, if the student answers incorrectly, guide him or her to read the text again. Questions: 1. Does the dog have feathers or fur? 2. What color is the dog? 3. Where is the dog? 4. What color is the doghouse? 5. Where is the ball? 6. What color is the ball? 7. What is the dog holding? Answers: 1. The dog has fur. 2. The dog is yellow. 3. The dog is next to his doghouse. 4. The doghouse is purple. 5. The ball is inside the doghouse. 6. The ball is orange. 7. The dog is holding a bone.

11. Ask the questions again in random order. Give each student a chance to answer correctly, in complete sentences.

12. Pass out pencils. Ask each comprehension question again. (See step 10 for questions and answers.) When a student answers correctly, write the sentence on the board. Say: "Copy the sentence onto your paper." Do this for each question and answer. Take pencils from them.

13. Pass out boxes of crayons. Say: "Choose one crayon." Make sure they choose only one. Take boxes of crayons from them. Then say: "Color the flowers." Make sure they color only the flowers. Take papers from them.

14. Give out reinforcers.

THE DOG
Sentence-Building Exercise 2

Materials:

photograph of dog, students' circle-in-circle charts and branch organizers, lined paper, tape, completed circle-in-circle chart on chart paper (from Lesson 55 sentence-building exercise), two pieces of blank chart paper, dry-erase marker, watercolor marker

Before the Lesson:

1. At http://fhautism.com/arc.html, find the circle-in-circle chart, branch organizer, and lined paper. Print one of each for each student, plus a few extras.

2. On the blank chart paper, draw the lined paper and branch organizer.

3. On the board, hang the completed circle-in-circle chart on chart paper (from Lesson 55 sentence-building exercise) and blank branch organizer.

4. Write the date on the board.

Teaching the Lesson

1. Gather the children in a circle. Hold up the photograph of the dog. Ask: "What animal is this?" If no one can identify the animal, ask an aide to answer, or answer the question yourself.

2. Ask: "Who can tell me something about the dog?" If no one answers, ask: "What can the dog do?" If no one answers, prompt the students to look at the circle-in-circle chart on the board. If no one answers, ask an aide to answer, or answer the question yourself. Possible answers include bark, wag his tail, dig. Students may come up with different answers. Ask the question several times, and allow different children to answer.

3. Ask: "What does the dog have? If no one answers, prompt the students to look at the circle-in-circle chart on the board. If no one answers, ask an aide to answer, or answer the question yourself. Possible answers include four legs, a tail, teeth.

Students may come up with different answers. Ask the question several times, and allow different children to answer.

4. Ask: "What does the dog like? If no one answers, prompt the students to look at the circle-in-circle chart on the board. If no one answers, ask an aide to answer, or answer the question yourself. Possible answers include dog food, bones, hamburger. Students may come up with different answers. Ask the question several times, and allow different children to answer.

5. Praise students and pass out reinforcers.

6. The children return to their desks. Pass out pencils and blank graphic organizers. On each desk, tape a circle-in-circle chart on the left and the branch organizer on the right.

7. Say: "Write your name on your paper." Make sure everyone writes his or her name. Then say: "Write the date. It is on the board." Make sure everyone writes the date.

8. Say: "Copy the words from the circle-in-circle chart on the board onto your circle-in-circle chart."

9. Say: "Now we will do the branch organizer." On the branch organizer on the board, write "Dog" on the top line and "Can," "Has," and "Likes" on the three spaces under the top line. Say: "Copy the words onto your charts."

10. Ask: "What can the dog do?" Point to the words on the circle-in-circle chart. Encourage students to look at their own chart. If no one answers, ask an aide to answer, or answer the question yourself. Ask the question several times, and allow different children to answer.

    If someone uses a nonsensical word, e.g., "dog food," say the whole sentence. Say: "The dog can dog food? Does that make sense? Let's look back in the circle and find something the dog can do."

11. Write students' answers on the branch organizer on the board. For each answer, say: "Write (the answer) under the word 'Can' on your branch organizer."

12. For each word that students write, say the whole sentence, e.g., "The dog can dig." As you say each word of the sentence, point to the corresponding word on the branch chart.

---

13. Ask: "What does the dog have?" Point to the words on the circle-in-circle chart. If no one answers, ask an aide to answer, or answer the question yourself. Ask the question several times, and allow different children to answer.

If someone uses a nonsensical word, e.g., "dig," say the whole sentence. Say: "The dog has dig? Does that make sense? Let's look back in the circle and find something the dog has."

14. Write students' answers on the branch chart. For each answer, say: "Write (the answer) under the word 'Has' on your branch organizer."

15. For each word that students write, say the whole sentence, e.g., "The dog has teeth." As you say each word of the sentence, point to the corresponding word on the branch chart.

16. Ask: "What does the dog like?" Point to the words on the circle-in-circle chart. If no one answers, ask an aide to answer, or answer the question yourself. Ask the question several times, and allow different children to answer.

If someone uses nonsensical words, e.g., "four legs," say the whole sentence. Say: "The dog likes four legs? Does that make sense? Let's look back in the circle and find something the dog likes."

17. Write students' answers on the branch organizer on the board. For each answer, say: "Write (the answer) under the word 'Likes' on your branch organizer."

18. For each word that students write, say the whole sentence, e.g., "The dog likes dog food." As you say each word of the sentence, point to the corresponding word on the branch chart.

19. Praise students, pass out reinforcers, and take a short break.

20. Draw a large version of the lined paper on your chart paper, using the watercolor marker. Tape the chart paper to the board. Pass out the lined paper. Tape one to each desk, next to the branch organizer.

21. Say: "It's time to make a sentence. Let's make a sentence from the first column of the branch organizer, using the word 'Can.'" (Example sentence: The dog can dig.) Point to the words on the branch chart on the board as you slowly say them, forming the sentence.

Lead students to make different sentences than they did in the first sentence-building exercise.

22. Write the sentence on your "lined paper" on the board.

23. Say: "Copy the sentence on the first line of your paper."

24. Say: "Today we are going to try making a longer sentence. We are going to use two words from the 'Has' column of the branch organizer. Let me show you how." Point to the words on the branch chart on the board as you slowly say them, forming the sentence. (Example sentence: The dog has teeth and four legs.)

Use only one compound phrase per exercise.

25. Write the sentence on your "lined paper" on the board.

26. Say: "Copy the sentence on the second line of your paper." Make sure they write on the lines and not in the blank space above. This is for the illustration.

27. Say: "Let's make a sentence from the third column of the branch organizer, using the word 'Likes.'" (Example sentence: The dog likes dog food.) Point to the words on the branch chart on the board as you slowly say them, forming the sentence.

28. Write the sentence on your "lined paper" on the board.

29. Say: "Copy the sentence on the third line of your paper."

When students become familiar with this process, they may choose any of the three words to make a sentence.

30. Say: "Now we will read our sentences aloud." Group students in pairs to read to each other, or let each child read aloud to you, an aide, or the whole class.

31. Praise students and pass out reinforcers.

32. Say: "Now we will draw a picture to go with our sentences." Lead students to read the first sentence and then draw a picture of it. Do this for each sentence, one sentence at a time at first. Monitor the drawings and try to limit them to drawing only one dog. If a higher-functioning child is drawing three dogs, clearly intending one dog for each sentence, without exhibiting difficulties, then that is okay. Later in the program, they may be able to remember two or three details at once and incorporate them all into one dog picture.

Students might be tempted to draw the same picture as in the first sentence-building exercise. Keep students connected to the meaning of the words. Remember, the illustration must reflect the information in the sentence.

33. Collect papers and pencils, praise students, and pass out reinforcers.

THE HORSE

Get the free print PDF of the horse photo and this page at http://fhautism.com/arc.html.

Name_____ Date _____

The boy is in front of the _____ horse. The boy's shirt is _____.
The boy's hat is _____. The horse is eating a _____ apple.
The horse feels happy.

1. Where is the boy?

_____

2. What color is the horse?

_____

THE HORSE —Worksheet 13, Blank

3. What color is the boy's shirt?

_____

4. What color is the boy's hat?

_____

5. What is the horse eating?

_____

6. What color is the apple?

_____

7. How does the horse feel?

_____

THE HORSE —Worksheet 13, Blank

THE HORSE
Worksheet 13, Variation 1

Materials:

Worksheet 13 (Variation 1), pencils, and boxes of crayons for each child

Color Variation 1:

Brown Horse
Red Shirt
Yellow Hat
Green Apple

Before the Lesson:

At http://fhautism.com/arc.html, find Worksheet 13 (Variation 1). Print one for each student, plus a few extras. Write the date on the board.

Teaching the Lesson

1. Distribute the worksheets and pencils to your students. Say: "Write your name on your paper." Make sure everyone writes his or her name. Then say: "Write the date. It is on the board." Make sure everyone writes the date. Take the pencils from them.

2. Say: "(student's name), please read the sentences at the top of the paper." Ask several students to read. If no one can read the passage, read it yourself, or have an aide read it.

3. Say: "We want to color the picture. What four crayons do we need?" Ask the question several times, and allow different children to answer. Then help them find the brown, red, yellow, and green crayons. Take the crayon boxes from them.

4. Say: "We will color the horse brown, the shirt red, the hat yellow, and the apple green. What color do we color the horse?" Ask the question several times, and allow different children to answer.

5. Say: "Color the horse." Make sure they color only the horse. Repeat the words "brown horse" as often as possible.

6. Say: "What color do we color the shirt? Let's look back at our story if we need a reminder." Ask the question several times, and allow different children to answer.

7. Say: "Color the shirt." Make sure they color only the shirt. Repeat the words "red shirt" as often as possible.

8. Say: "What color do we color the hat? Let's look back at our story if we need a reminder." Ask the question several times, and allow different children to answer.

9. Say: "Color the hat." Make sure they color only the hat. Repeat the words "yellow hat" as often as possible.

10. Say: "What color do we color the apple? Let's look back at our story if we need a reminder." Ask the question several times, and allow different children to answer.

11. Say: "Color the apple." Make sure they color only the apple. Repeat the words "green apple" as often as possible. Then take the crayons.

12. Ask comprehension questions. Lead students to answer orally, in a complete sentence. For each question, if the student answers incorrectly, guide him or her to read the text again. Questions: 1. Where is the boy? 2. What color is the horse? 3. What color is the boy's shirt? 4. What color is the boy's hat? 5. What is the horse eating? 6. What color is the apple? 7. How does the horse feel? Answers: 1. The boy is in front of the horse. 2. The horse is brown. 3. The boy's shirt is red. 4. The boy's hat is yellow. 5. The horse is eating an apple. 6. The apple is green. 7. The horse feels happy.

13. Ask the questions again in random order. Give each student a chance to answer correctly, in complete sentences.

14. Pass out pencils. Ask each comprehension question again. (See step 12 for questions and answers.) When a student answers correctly, write the sentence on the board. Say: "Copy the sentence onto your paper." Do this for each question and answer. Take pencils from them.

15. Give out reinforcers.

THE HORSE
Worksheet 13, Variation 2

Materials:

Worksheet 13 (Variation 2), pencils, and boxes of crayons for each child

Color Variation 2:

Black Horse
Orange Shirt
Blue Hat
Yellow Apple

Before the Lesson:

At http://fhautism.com/arc.html, find Worksheet 13 (Variation 2). Print one for each student, plus a few extras. Write the date on the board.

Teaching the Lesson

1. Distribute the worksheets and pencils to your students. Say: "Write your name on your paper." Make sure everyone writes his or her name. Then say: "Write the date. It is on the board." Make sure everyone writes the date. Take the pencils from them.

2. Say: "(student's name), please read the sentences at the top of the paper." Ask several students to read. If no one can read the passage, read it yourself, or have an aide read it.

3. Say: "We want to color the picture. What four crayons do we need?" Ask the question several times, and allow different children to answer. Then help them find the black, orange, blue, and yellow crayons. Take the crayon boxes from them.

4. Say: "We will color the horse black, the shirt orange, the hat blue, and the apple yellow. What color do we color the horse?" Ask the question several times, and allow different children to answer.

5. Say: "Color the horse." Make sure they color only the horse. Repeat the words "black horse" as often as possible.

6. Say: "What color do we color the shirt? Let's look back at our story if we need a reminder." Ask the question several times, and allow different children to answer.

7. Say: "Color the shirt." Make sure they color only the shirt. Repeat the words "orange shirt" as often as possible.

8. Say: "What color do we color the hat? Let's look back at our story if we need a reminder." Ask the question several times, and allow different children to answer.

9. Say: "Color the hat." Make sure they color only the hat. Repeat the words "blue hat" as often as possible.

10. Say: "What color do we color the apple? Let's look back at our story if we need a reminder." Ask the question several times, and allow different children to answer.

11. Say: "Color the apple." Make sure they color only the apple. Repeat the words "yellow apple" as often as possible. Then take the crayons.

12. Ask comprehension questions. Lead students to answer orally, in a complete sentence. For each question, if the student answers incorrectly, guide him or her to read the text again. Questions: 1. Where is the boy? 2. What color is the horse? 3. What color is the boy's shirt? 4. What color is the boy's hat? 5. What is the horse eating? 6. What color is the apple? 7. How does the horse feel? Answers: 1. The boy is in front of the horse. 2. The horse is black. 3. The boy's shirt is orange. 4. The boy's hat is blue. 5. The horse is eating an apple. 6. The apple is yellow. 7. The horse feels happy.

13. Ask the questions again in random order. Give each student a chance to answer correctly, in complete sentences.

14. Pass out pencils. Ask each comprehension question again. (See step 12 for questions and answers.) When a student answers correctly, write the sentence on the board. Say: "Copy the sentence onto your paper." Do this for each question and answer. Take pencils from them.

15. Give out reinforcers.

AUTISM & READING COMPREHENSION
© 2011 by Joseph Porter, M.Ed. Future Horizons, Inc.

THE HORSE
Worksheet 13, Variation 3

Materials:

Worksheet 13 (Variation 3), pencils, and boxes of crayons for each child

Color Variation 3:

Yellow Horse
Blue Shirt
Pink Hat
Red Apple

Before the Lesson:

At http://fhautism.com/arc.html, find Worksheet 13 (Variation 3). Print one for each student, plus a few extras. Write the date on the board.

Teaching the Lesson

1. Distribute the worksheets and pencils to your students. Say: "Write your name on your paper." Make sure everyone writes his or her name. Then say: "Write the date. It is on the board." Make sure everyone writes the date. Take the pencils from them.

2. Say: "(student's name), please read the sentences at the top of the paper." Ask several students to read. If no one can read the passage, read it yourself, or have an aide read it.

3. Say: "We want to color the picture. What four crayons do we need?" Ask the question several times, and allow different children to answer. Then help them find the yellow, blue, pink, and red crayons. Take the crayon boxes from them.

4. Say: "We will color the horse yellow, the shirt blue, the hat pink, and the apple red. What color do we color the horse?" Ask the question several times, and allow different children to answer.

5. Say: "Color the horse." Make sure they color only the horse. Repeat the words "yellow horse" as often as possible.

6. Say: "What color do we color the shirt? Let's look back at our story if we need a reminder." Ask the question several times, and allow different children to answer.

7. Say: "Color the shirt." Make sure they color only the shirt. Repeat the words "blue shirt" as often as possible.

8. Say: "What color do we color the hat? Let's look back at our story if we need a reminder." Ask the question several times, and allow different children to answer.

9. Say: "Color the hat." Make sure they color only the hat. Repeat the words "pink hat" as often as possible.

10. Say: "What color do we color the apple? Let's look back at our story if we need a reminder." Ask the question several times, and allow different children to answer.

11. Say: "Color the apple." Make sure they color only the apple. Repeat the words "red apple" as often as possible. Then take the crayons.

12. Ask comprehension questions. Lead students to answer orally, in a complete sentence. For each question, if the student answers incorrectly, guide him or her to read the text again. Questions: 1. Where is the boy? 2. What color is the horse? 3. What color is the boy's shirt? 4. What color is the boy's hat? 5. What is the horse eating? 6. What color is the apple? 7. How does the horse feel? Answers: 1. The boy is in front of the horse. 2. The horse is yellow. 3. The boy's shirt is blue. 4. The boy's hat is pink. 5. The horse is eating an apple. 6. The apple is red. 7. The horse feels happy.

13. Ask the questions again in random order. Give each student a chance to answer correctly, in complete sentences.

14. Pass out pencils. Ask each comprehension question again. (See step 12 for questions and answers.) When a student answers correctly, write the sentence on the board. Say: "Copy the sentence onto your paper." Do this for each question and answer. Take pencils from them.

15. Give out reinforcers.

THE HORSE
Worksheet 13, Variation 4

Materials:

Worksheet 13 (Variation 4), pencils, and boxes of crayons for each child

Color Variation 4:

Gray Horse
Green Shirt
Purple Hat
Pink Apple

Before the Lesson:

At http://fhautism.com/arc.html, find Worksheet 13 (Variation 4). Print one for each student, plus a few extras. Write the date on the board.

Teaching the Lesson

1. Distribute the worksheets and pencils to your students. Say: "Write your name on your paper." Make sure everyone writes his or her name. Then say: "Write the date. It is on the board." Make sure everyone writes the date. Take the pencils from them.

2. Say: "(student's name), please read the sentences at the top of the paper." Ask several students to read. If no one can read the passage, read it yourself, or have an aide read it.

3. Say: "We want to color the picture. What four crayons do we need?" Ask the question several times, and allow different children to answer. Then help them find the gray, green, purple, and pink crayons. Take the crayon boxes from them.

4. Say: "We will color the horse gray, the shirt green, the hat purple, and the apple pink. What color do we color the horse?" Ask the question several times, and allow different children to answer.

5. Say: "Color the horse." Make sure they color only the horse. Repeat the words "gray horse" as often as possible.

6. Say: "What color do we color the shirt? Let's look back at our story if we need a reminder." Ask the question several times, and allow different children to answer.

7. Say: "Color the shirt." Make sure they color only the shirt. Repeat the words "green shirt" as often as possible.

8. Say: "What color do we color the hat? Let's look back at our story if we need a reminder." Ask the question several times, and allow different children to answer.

9. Say: "Color the hat." Make sure they color only the hat. Repeat the words "purple hat" as often as possible.

10. Say: "What color do we color the apple? Let's look back at our story if we need a reminder." Ask the question several times, and allow different children to answer.

11. Say: "Color the apple." Make sure they color only the apple. Repeat the words "pink apple" as often as possible. Then take the crayons.

12. Ask comprehension questions. Lead students to answer orally, in a complete sentence. For each question, if the student answers incorrectly, guide him or her to read the text again. Questions: 1. Where is the boy? 2. What color is the horse? 3. What color is the boy's shirt? 4. What color is the boy's hat? 5. What is the horse eating? 6. What color is the apple? 7. How does the horse feel? Answers: 1. The boy is in front of the horse. 2. The horse is gray. 3. The boy's shirt is green. 4. The boy's hat is purple. 5. The horse is eating an apple. 6. The apple is pink. 7. The horse feels happy.

13. Ask the questions again in random order. Give each student a chance to answer correctly, in complete sentences.

14. Pass out pencils. Ask each comprehension question again. (See step 12 for questions and answers.) When a student answers correctly, write the sentence on the board. Say: "Copy the sentence onto your paper." Do this for each question and answer. Take pencils from them.

15. Give out reinforcers.

THE HORSE
Sentence-Building Exercise I

Materials:

photograph of horse, students' circle-in-circle charts and branch organizers, lined paper, tape, three pieces of chart paper, dry-erase marker, watercolor marker

Before the Lesson:

1. At http://fhautism.com/arc.html, find the circle-in-circle chart, branch organizer, and lined paper. Print one of each for each student, plus a few extras.

2. On the chart paper, draw a blank circle-in-circle chart, branch organizer, and lined paper.

3. On the board, hang a blank circle-in-circle chart on the left and a branch organizer on the right. Make them large enough to write all the words you will need.

4. Write the date on the board.

Teaching the Lesson

1. Gather the children in a circle. Hold up the photograph of the horse. Ask: "What animal is this?" If no one can identify the animal, ask an aide to answer, or answer the question yourself.

2. When a student says, "horse," write "horse" in the smaller, inner circle of the circle-in-circle chart.

3. Ask: "Who can tell me something about the horse?" If no one answers, ask: "What can the horse do?" If no one answers, prompt the students. Ask: "Can the horse ride a bike?" If no one answers, ask an aide to answer, or answer the question yourself. Possible answers include gallop, run, jump. Students may come up with different answers. Ask the question several times, and allow different children to answer. Write the answers in the large circle.

4. Ask: "What does the horse have? If no one answers, prompt the students. Ask: "Does the horse have fur or feathers?" Other good questions: "Does the horse have four eyes?" "Does the horse have wings?" If no one answers, ask an aide to answer, or answer the question yourself. Possible answers include four legs, a mane, a tail. Students may come up with different answers. Ask the question several times, and allow different children to answer. Write the answers in the large circle.

5. Ask: "What does the horse like? If no one answers, prompt the students with a guessing game. Say: "The horse likes to eat a red fruit. It is crunchy. It grows on trees. Sometimes we bake it in a pie. " Do this for the other two answers. If no one answers, ask an aide to answer, or answer the question yourself. Possible answers include apples, hay, carrots. Students may come up with different answers. Ask the question several times, and allow different children to answer. Write the answers in the large circle. NOTE: If students appear to be getting agitated or panicky, just tell them the answer.

6. Praise students and pass out reinforcers.

7. The children return to their desks. Pass out pencils and blank graphic organizers. On each desk, tape the circle-in-circle chart on the left and the branch organizer on the right.

8. Say: "Write your name on your paper." Make sure everyone writes his or her name. Then say: "Write the date. It is on the board." Make sure everyone writes the date.

9. Say: "Copy the words from the circle-in-circle chart on the board onto your circle-in-circle chart."

10. Say: "Now we will do the branch organizer." On the branch organizer on the board, write "Horse" on the top line and "Can," "Has," and "Likes" on the three spaces under the top line. Say: "Copy the words onto your charts."

11. Ask: "What can the horse do?" Point to the words on the circle-in-circle chart. Encourage students to look at their own chart. If no one answers, ask an aide to answer, or answer the question yourself. Ask the question several times, and allow different children to answer.

    If someone uses a nonsensical word, e.g., "apples," say the whole sentence. Say: "The horse can apples? Does that make sense? Let's look back in the circle and find something the horse can do."

12. Write students' answers on the branch organizer on the board. For each answer, say: "Write (the answer) under the word 'Can' on your branch organizer."

13. For each word that students write, say the whole sentence, e.g., "The horse can run." As you say each word of the sentence, point to the corresponding word on the branch chart. This way, they become familiar with the way we use the chart to form the sentences.

14. Ask: "What does the horse have?" Point to the words on the circle-in-circle chart. If no one answers, ask an aide to answer, or answer the question yourself. Ask the question several times, and allow different children to answer.

If someone uses a nonsensical word, e.g., "run," say the whole sentence. Say: "The horse has run? Does that make sense? Let's look back in the circle and find something the horse has."

15. Write students' answers on the branch organizer on the board. For each answer, say: "Write (the answer) under the word 'Has' on your branch organizer."

16. For each word that students write, say the whole sentence, e.g., "The horse has a mane." As you say each word of the sentence, point to the corresponding word on the branch chart.

17. Ask: "What does the horse like?" Point to the words on the circle-in-circle chart. If no one answers, ask an aide to answer, or answer the question yourself. Ask the question several times, and allow different children to answer.

If someone uses a nonsensical word, e.g., "four legs," say the whole sentence. Say: "The horse likes four legs? Does that make sense? Let's look back in the circle and find something the horse likes."

18. Write students' answers on the branch organizer on the board. For each answer, say: "Write (the answer) under the word 'Likes' on your branch organizer."

19. For each word that students write, say the whole sentence, e.g., "The horse likes apples." As you say each word of the sentence, point to the corresponding word on the branch chart.

20. Praise students, pass out reinforcers, and take a short break.

21. Draw a large version of the lined paper on your chart paper, using the watercolor marker. Tape the chart paper to the board. Pass out the lined paper. Tape one to each desk, next to the branch organizer.

22. Say: "It's time to make a sentence. Let's make a sentence from the first column of the branch organizer, using the word 'Can.'" (Example sentence: The horse can run.) Point to the words on the branch chart on the board as you slowly say them, forming the sentence.

23. Write the sentence on your "lined paper" on the board.

24. Say: "Copy the sentence on the first line of your paper."

25. Say: "Today we are going to try making a longer sentence. We are going to use two words from the 'Has' column of the branch organizer. Let me show you how." Point to the words on the branch chart on the board as you slowly say them, forming the sentence. (Example sentence: The horse has four legs and a mane.)

Use only one compound phrase per exercise.

26. Write the sentence on your "lined paper" on the board.

27. Say: "Copy the sentence on the second line of your paper." Make sure they write on the lines and not in the blank space above. This is for the illustration.

28. Say: "Let's make a sentence from the third column of the branch organizer, using the word 'Likes.'" (Example sentence: The horse likes apples.) Point to the words on the branch chart on the board as you slowly say them, forming the sentence.

29. Write the sentence on your "lined paper" on the board.

30. Say: "Copy the sentence on the third line of your paper."

When students become familiar with this process, they may choose any of the three words to make a sentence.

31. Say: "Now we will read our sentences aloud." Group students in pairs to read to each other, or let each child read aloud to you, an aide, or the whole class.

32. Praise students and pass out reinforcers.

33. Say: "Now we will draw a picture to go with our sentences." Lead students to read the first sentence and then draw a picture of it. Do this for each sentence, one sentence at a time at first. Monitor the drawings and try to limit them to drawing only one horse. If a higher-functioning child is drawing three horses, clearly intending one horse for each sentence, without exhibiting difficulties, then that is okay. Later in the program, they may be able to remember two or three details at once and incorporate them all into one horse picture.

34. Collect papers and pencils, praise students, and pass out reinforcers.

Name_____ Date _____

The boy is riding the _____ horse. The boy's hat is _____.
The boy's pants are _____. The _____ horse has a
mane and a long tail. The _____ horse is jumping over a fence.
The fence is _____.

1. What is the boy riding?

_____

2. What color is the boy's hat?

_____

THE HORSE —Worksheet 14, Blank

3. What color are the boy's pants?

_____

4. What color is the horse?

_____

5. Does the horse have a long tail or short tail?

_____

6. What is the horse jumping over?

_____

7. What color is the fence?

_____

THE HORSE —Worksheet 14, Blank

THE HORSE
Worksheet 14, Variation 1

Materials:

Worksheet 14 (Variation 1), pencils, and boxes of crayons for each child

Color Variation 1:

Brown Horse
Yellow Hat
Orange Pants
Red Fence

Before the Lesson:

At http://fhautism.com/arc.html, find Worksheet 14 (Variation 1). Print one for each student, plus a few extras. Write the date on the board.

Teaching the Lesson

1. Distribute the worksheets and pencils to your students. Say: "Write your name on your paper." Make sure everyone writes his or her name. Then say: "Write the date. It is on the board." Make sure everyone writes the date. Take the pencils from them.

2. Say: "(student's name), please read the sentences at the top of the paper." Ask several students to read. If no one can read the passage, read it yourself, or have an aide read it.

3. Say: "We want to color the picture. What four crayons do we need?" Ask the question several times, and allow different children to answer. Then help them find the brown, yellow, orange, and red crayons. Take the crayon boxes from them.

4. Say: "We will color the horse brown, the hat yellow, the pants orange, and the fence red. What color do we color the horse?" Ask the question several times, and allow different children to answer.

5. Say: "Color the horse." Make sure they color only the horse. Repeat the words "brown horse" as often as possible.

6. Say: "What color do we color the hat? Let's look back at our story if we need a reminder." Ask the question several times, and allow different children to answer.

7. Say: "Color the hat." Make sure they color only the hat. Repeat the words "yellow hat" as often as possible.

8. Say: "What color do we color the pants? Let's look back at our story if we need a reminder." Ask the question several times, and allow different children to answer.

9. Say: "Color the pants." Make sure they color only the pants. Repeat the words "orange pants" as often as possible.

10. Say: "What color do we color the fence? Let's look back at our story if we need a reminder." Ask the question several times, and allow different children to answer.

11. Say: "Color the fence." Make sure they color only the fence. Repeat the words "red fence" as often as possible. Then take the crayons.

12. Ask comprehension questions. Lead students to answer orally, in a complete sentence. For each question, if the student answers incorrectly, guide him or her to read the text again. Questions: 1. What is the boy riding? 2. What color is the boy's hat? 3. What color are the boy's pants? 4. What color is the horse? 5. Does the horse have a long tail or a short tail? 6. What is the horse jumping over? 7. What color is the fence? Answers: 1. The boy is riding the horse. 2. The boy's hat is yellow. 3. The boy's pants are orange. 4. The horse is brown. 5. The horse has a long tail. 6. The horse is jumping over a fence. 7. The fence is red.

13. Ask the questions again in random order. Give each student a chance to answer correctly, in complete sentences.

14. Pass out pencils. Ask each comprehension question again. (See step 12 for questions and answers.) When a student answers correctly, write the sentence on the board. Say: "Copy the sentence onto your paper." Do this for each question and answer. Take pencils from them.

15. Give out reinforcers.

THE HORSE
Worksheet 14, Variation 2

Materials:

Worksheet 14 (Variation 2), pencils, and boxes of crayons for each child

Color Variation 2:

Black Horse
Green Hat
Yellow Pants
Blue Fence

Before the Lesson:

At http://fhautism.com/arc.html, find Worksheet 14 (Variation 2). Print one for each student, plus a few extras. Write the date on the board.

Teaching the Lesson

1. Distribute the worksheets and pencils to your students. Say: "Write your name on your paper." Make sure everyone writes his or her name. Then say: "Write the date. It is on the board." Make sure everyone writes the date. Take the pencils from them.

2. Say: "(student's name), please read the sentences at the top of the paper." Ask several students to read. If no one can read the passage, read it yourself, or have an aide read it.

3. Say: "We want to color the picture. What four crayons do we need?" Ask the question several times, and allow different children to answer. Then help them find the black, green, yellow, and blue crayons. Take the crayon boxes from them.

4. Say: "We will color the horse black, the hat green, the pants yellow, and the fence blue. What color do we color the horse?" Ask the question several times, and allow different children to answer.

5. Say: "Color the horse." Make sure they color only the horse. Repeat the words "black horse" as often as possible.

6. Say: "What color do we color the hat? Let's look back at our story if we need a reminder." Ask the question several times, and allow different children to answer.

7.   Say: "Color the hat." Make sure they color only the hat. Repeat the words "green hat" as often as possible.

8.   Say: "What color do we color the pants? Let's look back at our story if we need a reminder." Ask the question several times, and allow different children to answer.

9.   Say: "Color the pants." Make sure they color only the pants. Repeat the words "yellow pants" as often as possible.

10.   Say: "What color do we color the fence? Let's look back at our story if we need a reminder." Ask the question several times, and allow different children to answer.

11.   Say: "Color the fence." Make sure they color only the fence. Repeat the words "blue fence" as often as possible. Then take the crayons.

12.   Ask comprehension questions. Lead students to answer orally, in a complete sentence. For each question, if the student answers incorrectly, guide him or her to read the text again. Questions: 1. What is the boy riding? 2. What color is the boy's hat? 3. What color are the boy's pants? 4. What color is the horse? 5. Does the horse have a long tail or a short tail? 6. What is the horse jumping over? 7. What color is the fence? Answers: 1. The boy is riding the horse. 2. The boy's hat is green. 3. The boy's pants are yellow. 4. The horse is black. 5. The horse has a long tail. 6. The horse is jumping over a fence. 7. The fence is blue.

13.   Ask the questions again in random order. Give each student a chance to answer correctly, in complete sentences.

14.   Pass out pencils. Ask each comprehension question again. (See step 12 for questions and answers.) When a student answers correctly, write the sentence on the board. Say: "Copy the sentence onto your paper." Do this for each question and answer. Take pencils from them.

15.   Give out reinforcers.

THE HORSE
Worksheet 14, Variation 3

Materials:

Worksheet 14 (Variation 3), pencils, and boxes of crayons for each child

Color Variation 3:

Yellow Horse
Orange Hat
Black Pants
Green Fence

Before the Lesson:

At http://fhautism.com/arc.html, find Worksheet 14 (Variation 3). Print one for each student, plus a few extras. Write the date on the board.

Teaching the Lesson

1. Distribute the worksheets and pencils to your students. Say: "Write your name on your paper." Make sure everyone writes his or her name. Then say: "Write the date. It is on the board." Make sure everyone writes the date. Take the pencils from them.

2. Say: "(student's name), please read the sentences at the top of the paper." Ask several students to read. If no one can read the passage, read it yourself, or have an aide read it.

3. Say: "We want to color the picture. What four crayons do we need?" Ask the question several times, and allow different children to answer. Then help them find the yellow, orange, black, and green crayons. Take the crayon boxes from them.

4. Say: "We will color the horse yellow, the hat orange, the pants black, and the fence green. What color do we color the horse?" Ask the question several times, and allow different children to answer.

5. Say: "Color the horse." Make sure they color only the horse. Repeat the words "yellow horse" as often as possible.

6. Say: "What color do we color the hat? Let's look back at our story if we need a reminder." Ask the question several times, and allow different children to answer.

7. Say: "Color the hat." Make sure they color only the hat. Repeat the words "orange hat" as often as possible.

8. Say: "What color do we color the pants? Let's look back at our story if we need a reminder." Ask the question several times, and allow different children to answer.

9. Say: "Color the pants." Make sure they color only the pants. Repeat the words "black pants" as often as possible.

10. Say: "What color do we color the fence? Let's look back at our story if we need a reminder." Ask the question several times, and allow different children to answer.

11. Say: "Color the fence." Make sure they color only the fence. Repeat the words "green fence" as often as possible. Then take the crayons.

12. Ask comprehension questions. Lead students to answer orally, in a complete sentence. For each question, if the student answers incorrectly, guide him or her to read the text again. Questions: 1. What is the boy riding? 2. What color is the boy's hat? 3. What color are the boy's pants? 4. What color is the horse? 5. Does the horse have a long tail or a short tail? 6. What is the horse jumping over? 7. What color is the fence? Answers: 1. The boy is riding the horse. 2. The boy's hat is orange. 3. The boy's pants are black. 4. The horse is yellow. 5. The horse has a long tail. 6. The horse is jumping over a fence. 7. The fence is green.

13. Ask the questions again in random order. Give each student a chance to answer correctly, in complete sentences.

14. Pass out pencils. Ask each comprehension question again. (See step 12 for questions and answers.) When a student answers correctly, write the sentence on the board. Say: "Copy the sentence onto your paper." Do this for each question and answer. Take pencils from them.

15. Give out reinforcers.

THE HORSE
Worksheet 14, Variation 4

Materials:

Worksheet 14 (Variation 4), pencils, and boxes of crayons for each child

Color Variation 4:

Gray Horse
Pink Hat
Purple Pants
Yellow Fence

Before the Lesson:

At http://fhautism.com/arc.html, find Worksheet 14 (Variation 4). Print one for each student, plus a few extras. Write the date on the board.

Teaching the Lesson

1. Distribute the worksheets and pencils to your students. Say: "Write your name on your paper." Make sure everyone writes his or her name. Then say: "Write the date. It is on the board." Make sure everyone writes the date. Take the pencils from them.

2. Say: "(student's name), please read the sentences at the top of the paper." Ask several students to read. If no one can read the passage, read it yourself, or have an aide read it.

3. Say: "We want to color the picture. What four crayons do we need?" Ask the question several times, and allow different children to answer. Then help them find the gray, pink, purple, and yellow crayons. Take the crayon boxes from them.

4. Say: "We will color the horse gray, the hat pink, the pants purple, and the fence yellow. What color do we color the horse?" Ask the question several times, and allow different children to answer.

5. Say: "Color the horse." Make sure they color only the horse. Repeat the words "gray horse" as often as possible.

6. Say: "What color do we color the hat? Let's look back at our story if we need a reminder." Ask the question several times, and allow different children to answer.

7. Say: "Color the hat." Make sure they color only the hat. Repeat the words "pink hat" as often as possible.

8. Say: "What color do we color the pants? Let's look back at our story if we need a reminder." Ask the question several times, and allow different children to answer.

9. Say: "Color the pants." Make sure they color only the pants. Repeat the words "purple pants" as often as possible.

10. Say: "What color do we color the fence? Let's look back at our story if we need a reminder." Ask the question several times, and allow different children to answer.

11. Say: "Color the fence." Make sure they color only the fence. Repeat the words "yellow fence" as often as possible. Then take the crayons.

12. Ask comprehension questions. Lead students to answer orally, in a complete sentence. For each question, if the student answers incorrectly, guide him or her to read the text again. Questions: 1. What is the boy riding? 2. What color is the boy's hat? 3. What color are the boy's pants? 4. What color is the horse? 5. Does the horse have a long tail or a short tail? 6. What is the horse jumping over? 7. What color is the fence? Answers: 1. The boy is riding the horse. 2. The boy's hat is pink. 3. The boy's pants are purple. 4. The horse is gray. 5. The horse has a long tail. 6. The horse is jumping over a fence. 7. The fence is yellow.

13. Ask the questions again in random order. Give each student a chance to answer correctly, in complete sentences.

14. Pass out pencils. Ask each comprehension question again. (See step 12 for questions and answers.) When a student answers correctly, write the sentence on the board. Say: "Copy the sentence onto your paper." Do this for each question and answer. Take pencils from them.

15. Give out reinforcers.

THE HORSE
Sentence-Building Exercise 2

Materials:

photograph of horse, students' circle-in-circle charts and branch organizers, lined paper, tape, completed circle-in-circle chart on chart paper (from Lesson 65 sentence-building exercise), two pieces of blank chart paper, dry-erase marker, watercolor marker

Before the Lesson:

1. At http://fhautism.com/arc.html, find the circle-in-circle chart, branch organizer, and lined paper. Print one of each for each student, plus a few extras.

2. On the blank chart paper, draw the lined paper and branch organizer.

3. On the board, hang the completed circle-in-circle chart on chart paper (from Lesson 65 sentence-building exercise) and blank branch organizer.

4. Write the date on the board.

Teaching the Lesson

1. Gather the children in a circle. Hold up the photograph of the horse. Ask: "What animal is this?" If no one can identify the animal, ask an aide to answer, or answer the question yourself.

2. Ask: "Who can tell me something about the horse?" If no one answers, ask: "What can the horse do?" If no one answers, prompt the students to look at the circle-in-circle chart on the board. If no one answers, ask an aide to answer, or answer the question yourself. Possible answers include gallop, run, jump. Students may come up with different answers. Ask the question several times, and allow different children to answer.

3. Ask: "What does the horse have? If no one answers, prompt the students to look at the circle-in-circle chart on the board. If no one answers, ask an aide to answer, or answer the question yourself. Possible answers include four legs, a mane, a tail. Ask the question several times, and allow different children to answer.

4. Ask: "What does the horse like? If no one answers, prompt the students to look at the circle-in-circle chart on the board. If no one answers, ask an aide to answer, or answer the question yourself. Possible answers include apples, hay, carrots. Ask the question several times, and allow different children to answer.

5. Praise students and pass out reinforcers.

6. The children return to their desks. Pass out pencils and blank graphic organizers. On each desk, tape a circle-in-circle chart on the left and the branch organizer on the right.

7. Say: "Write your name on your paper." Make sure everyone writes his or her name. Then say: "Write the date. It is on the board." Make sure everyone writes the date.

8. Say: "Copy the words from the circle-in-circle chart on the board onto your circle-in-circle chart."

9. Say: "Now we will do the branch organizer." On the branch organizer on the board, write "Horse" on the top line and "Can," "Has," and "Likes" on the three spaces under the top line. Say: "Copy the words onto your charts."

10. Ask: "What can the horse do?" Point to the words on the circle-in-circle chart. Encourage students to look at their own chart. If no one answers, ask an aide to answer, or answer the question yourself. Ask the question several times, and allow different children to answer.

    If someone uses a nonsensical word, e.g., "hay," say the whole sentence. Say: "The horse can hay? Does that make sense? Let's look back in the circle and find something the horse can do."

11. Write students' answers on the branch organizer on the board. For each answer, say: "Write (the answer) under the word 'Can' on your branch organizer."

12. For each word that students write, say the whole sentence, e.g., "The horse can gallop." As you say each word of the sentence, point to the corresponding word on the branch chart.

13. Ask: "What does the horse have?" Point to the words on the circle-in-circle chart. If no one answers, ask an aide to answer, or answer the question yourself. Ask the question several times, and allow different children to answer.

If someone uses a nonsensical word, e.g., "gallop," say the whole sentence. Say: "The horse has gallop? Does that make sense? Let's look back in the circle and find something the horse has."

14. Write students' answers on the branch chart. For each answer, say: "Write (the answer) under the word 'Has' on your branch organizer."

15. For each word that students write, say the whole sentence, e.g., "The horse has a long tail." As you say each word of the sentence, point to the corresponding word on the branch chart.

16. Ask: "What does the horse like?" Point to the words on the circle-in-circle chart. If no one answers, ask an aide to answer, or answer the question yourself. Ask the question several times, and allow different children to answer.

If someone uses nonsensical words, e.g., "a long tail," say the whole sentence. Say: "The horse likes a long tail? Does that make sense? Let's look back in the circle and find something the horse likes."

17. Write students' answers on the branch organizer on the board. For each answer, say: "Write (the answer) under the word 'Likes' on your branch organizer."

18. For each word that students write, say the whole sentence, e.g., "The horse likes hay." As you say each word of the sentence, point to the corresponding word on the branch chart.

19. Praise students, pass out reinforcers, and take a short break.

20. Draw a large version of the lined paper on your chart paper, using the watercolor marker. Tape the chart paper to the board. Pass out the lined paper. Tape one to each desk, next to the branch organizer.

21. Say: "Today we are going to try making a longer sentence. We are going to use two words from the 'Can' column of the branch organizer. Let me show you how." Point to the words on the branch chart on the board as you slowly say them, forming the sentence. (Example sentence: The horse can gallop and jump.)

Lead students to make different sentences than they did in the first sentence-building exercise. Use only one compound phrase per exercise.

22. Write the sentence on your "lined paper" on the board.

23. Say: "Copy the sentence on the first line of your paper."

24. Say: Let's make a sentence from the second column of the branch organizer, using the word 'Has.'" (Example sentence: The horse has a long tail.) Point to the words on the branch chart on the board as you slowly say them, forming the sentence.

25. Write the sentence on your "lined paper" on the board.

26. Say: "Copy the sentence on the second line of your paper."

27. Say: "Let's make a sentence from the third column of the branch organizer, using the word 'Likes.'" (Example sentence: The horse likes hay.) Point to the words on the branch chart on the board as you slowly say them, forming the sentence.

28. Write the sentence on your "lined paper" on the board.

29. Say: "Copy the sentence on the third line of your paper."

30. Say: "Now we will read our sentences aloud." Group students in pairs to read to each other, or let each child read aloud to you, an aide, or the whole class.

31. Praise students and pass out reinforcers.

32. Say: "Now we will draw a picture to go with our sentences." Lead students to read the sentences. Then encourage them to remember and draw two or three details at once and incorporate them all into one horse picture.

Students might be tempted to draw the same picture as in the first sentence-building exercise. Keep students connected to the meaning of the words.

33. Collect papers and pencils, praise students, and pass out reinforcers.

LEVEL 8

THE BIRDS

Get the free print PDF of the bird photo and this page at http://fhautism.com/arc.html.

Name_____ Date _____

There are three birds in the brown nest. They are eating _____ worms.

The bird on the left is _____. The bird on the right is _____.

The bird in the middle is _____. The birds feel happy.

1. Where are the birds?

_____

2. How many birds are in the nest?

_____

3. What color is the nest?

_____

THE BIRDS —Worksheet 15, Blank

4. What color are the worms?

_____

5. What color is the left bird?

_____

6. What color is the right bird?

_____

7. What color is the middle bird?

_____

8. How do the birds feel?

_____

THE BIRDS —Worksheet 15, Blank

THE BIRDS
Worksheet 15, Variation 1

Materials:

Worksheet 15 (Variation 1), pencils, and boxes of crayons for each child

Color Variation 1:

Brown Worms
Red Left Bird
Blue Right Bird
Yellow Middle Bird

Before the Lesson:

At http://fhautism.com/arc.html, find Worksheet 15 (Variation 1). Print one for each student, plus a few extras. Write the date on the board.

Teaching the Lesson

1. Distribute the worksheets and pencils to your students. Say: "Write your name on your paper." Make sure everyone writes his or her name. Then say: "Write the date. It is on the board." Make sure everyone writes the date. Take the pencils from them.

2. Say: "(student's name), please read the sentences at the top of the paper." Ask several students to read. If no one can read the passage, read it yourself, or have an aide read it.

3. Say: "We want to color the picture. What four crayons do we need?" Ask the question several times, and allow different children to answer. Then help them find the brown, red, blue, and yellow crayons. Take the crayon boxes from them.

4. Say: "We will color the worms brown, the left bird red, the right bird blue, and the middle bird yellow. What color do we color the worms?" Ask the question several times, and allow different children to answer.

5. Say: "Color the worms." Make sure they color only the worms. Repeat the words "brown worms" as often as possible.

6. Say: "What color do we color the left bird? Let's look back at our story if we need a reminder." Ask the question several times, and allow different children to answer.

7. Say: "Color the left bird." Make sure they color only the left bird. Repeat the words "red left bird" as often as possible.

8. Say: "What color do we color the right bird? Let's look back at our story if we need a reminder." Ask the question several times, and allow different children to answer.

9. Say: "Color the right bird." Make sure they color only the right bird. Repeat the words "blue right bird" as often as possible.

10. Say: "What color do we color the middle bird? Let's look back at our story if we need a reminder." Ask the question several times, and allow different children to answer.

11. Say: "Color the middle bird." Make sure they color only the middle bird. Repeat the words "yellow middle bird" as often as possible. Then take the crayons.

12. Ask comprehension questions. Lead students to answer orally, in a complete sentence. For each question, if the student answers incorrectly, guide him or her to read the text again. Questions: 1. Where are the birds? 2. How many birds are in the nest? 3. What color is the nest? 4. What color are the worms? 5. What color is the left bird? 6. What color is the right bird? 7. What color is the middle bird? 8. How do the birds feel? Answers: 1. The birds are in the nest. 2. There are three birds in the nest. 3. The nest is brown. 4. The worms are brown. 5. The left bird is red. 6. The right bird is blue. 7. The middle bird is yellow. 8. The birds feel happy.

13. Ask the questions again in random order. Give each student a chance to answer correctly, in complete sentences.

14. Pass out pencils. Ask each comprehension question again. (See step 12 for questions and answers.) When a student answers correctly, write the sentence on the board. Say: "Copy the sentence onto your paper." Do this for each question and answer. Take pencils from them.

15. Give out reinforcers.

THE BIRDS
Worksheet 15, Variation 2

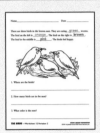

Materials:

Worksheet 15 (Variation 2), pencils, and boxes of crayons for each child

Color Variation 2:

Green Worms
Orange Left Bird
Brown Right Bird
Pink Middle Bird

Before the Lesson:

At http://fhautism.com/arc.html, find Worksheet 15 (Variation 2). Print one for each student, plus a few extras. Write the date on the board.

Teaching the Lesson

1. Distribute the worksheets and pencils to your students. Say: "Write your name on your paper." Make sure everyone writes his or her name. Then say: "Write the date. It is on the board." Make sure everyone writes the date. Take the pencils from them.

2. Say: "(student's name), please read the sentences at the top of the paper." Ask several students to read. If no one can read the passage, read it yourself, or have an aide read it.

3. Say: "We want to color the picture. What four crayons do we need?" Ask the question several times, and allow different children to answer. Then help them find the green, orange, brown, and pink crayons. Take the crayon boxes from them.

4. Say: "We will color the worms green, the left bird orange, the right bird brown, and the middle bird pink. What color do we color the worms?" Ask the question several times, and allow different children to answer.

5. Say: "Color the worms." Make sure they color only the worms. Repeat the words "green worms" as often as possible.

6. Say: "What color do we color the left bird? Let's look back at our story if we need a reminder." Ask the question several times, and allow different children to answer.

7. Say: "Color the left bird." Make sure they color only the left bird. Repeat the words "orange left bird" as often as possible.

8. Say: "What color do we color the right bird? Let's look back at our story if we need a reminder." Ask the question several times, and allow different children to answer.

9. Say: "Color the right bird." Make sure they color only the right bird. Repeat the words "brown right bird" as often as possible.

10. Say: "What color do we color the middle bird? Let's look back at our story if we need a reminder." Ask the question several times, and allow different children to answer.

11. Say: "Color the middle bird." Make sure they color only the middle bird. Repeat the words "pink middle bird" as often as possible. Then take the crayons.

12. Ask comprehension questions. Lead students to answer orally, in a complete sentence. For each question, if the student answers incorrectly, guide him or her to read the text again. Questions: 1. Where are the birds? 2. How many birds are in the nest? 3. What color is the nest? 4. What color are the worms? 5. What color is the left bird? 6. What color is the right bird? 7. What color is the middle bird? 8. How do the birds feel? Answers: 1. The birds are in the nest. 2. There are three birds in the nest. 3. The nest is brown. 4. The worms are green. 5. The left bird is orange. 6. The right bird is brown. 7. The middle bird is pink. 8. The birds feel happy.

13. Ask the questions again in random order. Give each student a chance to answer correctly, in complete sentences.

14. Pass out pencils. Ask each comprehension question again. (See step 12 for questions and answers.) When a student answers correctly, write the sentence on the board. Say: "Copy the sentence onto your paper." Do this for each question and answer. Take pencils from them.

15. Give out reinforcers.

THE BIRDS
Worksheet 15, Variation 3

Materials:

Worksheet 15 (Variation 3), pencils, and boxes of crayons for each child

Color Variation 3:

Pink Worms
Purple Left Bird
Green Right Bird
Brown Middle Bird

Before the Lesson:

At http://fhautism.com/arc.html, find Worksheet 15 (Variation 3). Print one for each student, plus a few extras. Write the date on the board.

Teaching the Lesson

1. Distribute the worksheets and pencils to your students. Say: "Write your name on your paper." Make sure everyone writes his or her name. Then say: "Write the date. It is on the board." Make sure everyone writes the date. Take the pencils from them.

2. Say: "(student's name), please read the sentences at the top of the paper." Ask several students to read. If no one can read the passage, read it yourself, or have an aide read it.

3. Say: "We want to color the picture. What four crayons do we need?" Ask the question several times, and allow different children to answer. Then help them find the pink, purple, green, and brown crayons. Take the crayon boxes from them.

4. Say: "We will color the worms pink, the left bird purple, the right bird green, and the middle bird brown. What color do we color the worms?" Ask the question several times, and allow different children to answer.

5. Say: "Color the worms." Make sure they color only the worms. Repeat the words "pink worms" as often as possible.

6. Say: "What color do we color the left bird? Let's look back at our story if we need a reminder." Ask the question several times, and allow different children to answer.

7. Say: "Color the left bird." Make sure they color only the left bird. Repeat the words "purple left bird" as often as possible.

8. Say: "What color do we color the right bird? Let's look back at our story if we need a reminder." Ask the question several times, and allow different children to answer.

9. Say: "Color the right bird." Make sure they color only the right bird. Repeat the words "green right bird" as often as possible.

10. Say: "What color do we color the middle bird? Let's look back at our story if we need a reminder." Ask the question several times, and allow different children to answer.

11. Say: "Color the middle bird." Make sure they color only the middle bird. Repeat the words "brown middle bird" as often as possible. Then take the crayons.

12. Ask comprehension questions. Lead students to answer orally, in a complete sentence. For each question, if the student answers incorrectly, guide him or her to read the text again. Questions: 1. Where are the birds? 2. How many birds are in the nest? 3. What color is the nest? 4. What color are the worms? 5. What color is the left bird? 6. What color is the right bird? 7. What color is the middle bird? 8. How do the birds feel? Answers: 1. The birds are in the nest. 2. There are three birds in the nest. 3. The nest is brown. 4. The worms are pink. 5. The left bird is purple. 6. The right bird is green. 7. The middle bird is brown. 8. The birds feel happy.

13. Ask the questions again in random order. Give each student a chance to answer correctly, in complete sentences.

14. Pass out pencils. Ask each comprehension question again. (See step 12 for questions and answers.) When a student answers correctly, write the sentence on the board. Say: "Copy the sentence onto your paper." Do this for each question and answer. Take pencils from them.

15. Give out reinforcers.

THE BIRDS
Worksheet 15, Variation 4

Materials:

Worksheet 15 (Variation 4), pencils, and boxes of crayons for each child

Color Variation 4:

Orange Worms
Blue Left Bird
Black Right Bird
Red Middle Bird

Before the Lesson:

At http://fhautism.com/arc.html, find Worksheet 15 (Variation 4). Print one for each student, plus a few extras. Write the date on the board.

Teaching the Lesson

1. Distribute the worksheets and pencils to your students. Say: "Write your name on your paper." Make sure everyone writes his or her name. Then say: "Write the date. It is on the board." Make sure everyone writes the date. Take the pencils from them.

2. Say: "(student's name), please read the sentences at the top of the paper." Ask several students to read. If no one can read the passage, read it yourself, or have an aide read it.

3. Say: "We want to color the picture. What four crayons do we need?" Ask the question several times, and allow different children to answer. Then help them find the orange, blue, black, and red crayons. Take the crayon boxes from them.

4. Say: "We will color the worms orange, the left bird blue, the right bird black, and the middle bird red. What color do we color the worms?" Ask the question several times, and allow different children to answer.

5. Say: "Color the worms." Make sure they color only the worms. Repeat the words "orange worms" as often as possible.

6. Say: "What color do we color the left bird? Let's look back at our story if we need a reminder." Ask the question several times, and allow different children to answer.

7. Say: "Color the left bird." Make sure they color only the left bird. Repeat the words "blue left bird" as often as possible.

8. Say: "What color do we color the right bird? Let's look back at our story if we need a reminder." Ask the question several times, and allow different children to answer.

9. Say: "Color the right bird." Make sure they color only the right bird. Repeat the words "black right bird" as often as possible.

10. Say: "What color do we color the middle bird? Let's look back at our story if we need a reminder." Ask the question several times, and allow different children to answer.

11. Say: "Color the middle bird." Make sure they color only the middle bird. Repeat the words "red middle bird" as often as possible. Then take the crayons.

12. Ask comprehension questions. Lead students to answer orally, in a complete sentence. For each question, if the student answers incorrectly, guide him or her to read the text again. Questions: 1. Where are the birds? 2. How many birds are in the nest? 3. What color is the nest? 4. What color are the worms? 5. What color is the left bird? 6. What color is the right bird? 7. What color is the middle bird? 8. How do the birds feel? Answers: 1. The birds are in the nest. 2. There are three birds in the nest. 3. The nest is brown. 4. The worms are orange. 5. The left bird is blue. 6. The right bird is black. 7. The middle bird is red. 8. The birds feel happy.

13. Ask the questions again in random order. Give each student a chance to answer correctly, in complete sentences.

14. Pass out pencils. Ask each comprehension question again. (See step 12 for questions and answers.) When a student answers correctly, write the sentence on the board. Say: "Copy the sentence onto your paper." Do this for each question and answer. Take pencils from them.

15. Give out reinforcers.

THE BIRDS
Sentence-Building Exercise 1

Materials:

photograph of bird, students' circle-in-circle charts and branch organizers, lined paper, tape, three pieces of chart paper, dry-erase marker, watercolor marker

Before the Lesson:

1. At http://fhautism.com/arc.html, find the circle-in-circle chart, branch organizer, and lined paper. Print one of each for each student, plus a few extras.

2. On the chart paper, draw a blank circle-in-circle chart, branch organizer, and lined paper.

3. On the board, hang a blank circle-in-circle chart on the left and a branch organizer on the right. Make them large enough to write all the words you will need.

4. Write the date on the board.

Teaching the Lesson

1. Gather the children in a circle. Hold up the photograph of the bird. Ask: "What animal is this?" If no one can identify the animal, ask an aide to answer, or answer the question yourself.

2. When a student says, "bird," write "bird" in the smaller, inner circle of the circle-in-circle chart.

3. Ask: "Who can tell me something about the bird?" If no one answers, ask: "What can the bird do?" If no one answers, prompt the students. Ask: "Can the bird ride a bike?" If no one answers, ask an aide to answer, or answer the question yourself. Possible answers include fly, chirp, lay an egg. Students may come up with different answers. Ask the question several times, and allow different children to answer. Write the answers in the large circle.

4. Ask: "What does the bird have? If no one answers, prompt the students. Ask: "Does the bird have fur or feathers?" or "Does the bird have four eyes?" If no one answers, ask an aide to answer, or answer the question yourself. Possible answers include wings, a beak, feathers. Students may come up with different answers. Ask the question several times, and allow different children to answer. Write the answers in the large circle.

5. Ask: "What does the bird like? If no one answers, prompt the students with a guessing game. Say: "The bird likes to eat a long, skinny animal. It digs in the dirt. It lives underground. Sometimes we put it on our hook when we go fishing." Do this for the other two answers. If no one answers, ask an aide to answer, or answer the question yourself. Possible answers include worms, bugs, seeds. Students may come up with different answers. Ask the question several times, and allow different children to answer. Write the answers in the large circle. NOTE: If students appear to be getting agitated or panicky, just tell them the answer.

6. Praise students and pass out reinforcers.

7. The children return to their desks. Pass out pencils and blank graphic organizers. On each desk, tape the circle-in-circle chart on the left and the branch organizer on the right.

8. Say: "Write your name on your paper." Make sure everyone writes his or her name. Then say: "Write the date. It is on the board." Make sure everyone writes the date.

9. Say: "Copy the words from the circle-in-circle chart on the board onto your circle-in-circle chart." They do not have to copy all of the words at first.

10. Say: "Now we will do the branch organizer." On the branch organizer on the board, write "Bird" on the top line and "Can," "Has," and "Likes" on the three spaces under the top line. Say: "Copy the words onto your charts."

11. Ask: "What can the bird do?" Point to the words on the circle-in-circle chart. Encourage students to look at their own chart. If no one answers, ask an aide to answer, or answer the question yourself. Ask the question several times, and allow different children to answer.

If someone uses a nonsensical word, e.g., "worms," say the whole sentence. Say: "The bird can worms? Does that make sense? Let's look back in the circle and find something the bird can do."

12. Write students' answers on the branch organizer on the board. For each answer, say: "Write (the answer) under the word 'Can' on your branch organizer."

13. For each word that students write, say the whole sentence, e.g., "The bird can fly." As you say each word of the sentence, point to the corresponding word on the branch chart.

14. Ask: "What does the bird have?" Point to the words on the circle-in-circle chart. If no one answers, ask an aide to answer, or answer the question yourself. Ask the question several times, and allow different children to answer.

If someone uses a nonsensical word, e.g., "fly," say the whole sentence. Say: "The bird has fly? Does that make sense? Let's look back in the circle and find something the bird has."

15. Write students' answers on the branch organizer on the board. For each answer, say: "Write (the answer) under the word 'Has' on your branch organizer."

16. For each word that students write, say the whole sentence, e.g., "The bird has feathers." As you say each word of the sentence, point to the corresponding word on the branch chart.

17. Ask: "What does the bird like?" Point to the words on the circle-in-circle chart. If no one answers, ask an aide to answer, or answer the question yourself. Ask the question several times, and allow different children to answer.

If someone uses a nonsensical word, e.g., "feathers," say the whole sentence. Say: "The bird likes feathers? Does that make sense? Let's look back in the circle and find something the bird likes."

18. Write students' answers on the branch organizer on the board. For each answer, say: "Write (the answer) under the word 'Likes' on your branch organizer."

19. For each word that students write, say the whole sentence, e.g., "The bird likes worms." As you say each word of the sentence, point to the corresponding word on the branch chart.

20. Praise students, pass out reinforcers, and take a short break.

21. Draw a large version of the lined paper on your chart paper, using the watercolor marker. Tape the chart paper to the board. Pass out the lined paper. Tape one to each desk, next to the branch organizer.

22. Say: "It's time to make a sentence. Let's make a sentence from the first column of the branch organizer, using the word 'Can.'" (Example sentence: The bird can fly.) Point to the words on the branch chart on the board as you slowly say them, forming the sentence.

23. Write the sentence on your "lined paper" on the board.

24. Say: "Copy the sentence on the first line of your paper."

25. Say: "Let's make a sentence from the second column of the branch organizer, using the word 'Has.'" (Example sentence: The bird has feathers.) Point to the words on the branch chart on the board as you slowly say them, forming the sentence.

26. Write the sentence on your "lined paper" on the board.

27. Say: "Copy the sentence on the second line of your paper."

28. Say: "Today we are going to try making a longer sentence. We are going to use two words from the 'Likes' column of the branch organizer. Let me show you how." Point to the words on the branch chart on the board as you slowly say them, forming the sentence. (Example sentence: The bird likes worms and bugs.)

    Use only one compound phrase per exercise.

29. Write the sentence on your "lined paper" on the board.

30. Say: "Copy the sentence on the third line of your paper."

31. Say: "Now we will read our sentences aloud." Group students in pairs to read to each other, or let each child read aloud to you, an aide, or the whole class.

32. Praise students and pass out reinforcers.

33. Say: "Now we will draw a picture to go with our sentences." Lead students to read the sentences. Then encourage them to remember and draw two or three details at once and incorporate them all into one bird picture.

34. Collect papers and pencils, praise students, and pass out reinforcers.

Name_____ Date _____

The birds have feathers. The _____ bird is sitting in the nest. The _____ bird is standing on the branch. The leaves on the branch are _____. The _____ bird is flying in the air. The _____ bird is laying an egg. The _____ bird is eating a worm. The _____ bird is chirping.

CHIRP

1. Do the birds have feathers or fur?

_____

2. Where is the _____ bird sitting?

_____

THE BIRDS —Worksheet 16, Blank

3. Where is the _____ bird standing?

_____

4. What color are the leaves on the branch?

_____

5. Where is the _____ bird flying?

_____

6. What is the _____ sitting bird doing?

_____

7. What is the _____ standing bird eating?

_____

8. What is the _____ flying bird doing?

_____

THE BIRDS —Worksheet 16, Blank

THE BIRDS
Worksheet 16, Variation 1

Materials:
Worksheet 16 (Variation 1), pencils, and boxes of crayons for each child

Color Variation 1:

Blue Nesting Bird
Yellow Standing Bird
Orange Leaves
Red Flying Bird

Before the Lesson:
At http://fhautism.com/arc.html, find Worksheet 16 (Variation 1). Print one for each student, plus a few extras. Write the date on the board.

Teaching the Lesson

1. Distribute the worksheets and pencils to your students. Say: "Write your name on your paper." Make sure everyone writes his or her name. Then say: "Write the date. It is on the board." Make sure everyone writes the date. Take the pencils from them.

2. Say: "(student's name), please read the sentences at the top of the paper." Ask several students to read. If no one can read the passage, read it yourself, or have an aide read it.

3. Say: "We want to color the picture. What four crayons do we need?" Ask the question several times, and allow different children to answer. Then help them find the blue, yellow, orange, and red crayons. Take the crayon boxes from them.

4. Say: "We will color the nesting bird blue, the standing bird yellow, the leaves orange, and the flying bird red. What color do we color the nesting bird?" Ask the question several times, and allow different children to answer.

5. Say: "Color the nesting bird." Make sure they color only the nesting bird. Repeat the words "blue nesting bird" as often as possible.

6. Say: "What color do we color the standing bird? Let's look back at our story if we need a reminder." Ask the question several times, and allow different children to answer.

7. Say: "Color the standing bird." Make sure they color only the standing bird. Repeat the words "yellow standing bird" as often as possible.

8. Say: "What color do we color the leaves? Let's look back at our story if we need a reminder." Ask the question several times, and allow different children to answer.

9. Say: "Color the leaves." Make sure they color only the leaves. Repeat the words "orange leaves" as often as possible.

10. Say: "What color do we color the flying bird? Let's look back at our story if we need a reminder." Ask the question several times, and allow different children to answer.

11. Say: "Color the flying bird." Make sure they color only the flying bird. Repeat the words "red flying bird" as often as possible. Then take the crayons.

12. Ask comprehension questions. Lead students to answer orally, in a complete sentence. For each question, if the student answers incorrectly, guide him or her to read the text again. Questions: 1. Do the birds have feathers or fur? 2. Where is the blue bird sitting? 3. Where is the yellow bird standing? 4. What color are the leaves on the branch? 5. Where is the red bird flying? 6. What is the blue sitting bird doing? 7. What is the yellow standing bird eating? 8. What is the red flying bird doing? Answers: 1. The birds have feathers. 2. The blue bird is sitting in the nest. 3. The yellow bird is standing on the branch. 4. The leaves on the branch are orange. 5. The red bird is flying in the air. 6. The blue sitting bird is laying an egg. 7. The yellow standing bird is eating a worm. 8. The red flying bird is chirping.

13. Ask the questions again in random order. Give each student a chance to answer correctly, in complete sentences.

14. Pass out pencils. Ask each comprehension question again. (See step 12 for questions and answers.) When a student answers correctly, write the sentence on the board. Say: "Copy the sentence onto your paper." Do this for each question and answer. Take pencils from them.

15. Give out reinforcers.

THE BIRDS
Worksheet 16, Variation 2

Materials:

Worksheet 16 (Variation 2), pencils, and boxes of crayons for each child

Color Variation 2:

Orange Nesting Bird
Red Standing Bird
Yellow Leaves
Blue Flying Bird

Before the Lesson:

At http://fhautism.com/arc.html, find Worksheet 16 (Variation 2). Print one for each student, plus a few extras. Write the date on the board.

Teaching the Lesson

1. Distribute the worksheets and pencils to your students. Say: "Write your name on your paper." Make sure everyone writes his or her name. Then say: "Write the date. It is on the board." Make sure everyone writes the date. Take the pencils from them.

2. Say: "(student's name), please read the sentences at the top of the paper." Ask several students to read. If no one can read the passage, read it yourself, or have an aide read it.

3. Say: "We want to color the picture. What four crayons do we need?" Ask the question several times, and allow different children to answer. Then help them find the orange, red, yellow, and blue crayons. Take the crayon boxes from them.

4. Say: "We will color the nesting bird orange, the standing bird red, the leaves yellow, and the flying bird blue. What color do we color the nesting bird?" Ask the question several times, and allow different children to answer.

5. Say: "Color the nesting bird." Make sure they color only the nesting bird. Repeat the words "orange nesting bird" as often as possible.

6. Say: "What color do we color the standing bird? Let's look back at our story if we need a reminder." Ask the question several times, and allow different children to answer.

7. Say: "Color the standing bird." Make sure they color only the standing bird. Repeat the words "red standing bird" as often as possible.

8. Say: "What color do we color the leaves? Let's look back at our story if we need a reminder." Ask the question several times, and allow different children to answer.

9. Say: "Color the leaves." Make sure they color only the leaves. Repeat the words "yellow leaves" as often as possible.

10. Say: "What color do we color the flying bird? Let's look back at our story if we need a reminder." Ask the question several times, and allow different children to answer.

11. Say: "Color the flying bird." Make sure they color only the flying bird. Repeat the words "blue flying bird" as often as possible. Then take the crayons.

12. Ask comprehension questions. Lead students to answer orally, in a complete sentence. For each question, if the student answers incorrectly, guide him or her to read the text again. Questions: 1. Do the birds have feathers or fur? 2. Where is the orange bird sitting? 3. Where is the red bird standing? 4. What color are the leaves on the branch? 5. Where is the blue bird flying? 6. What is the orange sitting bird doing? 7. What is the red standing bird eating? 8. What is the blue flying bird doing? Answers: 1. The birds have feathers. 2. The orange bird is sitting in the nest. 3. The red bird is standing on the branch. 4. The leaves on the branch are yellow. 5. The blue bird is flying in the air. 6. The orange sitting bird is laying an egg. 7. The red standing bird is eating a worm. 8. The blue flying bird is chirping.

13. Ask the questions again in random order. Give each student a chance to answer correctly, in complete sentences.

14. Pass out pencils. Ask each comprehension question again. (See step 12 for questions and answers.) When a student answers correctly, write the sentence on the board. Say: "Copy the sentence onto your paper." Do this for each question and answer. Take pencils from them.

15. Give out reinforcers.

AUTISM & READING COMPREHENSION
© 2011 by Joseph Porter, M.Ed. Future Horizons, Inc.

THE BIRDS
Worksheet 16, Variation 3

Materials:

Worksheet 16 (Variation 3), pencils, and boxes of crayons for each child

Color Variation 3:

Yellow Nesting Bird
Blue Standing Bird
Green Leaves
Orange Flying Bird

Before the Lesson:

At http://fhautism.com/arc.html, find Worksheet 16 (Variation 3). Print one for each student, plus a few extras. Write the date on the board.

Teaching the Lesson

1. Distribute the worksheets and pencils to your students. Say: "Write your name on your paper." Make sure everyone writes his or her name. Then say: "Write the date. It is on the board." Make sure everyone writes the date. Take the pencils from them.

2. Say: "(student's name), please read the sentences at the top of the paper." Ask several students to read. If no one can read the passage, read it yourself, or have an aide read it.

3. Say: "We want to color the picture. What four crayons do we need?" Ask the question several times, and allow different children to answer. Then help them find the yellow, blue, green, and orange crayons. Take the crayon boxes from them.

4. Say: "We will color the nesting bird yellow, the standing bird blue, the leaves green, and the flying bird orange. What color do we color the nesting bird?" Ask the question several times, and allow different children to answer.

5. Say: "Color the nesting bird." Make sure they color only the nesting bird. Repeat the words "yellow nesting bird" as often as possible.

6. Say: "What color do we color the standing bird? Let's look back at our story if we need a reminder." Ask the question several times, and allow different children to answer.

Get the free print PDF of this page at http://fhautism.com/arc.html. **277**

7. Say: "Color the standing bird." Make sure they color only the standing bird. Repeat the words "blue standing bird" as often as possible.

8. Say: "What color do we color the leaves? Let's look back at our story if we need a reminder." Ask the question several times, and allow different children to answer.

9. Say: "Color the leaves." Make sure they color only the leaves. Repeat the words "green leaves" as often as possible.

10. Say: "What color do we color the flying bird? Let's look back at our story if we need a reminder." Ask the question several times, and allow different children to answer.

11. Say: "Color the flying bird." Make sure they color only the flying bird. Repeat the words "orange flying bird" as often as possible. Then take the crayons.

12. Ask comprehension questions. Lead students to answer orally, in a complete sentence. For each question, if the student answers incorrectly, guide him or her to read the text again. Questions: 1. Do the birds have feathers or fur? 2. Where is the yellow bird sitting? 3. Where is the blue bird standing? 4. What color are the leaves on the branch? 5. Where is the orange bird flying? 6. What is the yellow sitting bird doing? 7. What is the blue standing bird eating? 8. What is the orange flying bird doing? Answers: 1. The birds have feathers. 2. The yellow bird is sitting in the nest. 3. The blue bird is standing on the branch. 4. The leaves on the branch are green. 5. The orange bird is flying in the air. 6. The yellow sitting bird is laying an egg. 7. The blue standing bird is eating a worm. 8. The orange flying bird is chirping.

13. Ask the questions again in random order. Give each student a chance to answer correctly, in complete sentences.

14. Pass out pencils. Ask each comprehension question again. (See step 12 for questions and answers.) When a student answers correctly, write the sentence on the board. Say: "Copy the sentence onto your paper." Do this for each question and answer. Take pencils from them.

15. Give out reinforcers.

THE BIRDS
Worksheet 16, Variation 4

Materials:

Worksheet 16 (Variation 4), pencils, and boxes of crayons for each child

Color Variation 4:

Red Nesting Bird
Orange Standing Bird
Brown Leaves
Yellow Flying Bird

✔ ## Before the Lesson:

At http://fhautism.com/arc.html, find Worksheet 16 (Variation 4). Print one for each student, plus a few extras. Write the date on the board.

Teaching the Lesson

1. Distribute the worksheets and pencils to your students. Say: "Write your name on your paper." Make sure everyone writes his or her name. Then say: "Write the date. It is on the board." Make sure everyone writes the date. Take the pencils from them.

2. Say: "(student's name), please read the sentences at the top of the paper." Ask several students to read. If no one can read the passage, read it yourself, or have an aide read it.

3. Say: "We want to color the picture. What four crayons do we need?" Ask the question several times, and allow different children to answer. Then help them find the red, orange, brown, and yellow crayons. Take the crayon boxes from them.

4. Say: "We will color the nesting bird red, the standing bird orange, the leaves brown, and the flying bird yellow. What color do we color the nesting bird?" Ask the question several times, and allow different children to answer.

5. Say: "Color the nesting bird." Make sure they color only the nesting bird. Repeat the words "red nesting bird" as often as possible.

6. Say: "What color do we color the standing bird? Let's look back at our story if we need a reminder." Ask the question several times, and allow different children to answer.

---

7. Say: "Color the standing bird." Make sure they color only the standing bird. Repeat the words "orange standing bird" as often as possible.

8. Say: "What color do we color the leaves? Let's look back at our story if we need a reminder." Ask the question several times, and allow different children to answer.

9. Say: "Color the leaves." Make sure they color only the leaves. Repeat the words "brown leaves" as often as possible.

10. Say: "What color do we color the flying bird? Let's look back at our story if we need a reminder." Ask the question several times, and allow different children to answer.

11. Say: "Color the flying bird." Make sure they color only the flying bird. Repeat the words "yellow flying bird" as often as possible. Then take the crayons.

12. Ask comprehension questions. Lead students to answer orally, in a complete sentence. For each question, if the student answers incorrectly, guide him or her to read the text again. Questions: 1. Do the birds have feathers or fur? 2. Where is the red bird sitting? 3. Where is the orange bird standing? 4. What color are the leaves on the branch? 5. Where is the yellow bird flying? 6. What is the red sitting bird doing? 7. What is the orange standing bird eating? 8. What is the yellow flying bird doing? Answers: 1. The birds have feathers. 2. The red bird is sitting in the nest. 3. The orange bird is standing on the branch. 4. The leaves on the branch are brown. 5. The yellow bird is flying in the air. 6. The red sitting bird is laying an egg. 7. The orange standing bird is eating a worm. 8. The yellow flying bird is chirping.

13. Ask the questions again in random order. Give each student a chance to answer correctly, in complete sentences.

14. Pass out pencils. Ask each comprehension question again. (See step 12 for questions and answers.) When a student answers correctly, write the sentence on the board. Say: "Copy the sentence onto your paper." Do this for each question and answer. Take pencils from them.

15. Give out reinforcers.

THE BIRDS
Sentence-Building Exercise 2

Materials:

photograph of bird, students' circle-in-circle charts and branch organizers, lined paper, tape, completed circle-in-circle chart on chart paper (from Lesson 75 sentence-building exercise), two pieces of blank chart paper, dry-erase marker, watercolor marker

Before the Lesson:

1. At http://fhautism.com/arc.html, find the circle-in-circle chart, branch organizer, and lined paper. Print one of each for each student, plus a few extras.

2. On the blank chart paper, draw the lined paper and branch organizer.

3. On the board, hang the completed circle-in-circle chart on chart paper (from Lesson 75 sentence-building exercise) and blank branch organizer.

4. Write the date on the board.

Teaching the Lesson

1. Gather the children in a circle. Hold up the photograph of the bird. Ask: "What animal is this?" If no one can identify the animal, ask an aide to answer, or answer the question yourself.

2. Ask: "Who can tell me something about the bird?" If no one answers, ask: "What can the bird do?" If no one answers, prompt the students to look at the circle-in-circle chart on the board. If no one answers, ask an aide to answer, or answer the question yourself. Possible answers include fly, chirp, lay an egg. Ask the question several times, and allow different children to answer.

3. Ask: "What does the bird have? If no one answers, prompt the students to look at the circle-in-circle chart on the board. If no one answers, ask an aide to answer, or answer the question yourself. Possible answers include wings, beak, feathers. Ask the question several times, and allow different children to answer.

4. Ask: "What does the bird like? If no one answers, prompt the students to look at the circle-in-circle chart on the board. If no one answers, ask an aide to answer, or answer the question yourself. Possible answers include worms, bugs, seeds. Ask the question several times, and allow different children to answer.

5. Praise students and pass out reinforcers.

6. The children return to their desks. Pass out pencils and blank graphic organizers. On each desk, tape a circle-in-circle chart on the left and the branch organizer on the right.

7. Say: "Write your name on your paper." Make sure everyone writes his or her name. Then say: "Write the date. It is on the board." Make sure everyone writes the date.

8. Say: "Copy the words from the circle-in-circle chart on the board onto your circle-in-circle chart." They do not have to copy all of the words at first.

9. Say: "Now we will do the branch organizer." On the branch organizer on the board, write "Bird" on the top line and "Can," "Has," and "Likes" on the three spaces under the top line. Say: "Copy the words onto your charts."

10. Ask: "What can the bird do?" Point to the words on the circle-in-circle chart. Encourage students to look at their own chart. If no one answers, ask an aide to answer, or answer the question yourself. Ask the question several times, and allow different children to answer.

    If someone uses a nonsensical word, e.g., "seeds," say the whole sentence. Say: "The bird can seeds? Does that make sense? Let's look back in the circle and find something the bird can do."

11. Write students' answers on the branch organizer on the board. For each answer, say: "Write (the answer) under the word 'Can' on your branch organizer."

12. For each word that students write, say the whole sentence, e.g., "The bird can lay an egg." As you say each word of the sentence, point to the corresponding word on the branch chart.

13. Ask: "What does the bird have?" Point to the words on the circle-in-circle chart. If no one answers, ask an aide to answer, or answer the question yourself. Ask the question several times, and allow different children to answer.

If someone uses a nonsensical word, e.g., "chirp," say the whole sentence. Say: "The bird has chirp? Does that make sense? Let's look back in the circle and find something the bird has."

14. Write students' answers on the branch chart. For each answer, say: "Write (the answer) under the word 'Has' on your branch organizer."

15. For each word that students write, say the whole sentence, e.g., "The bird has a beak." As you say each word of the sentence, point to the corresponding word on the branch chart.

16. Ask: "What does the bird like?" Point to the words on the circle-in-circle chart. If no one answers, ask an aide to answer, or answer the question yourself. Ask the question several times, and allow different children to answer.

If someone uses nonsensical words, e.g., "a beak," say the whole sentence. Say: "The bird likes a beak? Does that make sense? Let's look back in the circle and find something the bird likes."

17. Write students' answers on the branch organizer on the board. For each answer, say: "Write (the answer) under the word 'Likes' on your branch organizer."

18. For each word that students write, say the whole sentence, e.g., "The bird likes seeds." As you say each word of the sentence, point to the corresponding word on the branch chart.

19. Praise students, pass out reinforcers, and take a short break.

20. Draw a large version of the lined paper on your chart paper, using the watercolor marker. Tape the chart paper to the board. Pass out the lined paper. Tape one to each desk, next to the branch organizer.

21. Say: "It's time to make a sentence. Let's make a sentence from the first column of the branch organizer, using the word 'Can.'" (Example sentence: The bird can lay an egg.) Point to the words on the branch chart on the board as you slowly say them, forming the sentence.

Lead students to make different sentences than they did in the first sentence-building exercise. Use only one compound phrase per exercise.

22. Write the sentence on your "lined paper" on the board.

23. Say: "Copy the sentence on the first line of your paper."

24. Say: "Today we are going to try making a longer sentence. We are going to use two words from the 'Has' column of the branch organizer. Let me show you how." Point to the words on the branch chart on the board as you slowly say them, forming the sentence. (Example sentence: The bird has a beak and feathers.)

Use only one compound phrase per exercise.

25. Write the sentence on your "lined paper" on the board.

26. Say: "Copy the sentence on the second line of your paper." Make sure they write on the lines and not in the blank space above. This is for the illustration.

27. Say: "Let's make a sentence from the third column of the branch organizer, using the word 'Likes.'" (Example sentence: The bird likes seeds.) Point to the words on the branch chart on the board as you slowly say them, forming the sentence.

28. Write the sentence on your "lined paper" on the board.

29. Say: "Copy the sentence on the third line of your paper."

30. Say: "Now we will read our sentences aloud." Group students in pairs to read to each other, or let each child read aloud to you, an aide, or the whole class.

31. Praise students and pass out reinforcers.

32. Say: "Now we will draw a picture to go with our sentences." Lead students to read the sentences. Then encourage them to remember and draw two or three details at once and incorporate them all into one bird picture.

33. Collect papers and pencils, praise students, and pass out reinforcers.

LEVEL 9

THE
LIZARD

Get the free print PDF of the lizard photo and this page at http://fhautism.com/arc.html.

Name_____ Date _____

The _____ lizard is on the rock.

He is wearing a birthday hat on his head.

The birthday hat is _____.

The lizard is eating birthday cake.

The cake is _____.

The lizard feels excited.

He is holding a _____ balloon.

1. Where is the lizard?

_____

2. What color is the lizard?

_____

3. What is the lizard wearing on his head?

_____

THE LIZARD —Worksheet 17, Blank

AUTISM & READING COMPREHENSION
© 2011 by Joseph Porter, M.Ed. Future Horizons, Inc.

4. What color is the birthday hat?

_____

5. What is the lizard eating?

_____

6. What color is the cake?

_____

7. How does the lizard feel?

_____

8. What is the lizard holding?

_____

9. What color is the balloon?

_____

THE LIZARD —Worksheet 17, Blank

THE LIZARD
Worksheet 17, Variation 1

Materials:

Worksheet 17 (Variation 1), pencils, and boxes of crayons for each child

Color Variation 1:

Green Lizard
Red Birthday Hat
Pink Cake
Purple Balloon

✔ Before the Lesson:

At http://fhautism.com/arc.html, find Worksheet 17 (Variation 1). Print one for each student, plus a few extras. Write the date on the board.

Teaching the Lesson

1. Distribute the worksheets and pencils to your students. Say: "Write your name on your paper." Make sure everyone writes his or her name. Then say: "Write the date. It is on the board." Make sure everyone writes the date. Take the pencils from them.

2. Say: "(student's name), please read the sentences at the top of the paper." Ask several students to read. If no one can read the passage, read it yourself, or have an aide read it.

3. Say: "We want to color the picture. What four crayons do we need?" Ask the question several times, and allow different children to answer. Then help them find the green, red, pink, and purple crayons. Take the crayon boxes from them.

4. Say: "We will color the lizard green, the birthday hat red, the cake pink, and the balloon purple. What color do we color the lizard?" Ask the question several times, and allow different children to answer.

5. Say: "Color the lizard." Make sure they color only the lizard. Repeat the words "green lizard" as often as possible.

6. Say: "What color do we color the birthday hat? Let's look back at our story if we need a reminder." Ask the question several times, and allow different children to answer.

7. Say: "Color the birthday hat." Make sure they color only the birthday hat. Repeat the words "red birthday hat" as often as possible.

8. Say: "What color do we color the cake? Let's look back at our story if we need a reminder." Ask the question several times, and allow different children to answer.

9. Say: "Color the cake." Make sure they color only the cake. Repeat the words "pink cake" as often as possible.

10. Say: "What color do we color the balloon? Let's look back at our story if we need a reminder." Ask the question several times, and allow different children to answer.

11. Say: "Color the balloon." Make sure they color only the balloon. Repeat the words "purple balloon" as often as possible. Then take the crayons.

12. Ask comprehension questions. Lead students to answer orally, in a complete sentence. For each question, if the student answers incorrectly, guide him or her to read the text again. Questions: 1. Where is the lizard? 2. What color is the lizard? 3. What is the lizard wearing on his head? 4. What color is the birthday hat? 5. What is the lizard eating? 6. What color is the cake? 7. How does the lizard feel? 8. What is the lizard holding? 9. What color is the balloon? Answers: 1. The lizard is on the rock. 2. The lizard is green. 3. The lizard is wearing a birthday hat on his head. 4. The birthday hat is red. 5. The lizard is eating birthday cake. 6. The cake is pink. 7. The lizard feels excited. 8. The lizard is holding a balloon. 9. The balloon is purple.

13. Ask the questions again in random order. Give each student a chance to answer correctly, in complete sentences.

14. Pass out pencils. Ask each comprehension question again. (See step 12 for questions and answers.) When a student answers correctly, write the sentence on the board. Say: "Copy the sentence onto your paper." Do this for each question and answer. Take pencils from them.

15. Pass out boxes of crayons. Say: "Choose one crayon." Make sure they choose only one. Take boxes of crayons from them. Then say: "Color the rock." Make sure they color only the rock. Take papers from them.

16. Give out reinforcers.

AUTISM & READING COMPREHENSION
© 2011 by Joseph Porter, M.Ed. Future Horizons, Inc.

THE LIZARD
Worksheet 17, Variation 2

Materials:

Worksheet 17 (Variation 2), pencils, and boxes of crayons for each child

Color Variation 2:

Yellow Lizard
Green Birthday Hat
Purple Cake
Red Balloon

Before the Lesson:

At http://fhautism.com/arc.html, find Worksheet 17 (Variation 2). Print one for each student, plus a few extras. Write the date on the board.

Teaching the Lesson

1. Distribute the worksheets and pencils to your students. Say: "Write your name on your paper." Make sure everyone writes his or her name. Then say: "Write the date. It is on the board." Make sure everyone writes the date. Take the pencils from them.

2. Say: "(student's name), please read the sentences at the top of the paper." Ask several students to read. If no one can read the passage, read it yourself, or have an aide read it.

3. Say: "We want to color the picture. What four crayons do we need?" Ask the question several times, and allow different children to answer. Then help them find the yellow, green, purple, and red crayons. Take the crayon boxes from them.

4. Say: "We will color the lizard yellow, the birthday hat green, the cake purple, and the balloon red. What color do we color the lizard?" Ask the question several times, and allow different children to answer.

5. Say: "Color the lizard." Make sure they color only the lizard. Repeat the words "yellow lizard" as often as possible.

6. Say: "What color do we color the birthday hat? Let's look back at our story if we need a reminder." Ask the question several times, and allow different children to answer.

7. Say: "Color the birthday hat." Make sure they color only the birthday hat. Repeat the words "green birthday hat" as often as possible.

8. Say: "What color do we color the cake? Let's look back at our story if we need a reminder." Ask the question several times, and allow different children to answer.

9. Say: "Color the cake." Make sure they color only the cake. Repeat the words "purple cake" as often as possible.

10. Say: "What color do we color the balloon? Let's look back at our story if we need a reminder." Ask the question several times, and allow different children to answer.

11. Say: "Color the balloon." Make sure they color only the balloon. Repeat the words "red balloon" as often as possible. Then take the crayons.

12. Ask comprehension questions. Lead students to answer orally, in a complete sentence. For each question, if the student answers incorrectly, guide him or her to read the text again. Questions: 1. Where is the lizard? 2. What color is the lizard? 3. What is the lizard wearing on his head? 4. What color is the birthday hat? 5. What is the lizard eating? 6. What color is the cake? 7. How does the lizard feel? 8. What is the lizard holding? 9. What color is the balloon? Answers: 1. The lizard is on the rock. 2. The lizard is yellow. 3. The lizard is wearing a birthday hat on his head. 4. The birthday hat is green. 5. The lizard is eating birthday cake. 6. The cake is purple. 7. The lizard feels excited. 8. The lizard is holding a balloon. 9. The balloon is red.

13. Ask the questions again in random order. Give each student a chance to answer correctly, in complete sentences.

14. Pass out pencils. Ask each comprehension question again. (See step 12 for questions and answers.) When a student answers correctly, write the sentence on the board. Say: "Copy the sentence onto your paper." Do this for each question and answer. Take pencils from them.

15. Pass out boxes of crayons. Say: "Choose one crayon." Make sure they choose only one. Take boxes of crayons from them. Then say: "Color the rock." Make sure they color only the rock. Take papers from them.

16. Give out reinforcers.

THE LIZARD
Worksheet 17, Variation 3

Materials:

Worksheet 17 (Variation 3), pencils, and boxes of crayons for each child

Color Variation 3:

Orange Lizard
Pink Birthday Hat
Yellow Cake
Blue Balloon

Before the Lesson:

At http://fhautism.com/arc.html, find Worksheet 17 (Variation 3). Print one for each student, plus a few extras. Write the date on the board.

Teaching the Lesson

1. Distribute the worksheets and pencils to your students. Say: "Write your name on your paper." Make sure everyone writes his or her name. Then say: "Write the date. It is on the board." Make sure everyone writes the date. Take the pencils from them.

2. Say: "(student's name), please read the sentences at the top of the paper." Ask several students to read. If no one can read the passage, read it yourself, or have an aide read it.

3. Say: "We want to color the picture. What four crayons do we need?" Ask the question several times, and allow different children to answer. Then help them find the orange, pink, yellow, and blue crayons. Take the crayon boxes from them.

4. Say: "We will color the lizard orange, the birthday hat pink, the cake yellow, and the balloon blue. What color do we color the lizard?" Ask the question several times, and allow different children to answer.

5. Say: "Color the lizard." Make sure they color only the lizard. Repeat the words "orange lizard" as often as possible.

6. Say: "What color do we color the birthday hat? Let's look back at our story if we need a reminder." Ask the question several times, and allow different children to answer.

7. Say: "Color the birthday hat." Make sure they color only the birthday hat. Repeat the words "pink birthday hat" as often as possible.

8. Say: "What color do we color the cake? Let's look back at our story if we need a reminder." Ask the question several times, and allow different children to answer.

9. Say: "Color the cake." Make sure they color only the cake. Repeat the words "yellow cake" as often as possible.

10. Say: "What color do we color the balloon? Let's look back at our story if we need a reminder." Ask the question several times, and allow different children to answer.

11. Say: "Color the balloon." Make sure they color only the balloon. Repeat the words "blue balloon" as often as possible. Then take the crayons.

12. Ask comprehension questions. Lead students to answer orally, in a complete sentence. For each question, if the student answers incorrectly, guide him or her to read the text again. Questions: 1. Where is the lizard? 2. What color is the lizard? 3. What is the lizard wearing on his head? 4. What color is the birthday hat? 5. What is the lizard eating? 6. What color is the cake? 7. How does the lizard feel? 8. What is the lizard holding? 9. What color is the balloon? Answers: 1. The lizard is on the rock. 2. The lizard is orange. 3. The lizard is wearing a birthday hat on his head. 4. The birthday hat is pink. 5. The lizard is eating birthday cake. 6. The cake is yellow. 7. The lizard feels excited. 8. The lizard is holding a balloon. 9. The balloon is blue.

13. Ask the questions again in random order. Give each student a chance to answer correctly, in complete sentences.

14. Pass out pencils. Ask each comprehension question again. (See step 12 for questions and answers.) When a student answers correctly, write the sentence on the board. Say: "Copy the sentence onto your paper." Do this for each question and answer. Take pencils from them.

15. Pass out boxes of crayons. Say: "Choose one crayon." Make sure they choose only one. Take boxes of crayons from them. Then say: "Color the rock." Make sure they color only the rock. Take papers from them.

16. Give out reinforcers.

THE LIZARD
Worksheet 17, Variation 4

Materials:

Worksheet 17 (Variation 4), pencils, and boxes of crayons for each child

Color Variation 4:

Brown Lizard
Yellow Birthday Hat
Green Cake
Orange Balloon

Before the Lesson:

At http://fhautism.com/arc.html, find Worksheet 17 (Variation 4). Print one for each student, plus a few extras. Write the date on the board.

Teaching the Lesson

1. Distribute the worksheets and pencils to your students. Say: "Write your name on your paper." Make sure everyone writes his or her name. Then say: "Write the date. It is on the board." Make sure everyone writes the date. Take the pencils from them.

2. Say: "(student's name), please read the sentences at the top of the paper." Ask several students to read. If no one can read the passage, read it yourself, or have an aide read it.

3. Say: "We want to color the picture. What four crayons do we need?" Ask the question several times, and allow different children to answer. Then help them find the brown, yellow, green, and orange crayons. Take the crayon boxes from them.

4. Say: "We will color the lizard brown, the birthday hat yellow, the cake green, and the balloon orange. What color do we color the lizard?" Ask the question several times, and allow different children to answer.

5. Say: "Color the lizard." Make sure they color only the lizard. Repeat the words "brown lizard" as often as possible.

6. Say: "What color do we color the birthday hat? Let's look back at our story if we need a reminder." Ask the question several times, and allow different children to answer.

7. Say: "Color the birthday hat." Make sure they color only the birthday hat. Repeat the words "yellow birthday hat" as often as possible.

8. Say: "What color do we color the cake? Let's look back at our story if we need a reminder." Ask the question several times, and allow different children to answer.

9. Say: "Color the cake." Make sure they color only the cake. Repeat the words "green cake" as often as possible.

10. Say: "What color do we color the balloon? Let's look back at our story if we need a reminder." Ask the question several times, and allow different children to answer.

11. Say: "Color the balloon." Make sure they color only the balloon. Repeat the words "orange balloon" as often as possible. Then take the crayons.

12. Ask comprehension questions. Lead students to answer orally, in a complete sentence. For each question, if the student answers incorrectly, guide him or her to read the text again. Questions: 1. Where is the lizard? 2. What color is the lizard? 3. What is the lizard wearing on his head? 4. What color is the birthday hat? 5. What is the lizard eating? 6. What color is the cake? 7. How does the lizard feel? 8. What is the lizard holding? 9. What color is the balloon? Answers: 1. The lizard is on the rock. 2. The lizard is brown. 3. The lizard is wearing a birthday hat on his head. 4. The birthday hat is yellow. 5. The lizard is eating birthday cake. 6. The cake is green. 7. The lizard feels excited. 8. The lizard is holding a balloon. 9. The balloon is orange.

13. Ask the questions again in random order. Give each student a chance to answer correctly, in complete sentences.

14. Pass out pencils. Ask each comprehension question again. (See step 12 for questions and answers.) When a student answers correctly, write the sentence on the board. Say: "Copy the sentence onto your paper." Do this for each question and answer. Take pencils from them.

15. Pass out boxes of crayons. Say: "Choose one crayon." Make sure they choose only one. Take boxes of crayons from them. Then say: "Color the rock." Make sure they color only the rock. Take papers from them.

16. Give out reinforcers.

THE LIZARD
Sentence-Building Exercise I

Materials:

photograph of lizard, students' circle-in-circle charts and branch organizers, lined paper, tape, three pieces of chart paper, dry-erase marker, watercolor marker

Before the Lesson:

1. At http://fhautism.com/arc.html, find the circle-in-circle chart, branch organizer, and lined paper. Print one of each for each student, plus a few extras.

2. On the chart paper, draw a blank circle-in-circle chart, branch organizer, and lined paper.

3. On the board, hang a blank circle-in-circle chart on the left and a branch organizer on the right. Make them large enough to write all the words you will need.

4. Write the date on the board.

Teaching the Lesson

1. Gather the children in a circle. Hold up the photograph of the lizard. Ask: "What animal is this?" If no one can identify the animal, ask an aide to answer, or answer the question yourself.

2. When a student says, "lizard," write "lizard" in the smaller, inner circle of the circle-in-circle chart.

3. Ask: "Who can tell me something about the lizard?" If no one answers, ask: "What can the lizard do?" If no one answers, prompt the students. Ask: "Can the lizard ride a bike?" If no one answers, ask an aide to answer, or answer the question yourself. Possible answers include climb, run, lie in the sun. Ask the question several times, and allow different children to answer. Write the answers in the large circle.

4. Ask: "What does the lizard have? If no one answers, prompt the students. Ask: "Does the lizard have four eyes?" If no one answers, ask an aide to answer, or answer the question yourself. Possible answers include four legs, a long tail, a tongue. Ask the question several times, and allow different children to answer. Write the answers in the large circle.

5. Ask: "What does the lizard like? If no one answers, prompt the students with a guessing game. Say: "The lizard likes to eat an animal with six legs. It sometimes has wings. It has three body parts. Sometimes we call them insects." Do this for the other two answers. If no one answers, ask an aide to answer, or answer the question yourself. Possible answers include leaves, bugs, worms. Ask the question several times, and allow different children to answer. Write the answers in the large circle.

6. Praise students and pass out reinforcers.

7. The children return to their desks. Pass out pencils and blank graphic organizers. On each desk, tape the circle-in-circle chart on the left and the branch organizer on the right.

8. Say: "Write your name on your paper." Make sure everyone writes his or her name. Then say: "Write the date. It is on the board." Make sure everyone writes the date.

9. Say: "Copy the words from the circle-in-circle chart on the board onto your circle-in-circle chart."

10. Say: "Now we will do the branch organizer." On the branch organizer on the board, write "Lizard" on the top line and "Can," "Has," and "Likes" on the three spaces under the top line. Say: "Copy the words onto your charts."

11. Ask: "What can the lizard do?" Point to the words on the circle-in-circle chart. Encourage students to look at their own chart. If no one answers, ask an aide to answer, or answer the question yourself. Ask the question several times, and allow different children to answer.

If someone uses a nonsensical word, e.g., "bugs," say the whole sentence. Say: "The lizard can bugs? Does that make sense? Let's look back in the circle and find something the lizard can do."

12. Write students' answers on the branch organizer on the board. For each answer, say: "Write (the answer) under the word 'Can' on your branch organizer."

13. For each word that students write, say the whole sentence, e.g., "The lizard can run." As you say each word of the sentence, point to the corresponding word on the branch chart.

14. Ask: "What does the lizard have?" Point to the words on the circle-in-circle chart. If no one answers, ask an aide to answer, or answer the question yourself. Ask the question several times, and allow different children to answer.

If someone uses a nonsensical word, e.g., "run," say the whole sentence. Say: "The lizard has run? Does that make sense? Let's look back in the circle and find something the lizard has."

15. Write students' answers on the branch organizer on the board. For each answer, say: "Write (the answer) under the word 'Has' on your branch organizer."

16. For each word that students write, say the whole sentence, e.g., "The lizard has a tongue." As you say each word of the sentence, point to the corresponding word on the branch chart.

17. Ask: "What does the lizard like?" Point to the words on the circle-in-circle chart. If no one answers, ask an aide to answer, or answer the question yourself. Ask the question several times, and allow different children to answer.

If someone uses a nonsensical word, e.g., "a tongue," say the whole sentence. Say: "The lizard likes a tongue? Does that make sense? Let's look back in the circle and find something the lizard likes."

18. Write students' answers on the branch organizer on the board. For each answer, say: "Write (the answer) under the word 'Likes' on your branch organizer."

19. For each word that students write, say the whole sentence, e.g., "The lizard likes bugs." As you say each word of the sentence, point to the corresponding word on the branch chart.

20. Praise students, pass out reinforcers, and take a short break.

21. Draw a large version of the lined paper on your chart paper, using the watercolor marker. Tape the chart paper to the board. Pass out the lined paper. Tape one to each desk, next to the branch organizer.

22. Say: "It's time to make a sentence. Let's make a sentence from the first column of the branch organizer, using the word 'Can.'" (Example sentence: The lizard can run.) Point to the words on the branch chart on the board as you slowly say them, forming the sentence.

23. Write the sentence on your "lined paper" on the board.

24. Say: "Copy the sentence on the first line of your paper."

25. Say: "Let's make a sentence from the second column of the branch organizer, using the word 'Has.'" (Example sentence: The lizard has a tongue.) Point to the words on the branch chart on the board as you slowly say them, forming the sentence.

26. Write the sentence on your "lined paper" on the board.

27. Say: "Copy the sentence on the second line of your paper."

28. Say: "Today we are going to try making a longer sentence. We are going to use two words from the 'Likes" column of the branch organizer. Let me show you how." Point to the words on the branch chart on the board as you slowly say them, forming the sentence. (Example sentence: The lizard likes leaves and bugs.)

Use only one compound phrase per exercise.

29. Write the sentence on your "lined paper" on the board.

30. Say: "Copy the sentence on the third line of your paper."

31. Say: "Now we will read our sentences aloud." Group students in pairs to read to each other, or let each child read aloud to you, an aide, or the whole class.

32. Praise students and pass out reinforcers.

33. Say: "Now we will draw a picture to go with our sentences." Lead students to read the sentences. Then encourage them to remember and draw two or three details at once and incorporate them all into one lizard picture.

34. Collect papers and pencils, praise students, and pass out reinforcers.

Name_____ Date _____

The _____ lizard has four legs and a long tail.

The lizard is climbing up the tree.

The leaves are _____.

The tree is _____.

The lizard likes to eat leaves.

The lizard caught a bug with his tongue.

The bug is _____.

1. What color is the lizard?

_____

2. How many legs does the lizard have?

_____

3. Does the lizard have a short tail or long tail?

_____

THE LIZARD —Worksheet 18, Blank

AUTISM & READING COMPREHENSION
© 2011 by Joseph Porter, M.Ed. Future Horizons, Inc.

4. Where is the lizard climbing?

_____

5. What color are the leaves?

_____

6. What color is the tree?

_____

7. What does the lizard like to eat?

_____

8. What did the lizard catch with his tongue?

_____

9. What color is the bug?

_____

THE LIZARD —Worksheet 18, Blank

THE LIZARD
Worksheet 18, Variation 1

Materials:

Worksheet 18 (Variation 1), pencils, and boxes of crayons for each child

Color Variation 1:

Green Lizard
Yellow Tree
Orange Leaves
Purple Bug

Before the Lesson:

At http://fhautism.com/arc.html, find Worksheet 18 (Variation 1). Print one for each student, plus a few extras. Write the date on the board.

Teaching the Lesson

1. Distribute the worksheets and pencils to your students. Say: "Write your name on your paper." Make sure everyone writes his or her name. Then say: "Write the date. It is on the board." Make sure everyone writes the date. Take the pencils from them.

2. Say: "(student's name), please read the sentences at the top of the paper." Ask several students to read. If no one can read the passage, read it yourself, or have an aide read it.

3. Say: "We want to color the picture. What four crayons do we need?" Ask the question several times, and allow different children to answer. Then help them find the green, yellow, orange, and purple crayons. Take the crayon boxes from them.

4. Say: "We will color the lizard green, the tree yellow, the leaves orange, and the bug purple. What color do we color the lizard?" Ask the question several times, and allow different children to answer.

5. Say: "Color the lizard." Make sure they color only the lizard. Repeat the words "green lizard" as often as possible.

6. Say: "What color do we color the tree? Let's look back at our story if we need a reminder." Ask the question several times, and allow different children to answer.

---

7. Say: "Color the tree." Make sure they color only the tree. Repeat the words "yellow tree" as often as possible.

8. Say: "What color do we color the leaves? Let's look back at our story if we need a reminder." Ask the question several times, and allow different children to answer.

9. Say: "Color the leaves." Make sure they color only the leaves. Repeat the words "orange leaves" as often as possible.

10. Say: "What color do we color the bug? Let's look back at our story if we need a reminder." Ask the question several times, and allow different children to answer.

11. Say: "Color the bug." Make sure they color only the bug. Repeat the words "purple bug" as often as possible. Then take the crayons.

12. Ask comprehension questions. Lead students to answer orally, in a complete sentence. For each question, if the student answers incorrectly, guide him or her to read the text again. Questions: 1. What color is the lizard? 2. How many legs does the lizard have? 3. Does the lizard have a long tail or a short tail? 4. Where is the lizard climbing? 5. What color are the leaves? 6. What color is the tree? 7. What does the lizard like to eat? 8. What did the lizard catch with his tongue? 9. What color is the bug? Answers: 1. The lizard is green. 2. The lizard has four legs. 3. The lizard has a long tail. 4. The lizard is climbing up the tree. 5. The leaves are orange. 6. The tree is yellow. 7. The lizard likes to eat leaves. 8. The lizard caught a bug with his tongue. 9. The bug is purple.

13. Ask the questions again in random order. Give each student a chance to answer correctly, in complete sentences.

14. Pass out pencils. Ask each comprehension question again. (See step 12 for questions and answers.) When a student answers correctly, write the sentence on the board. Say: "Copy the sentence onto your paper." Do this for each question and answer. Take pencils from them.

15. Give out reinforcers.

THE LIZARD
Worksheet 18, Variation 2

Materials:

Worksheet 18 (Variation 2), pencils, and boxes of crayons for each child

Color Variation 2:

Orange Lizard
Brown Tree
Red Leaves
Green Bug

✔

Before the Lesson:

At http://fhautism.com/arc.html, find Worksheet 18 (Variation 2). Print one for each student, plus a few extras. Write the date on the board.

Teaching the Lesson

1. Distribute the worksheets and pencils to your students. Say: "Write your name on your paper." Make sure everyone writes his or her name. Then say: "Write the date. It is on the board." Make sure everyone writes the date. Take the pencils from them.

2. Say: "(student's name), please read the sentences at the top of the paper." Ask several students to read. If no one can read the passage, read it yourself, or have an aide read it.

3. Say: "We want to color the picture. What four crayons do we need?" Ask the question several times, and allow different children to answer. Then help them find the orange, brown, red, and green crayons. Take the crayon boxes from them.

4. Say: "We will color the lizard orange, the tree brown, the leaves red, and the bug green. What color do we color the lizard?" Ask the question several times, and allow different children to answer.

5. Say: "Color the lizard." Make sure they color only the lizard. Repeat the words "orange lizard" as often as possible.

6. Say: "What color do we color the tree? Let's look back at our story if we need a reminder." Ask the question several times, and allow different children to answer.

---

7. Say: "Color the tree." Make sure they color only the tree. Repeat the words "brown tree" as often as possible.

8. Say: "What color do we color the leaves? Let's look back at our story if we need a reminder." Ask the question several times, and allow different children to answer.

9. Say: "Color the leaves." Make sure they color only the leaves. Repeat the words "red leaves" as often as possible.

10. Say: "What color do we color the bug? Let's look back at our story if we need a reminder." Ask the question several times, and allow different children to answer.

11. Say: "Color the bug." Make sure they color only the bug. Repeat the words "green bug" as often as possible. Then take the crayons.

12. Ask comprehension questions. Lead students to answer orally, in a complete sentence. For each question, if the student answers incorrectly, guide him or her to read the text again. Questions: 1. What color is the lizard? 2. How many legs does the lizard have? 3. Does the lizard have a long tail or a short tail? 4. Where is the lizard climbing? 7. What does the lizard like to eat? 8. What did the lizard catch with his tongue? 9. What color is the bug? Answers: 1. The lizard is orange. 2. The lizard has four legs. 3. The lizard has a long tail. 4. The lizard is climbing up the tree. 5. The leaves are red. 6. The tree is brown. 7. The lizard likes to eat leaves. 8. The lizard caught a bug with his tongue. 9. The bug is green.

13. Ask the questions again in random order. Give each student a chance to answer correctly, in complete sentences.

14. Pass out pencils. Ask each comprehension question again. (See step 12 for questions and answers.) When a student answers correctly, write the sentence on the board. Say: "Copy the sentence onto your paper." Do this for each question and answer. Take pencils from them.

15. Give out reinforcers.

THE LIZARD
Worksheet 18, Variation 3

Materials:

Worksheet 18 (Variation 3), pencils, and boxes of crayons for each child

Color Variation 3:

Purple Lizard
Gray Tree
Yellow Leaves
Orange Bug

✓

Before the Lesson:

At http://fhautism.com/arc.html, find Worksheet 18 (Variation 3). Print one for each student, plus a few extras. Write the date on the board.

Teaching the Lesson

1. Distribute the worksheets and pencils to your students. Say: "Write your name on your paper." Make sure everyone writes his or her name. Then say: "Write the date. It is on the board." Make sure everyone writes the date. Take the pencils from them.

2. Say: "(student's name), please read the sentences at the top of the paper." Ask several students to read. If no one can read the passage, read it yourself, or have an aide read it.

3. Say: "We want to color the picture. What four crayons do we need?" Ask the question several times, and allow different children to answer. Then help them find the purple, gray, yellow, and orange crayons. Take the crayon boxes from them.

4. Say: "We will color the lizard purple, the tree gray, the leaves yellow, and the bug orange. What color do we color the lizard?" Ask the question several times, and allow different children to answer.

5. Say: "Color the lizard." Make sure they color only the lizard. Repeat the words "purple lizard" as often as possible.

6. Say: "What color do we color the tree? Let's look back at our story if we need a reminder." Ask the question several times, and allow different children to answer.

7. Say: "Color the tree." Make sure they color only the tree. Repeat the words "gray tree" as often as possible.

8. Say: "What color do we color the leaves? Let's look back at our story if we need a reminder." Ask the question several times, and allow different children to answer.

9. Say: "Color the leaves." Make sure they color only the leaves. Repeat the words "yellow leaves" as often as possible.

10. Say: "What color do we color the bug? Let's look back at our story if we need a reminder." Ask the question several times, and allow different children to answer.

11. Say: "Color the bug." Make sure they color only the bug. Repeat the words "orange bug" as often as possible. Then take the crayons.

12. Ask comprehension questions. Lead students to answer orally, in a complete sentence. For each question, if the student answers incorrectly, guide him or her to read the text again. Questions: 1. What color is the lizard? 2. How many legs does the lizard have? 3. Does the lizard have a long tail or a short tail? 4. Where is the lizard climbing? 5. What color are the leaves? 6. What color is the tree? 7. What does the lizard like to eat? 8. What did the lizard catch with his tongue? 9. What color is the bug? Answers: 1. The lizard is purple. 2. The lizard has four legs. 3. The lizard has a long tail. 4. The lizard is climbing up the tree. 5. The leaves are yellow. 6. The tree is gray. 7. The lizard likes to eat leaves. 8. The lizard caught a bug with his tongue. 9. The bug is orange.

13. Ask the questions again in random order. Give each student a chance to answer correctly, in complete sentences.

14. Pass out pencils. Ask each comprehension question again. (See step 12 for questions and answers.) When a student answers correctly, write the sentence on the board. Say: "Copy the sentence onto your paper." Do this for each question and answer. Take pencils from them.

15. Give out reinforcers.

THE LIZARD
Worksheet 18, Variation 4

Materials:

Worksheet 18 (Variation 4), pencils, and boxes of crayons for each child

Color Variation 4:

Red Lizard
Orange Tree
Green Leaves
Pink Bug

Before the Lesson:

At http://fhautism.com/arc.html, find Worksheet 18 (Variation 4). Print one for each student, plus a few extras. Write the date on the board.

Teaching the Lesson

1. Distribute the worksheets and pencils to your students. Say: "Write your name on your paper." Make sure everyone writes his or her name. Then say: "Write the date. It is on the board." Make sure everyone writes the date. Take the pencils from them.

2. Say: "(student's name), please read the sentences at the top of the paper." Ask several students to read. If no one can read the passage, read it yourself, or have an aide read it.

3. Say: "We want to color the picture. What four crayons do we need?" Ask the question several times, and allow different children to answer. Then help them find the red, orange, green, and pink crayons. Take the crayon boxes from them.

4. Say: "We will color the lizard red, the tree orange, the leaves green, and the bug pink. What color do we color the lizard?" Ask the question several times, and allow different children to answer.

5. Say: "Color the lizard." Make sure they color only the lizard. Repeat the words "red lizard" as often as possible.

6. Say: "What color do we color the tree? Let's look back at our story if we need a reminder." Ask the question several times, and allow different children to answer.

7. Say: "Color the tree." Make sure they color only the tree. Repeat the words "orange tree" as often as possible.

8. Say: "What color do we color the leaves? Let's look back at our story if we need a reminder." Ask the question several times, and allow different children to answer.

9. Say: "Color the leaves." Make sure they color only the leaves. Repeat the words "green leaves" as often as possible.

10. Say: "What color do we color the bug? Let's look back at our story if we need a reminder." Ask the question several times, and allow different children to answer.

11. Say: "Color the bug." Make sure they color only the bug. Repeat the words "pink bug" as often as possible. Then take the crayons.

12. Ask comprehension questions. Lead students to answer orally, in a complete sentence. For each question, if the student answers incorrectly, guide him or her to read the text again. Questions: 1. What color is the lizard? 2. How many legs does the lizard have? 3. Does the lizard have a long tail or a short tail? 4. Where is the lizard climbing? 5. What color are the leaves? 6. What color is the tree? 7. What does the lizard like to eat? 8. What did the lizard catch with his tongue? 9. What color is the bug? Answers: 1. The lizard is red. 2. The lizard has four legs. 3. The lizard has a long tail. 4. The lizard is climbing up the tree. 5. The leaves are green. 6. The tree is orange. 7. The lizard likes to eat leaves. 8. The lizard caught a bug with his tongue. 9. The bug is pink.

13. Ask the questions again in random order. Give each student a chance to answer correctly, in complete sentences.

14. Pass out pencils. Ask each comprehension question again. (See step 12 for questions and answers.) When a student answers correctly, write the sentence on the board. Say: "Copy the sentence onto your paper." Do this for each question and answer. Take pencils from them.

15. Give out reinforcers.

THE LIZARD
Sentence-Building Exercise 2

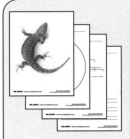

Materials:

photograph of lizard, students' circle-in-circle charts and branch organizers, lined paper, tape, completed circle-in-circle chart on chart paper (from Lesson 85 sentence-building exercise), two pieces of blank chart paper, dry-erase marker, watercolor marker

Before the Lesson:

1. At http://fhautism.com/arc.html, find the circle-in-circle chart, branch organizer, and lined paper. Print one of each for each student, plus a few extras.

2. On the blank chart paper, draw the lined paper and branch organizer.

3. On the board, hang the completed circle-in-circle chart on chart paper (from Lesson 85 sentence-building exercise) and blank branch organizer.

4. Write the date on the board.

Teaching the Lesson

1. Gather the children in a circle. Hold up the photograph of the lizard. Ask: "What animal is this?" If no one can identify the animal, ask an aide to answer, or answer the question yourself.

2. Ask: "Who can tell me something about the lizard?" If no one answers, ask: "What can the lizard do?" If no one answers, prompt the students to look at the circle-in-circle chart on the board. If no one answers, ask an aide to answer, or answer the question yourself. Possible answers include climb, run, lie in the sun. Ask the question several times, and allow different children to answer.

3. Ask: "What does the lizard have? If no one answers, prompt the students to look at the circle-in-circle chart on the board. If no one answers, ask an aide to answer, or answer the question yourself. Possible answers include four legs, a long tail, a tongue. Ask the question several times, and allow different children to answer.

4. Ask: "What does the lizard like? If no one answers, prompt the students to look at the circle-in-circle chart on the board. If no one answers, ask an aide to answer, or answer the question yourself. Possible answers include leaves, bugs, worms. Ask the question several times, and allow different children to answer.

5. Praise students and pass out reinforcers.

6. The children return to their desks. Pass out pencils and blank graphic organizers. On each desk, tape a circle-in-circle chart on the left and the branch organizer on the right.

7. Say: "Write your name on your paper." Make sure everyone writes his or her name. Then say: "Write the date. It is on the board." Make sure everyone writes the date.

8. Say: "Copy the words from the circle-in-circle chart on the board onto your circle-in-circle chart."

9. Say: "Now we will do the branch organizer." On the branch organizer on the board, write "Lizard" on the top line and "Can," "Has," and "Likes" on the three spaces under the top line. Say: "Copy the words onto your charts."

10. Ask: "What can the lizard do?" Point to the words on the circle-in-circle chart. Encourage students to look at their own chart. If no one answers, ask an aide to answer, or answer the question yourself. Ask the question several times, and allow different children to answer.

If someone uses a nonsensical word, e.g., "worms," say the whole sentence. Say: "The lizard can worms? Does that make sense? Let's look back in the circle and find something the lizard can do."

11. Write students' answers on the branch organizer on the board. For each answer, say: "Write (the answer) under the word 'Can' on your branch organizer."

12. For each word that students write, say the whole sentence, e.g., "The lizard can climb." As you say each word of the sentence, point to the corresponding word on the branch chart.

13. Ask: "What does the lizard have?" Point to the words on the circle-in-circle chart. If no one answers, ask an aide to answer, or answer the question yourself. Ask the question several times, and allow different children to answer.

If someone uses a nonsensical word, e.g., "climb," say the whole sentence. Say: "The lizard has climb? Does that make sense? Let's look back in the circle and find something the lizard has."

14. Write students' answers on the branch chart. For each answer, say: "Write (the answer) under the word 'Has' on your branch organizer."

15. For each word that students write, say the whole sentence, e.g., "The lizard has four legs." As you say each word of the sentence, point to the corresponding word on the branch chart.

16. Ask: "What does the lizard like?" Point to the words on the circle-in-circle chart. If no one answers, ask an aide to answer, or answer the question yourself. Ask the question several times, and allow different children to answer.

If someone uses nonsensical words, e.g., "four legs," say the whole sentence. Say: "The lizard likes four legs? Does that make sense? Let's look back in the circle and find something the lizard likes."

17. Write students' answers on the branch organizer on the board. For each answer, say: "Write (the answer) under the word 'Likes' on your branch organizer."

18. For each word that students write, say the whole sentence, e.g., "The lizard likes worms." As you say each word of the sentence, point to the corresponding word on the branch chart.

19. Praise students, pass out reinforcers, and take a short break.

20. Draw a large version of the lined paper on your chart paper, using the watercolor marker. Tape the chart paper to the board. Pass out the lined paper. Tape one to each desk, next to the branch organizer.

21. Say: "It's time to make a sentence. Let's make a sentence from the first column of the branch organizer, using the word 'Can.'" (Example sentence: The lizard can climb.) Point to the words on the branch chart on the board as you slowly say them, forming the sentence.

Lead students to make different sentences than they did in the first sentence-building exercise. Use only one compound phrase per exercise.

22. Write the sentence on your "lined paper" on the board.

23. Say: "Copy the sentence on the first line of your paper."

24. Say: "Today we are going to try making a longer sentence. We are going to use two words from the 'Has' column of the branch organizer. Let me show you how." Point to the words on the branch chart on the board as you slowly say them, forming the sentence. (Example sentence: The lizard has four legs and a long tail.)

Use only one compound phrase per exercise.

25. Write the sentence on your "lined paper" on the board.

26. Say: "Copy the sentence on the second line of your paper."

27. Say: "Let's make a sentence from the third column of the branch organizer, using the word 'Likes.'" (Example sentence: The lizard likes worms.) Point to the words on the branch chart on the board as you slowly say them, forming the sentence.

28. Write the sentence on your "lined paper" on the board.

29. Say: "Copy the sentence on the third line of your paper."

30. Say: "Now we will read our sentences aloud." Group students in pairs to read to each other, or let each child read aloud to you, an aide, or the whole class.

31. Praise students and pass out reinforcers.

32. Say: "Now we will draw a picture to go with our sentences." Lead students to read the sentences. Then encourage them to remember and draw two or three details at once and incorporate them all into one lizard picture.

33. Collect papers and pencils, praise students, and pass out reinforcers.

SUPPLEMENTAL RESOURCES AND ACTIVITIES

You can help bolster your students' familiarity with each animal through a variety of activities. I scoured the Internet to come up with a list of classroom activities for each of the nine animals. The websites for each animal contain art projects on a variety of levels, printables, coloring pages, and even entire themes. I've also included a list of picture books, songs, rhymes, and finger plays for each animal. Unfortunately, the lizard has not inspired many songs or poems. If the web addresses are too cumbersome to type, do a search. Type the name of the animal with the words "preschool," "theme" or "crafts."

THE CAT

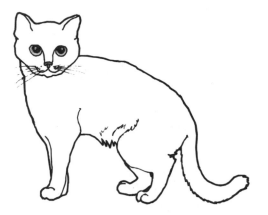

Websites

http://www.first-school.ws/theme/animals/pets/cat.htm

http://stepbystepcc.com/animals/cats.html

http://www.enchantedlearning.com/crafts/cat/

http://www.dltk-kids.com/animals/mpapercat.htm

http://familycrafts.about.com/od/catcrafts/Cat_Craft_Projects.htm

http://www.daniellesplace.com/html/catcrafts.html

http://www.ziggityzoom.com/activities.php?a=36

http://www.preschooleducation.com/shousepets.shtml

Picture Books

The Aristocats
By Louise Gikow

The Baby Blue Cat and the Dirty Dog Brothers
By Ainslie Pryor

Bad Kitty
By Nick Bruel

Bad Kitty Gets a Bath
By Nick Bruel

Bijou, Bonbon and Beau: The Kittens Who Danced for Degas
By Joan Sweeney

Black Cat
By Christopher Myers

The Cat Barked
By Lydia Monks

The Cat in the Hat
By Dr. Seuss

Cat, What Is That?
By Tony Johnston

Catwings
By Ursula K. Le Guin

Comet's Nine Lives
By Jan Brett

The Cookie-Store Cat
By Cynthia Rylant

Elemenopeo
By Harriet Ziefert

Francis the Scaredy Cat
By Ed Boxall

The Grannyman
By Judy Schachner

Happy Birthday, Bad Kitty
By Nick Bruel

Have You Seen My Cat?
By Eric Carle

Hi, Cat!
By Ezra Jack Keats

Hondo & Fabian
By Peter McCarty

Katje, the Windmill Cat
By Gretchen Woelfle

A Kitten Tale
By Eric Rohmann

Kitten's First Full Moon
By Kevin Henkes

A Kitten's Year
By Nancy Raines Day

Kittycat Lullaby
By Eileen Spinelli

Koko's Kitten
By Dr. Francine Patterson

Leo the Late Bloomer
By Robert Kraus

Like Likes Like
By Chris Raschka

Millions of Cats
By Wanda Gág

Mog the Forgetful Cat
By Judith Kerr

Mommy Mine
By Tim Warnes

Orlando (the Marmalade Cat) Buys a Farm
By Kathleen Hale

The Owl and the Pussycat
By Edward Lear

Papa Gatto: An Italian Fairy Tale
By Ruth Sanderson

Papa Piccolo
By Carol Talley

Puss in Boots
By Charles Perrault

Sagwa, The Chinese Siamese Cat
By Amy Tan

Santa's Snow Cat
By Sue Stainton

Six-Dinner Sid
By Inga Moore

Skippyjon Jones
By Judy Schachner

Skippyjon Jones and the Big Bones
By Judy Schachner

Skippyjon Jones in Mummy Trouble
By Judy Schachner

Skippyjon Jones in the Doghouse
By Judy Schachner

Splat the Cat
By Rob Scotton

The Tale of Ginger and Pickles
By Beatrix Potter

The Tale of Samuel Whiskers; or, The Roly-Poly Pudding
By Beatrix Potter

The Tale of Tom Kitten
By Beatrix Potter

Three Little Kittens
By Paul Galdone

Why Do Cats Meow?
By Joan Holub

Songs and Rhymes

"Soft Kitty"
Soft kitty, warm kitty
Little ball of fur
Lazy kitty, pretty kitty
Purr, purr, purr

"Five Kittens"
Five little kittens standing in a row. (Hold up five fingers)
They nod their heads to the children so. (Bend fingers)
They run to the left; they run to the right. (Run fingers to the left and then to the right)
They stand up and stretch in the bright sunlight. (Stretch fingers out tall)
Along comes a dog who's in for some fun. (Hold up one finger from opposite hand)
MEOW! See those little kittens run! (Let fingers run)

"I Have a Pet" (Sing to the tune of "BINGO")
I have a cat who's cuddly soft
And Beau-Jo is her name, oh!
Beau-jo is her name, Beau-jo is her name, Beau-jo is her name,
I love to rub her ears.

"Kitty, Kitty"
I have a little kitty, (Extend first and fourth fingers like ears)
He is as quick as he can be. (Make a quick sideways motion with one hand)
He jumps upon my lap, (Cup one hand in palm of other)
And purrs a song to me. (Make purring sound)

"Four Little Kittens"

One, two, three, four—four little kittens running through the door! (Make fingers run

Four, three, two, one—four little kittens, see how fast they run! (Put fingers behind back, hide all, and "run" again)

One, two, three, four, 'Bye little kittens, running to the store! (Wave with both hands)

"My Kitty Cat"

I have a kitty cat named Puff. (Hold up one thumb)

He's round and soft as a ball of fluff. (Make a circle with finger and thumb of other hand

Each day he laps up all his milk.

And his fur is soft as silk. (Stroke thumb with other hand)

When he's happy you will know,

For his fluffy tail swings to and fro. (Wiggle little finger)

"Lonely Kitten"

I'm just a lonely little kitten, as lonely as can be (Make fist of left hand, thumb for head and little finger for tail)

Won't somebody come and be a friend to me? (Right hand moves toward left with walking motion of index and middle fingers. When they meet, enclose fist in right hand.)

"I Know a Cat" (Sing to the tune of "BINGO")

I know a cat with perky ears, and Kitty is her name-o.

K-I-T-T-Y, K-I-T-T-Y, K-I-T-T-Y,

And Kitty is her name-o.

She makes a sound and it's "meow,"

And Kitty is her name-o.

K-I-T-T-Y, K-I-T-T-Y, K-I-T-T-Y,

And Kitty is her name-o.

"My Kitten" (Sing to the tune of "Sing a Song of Sixpence")

I have a little kitten,

She's black and white and gray.

When I try to cuddle her,

She always wants to play,

So I drag a piece of yarn

Across the kitchen floor.

She thinks it is a little mouse

To chase right out the door.

"I'm a Little Cat" (Sing to the tune of "I'm a Little Teapot")

I'm a little cat.

Soft and furry.

I'll be your friend.

So don't you worry.

Right up on your lap I like to hop.

I'll purr, purr, purr and never stop.

"Mrs. Kitty's Dinner"

Mrs. Kitty, sleek and fat (Put thumb up with fingers folded on right hand)

With her kittens four. (Hold up four fingers on right hand)

Went to sleep upon the mat (Make a fist)

By the kitchen door.

Mrs. Kitty heard a noise.

Up she jumped in glee. (Thumb up on right hand)

Kittens, maybe that's a mouse? (All five fingers on right hand up)

Let's go and see!

Creeping, creeping, creeping on, (Slowly sneaking with five fingers on floor)

Silently they stole.

But the little mouse had gone (Mouse is thumb on left hand)

Back into his hole.

"Pussycat Creeping"

Pussycat creeping and crawling along.(Right hand fingers creeping along)

Little bird chirping and singing a happy little song.(Left hand sitting on left shoulder)

Up jumps pussy, right into the tree.(Right hand onto left shoulder)

Away flies the bird so glad to be free.(Left hand flies away)

"Little Kitten" (Sing to the tune of "I Have a Little Dreidel")

I have a little kitten

With soft and shiny fur.

And when I pet my kitten,

She goes purr, purr, purr, purr.

Oh kitten, kitten, kitten

With soft and shiny fur.

I love to pet my kitten,

And hear her purr, purr, purr

"Carrie Had a Little Cat" (Sing to the tune of "Mary had a Little Lamb";
Substitute child's name)
Carrie had a little cat, little cat, little cat.
Carrie had a little cat,
Its fur was white as snow.
Everywhere that Carrie went, Carrie went, Carrie went,
The cat was sure to go.
It followed her to school one day, school one day, school one day.
Oh, yes, the cat knew how.
It made the children laugh and play, laugh and play, laugh and play
To hear the cat meow

"Two Little Kittens" (Sing to the tune of "Two Little Blackbirds")
Two little kittens sitting on a hill,
One named Jack and one named Jill.
Run away Jack, run away Jill.
Come back Jack, come back Jill.
Two little kittens sitting on a hill,
One named Jack and one named Jill.

"Transition Song"
See the kitties
Sleeping, sleeping.
See the kitties
Sleeping all day long.
Are they ill?
They're so still.
Wake up little kitties, go to ... (snack, table toys, etc.)

"This Kitty"
(Start by holding up all 5 fingers. At each line take one away. On the last line have the final
finger run through a hole made by the left hand.)
This kitty said, "I smell a mouse."
This kitty said, "Let's hunt through the house."
This kitty said, "Let's go creepy creep."
This kitty said, "Is the mouse asleep?"
This kitty said, "Meow, meow, I saw him go through
This hole just now."

"Counting Cats"
One cat napping in the sun.
Two cats playing pounce and run.
Three cats eating from one dish.
Four cats fishing for a fish.
Five cats prancing on a fence.
Six cats peeking under paper tents.
Seven cats blinking crossed blue eyes.
Eight cats chasing butterflies.
Nine cats cuddled tail to head.
Ten cats bouncing on my bed.

"My Cat Says Meow" (Sing to the tune of "The Farmer in the Dell")
My cat says, "Meow,"
My cat says, "Meow."
She likes to purr and run and play.
My cat says, "Meow."

THE RABBIT

Websites

http://www.first-school.ws/theme/animals/wild/rabbit.htm

http://www.everythingpreschool.com/themes/rabbit/index.htm

http://www.dltk-kids.com/animals/mpaperrabbit.htm

http://www.dltk-kids.com/animals/mbunny_basket.htm

http://www.dltk-kids.com/animals/m-ears.htm

http://www.enchantedlearning.com/subjects/mammals/farm/Rabbitprintout.shtml

Picture Books

The ABC Bunny
By Wanda Gág

Beck's Bunny Secret
By Tennant Redbank

The Bunny Book
By Patricia M. Scarry and Richard Scarry

Bunny Cakes
By Rosemary Wells

Bunny Days
By Tao Nyeu

Bunny Fairy Tales (Max and Ruby)
By Samantha Schutz and Katie Carella

Bunny Money
By Rosemary Wells

Busy Bunnies
By John Schindel

The Country Bunny and the Little Gold Shoes
By Du Bose Heyward

Emmaline and the Bunny
By Katherine Hannigan

Grandpa Bunny
By Golden Books

Home for a Bunny
By Margaret Wise Brown

I Am a Bunny
By Ole Risom

It's Not Easy Being a Bunny
By Marilyn Sadler

Little Bunny Follows His Nose
By Katherine Howard

Little Bunny Foo Foo: Told and Sung by the Good Fairy
By Paul Brett Johnson

The Little Rabbit
By Judy Dunn

Pat the Bunny
By Dorothy Kunhardt

Quiet Bunny
By Lisa McCue

Rabbit Magic
By Holly Webb

The Rabbits
By John Marsden

Rabbits and Raindrops
By Jim Arnosky

The Runaway Bunny
By Margaret Wise Brown

Sleepy Bunny
By Golden Books

Snuggle Bunnies
By L.C. Falken and Lisa McCue

So Many Bunnies: A Bedtime ABC and Counting Book
By Rick Walton

The Story of the Rabbit Children
By Sibylle von Olfers

The Tale of Benjamin Bunny
By Beatrix Potter

The Tale of the Flopsy Bunnies
By Beatrix Potter

The Tale of Peter Rabbit
By Beatrix Potter

That's Not My Bunny: Its Tail Is Too Fluffy
By Fiona Watt

The Velveteen Rabbit
By Margery Williams

White Rabbit's Color Book
By Alan Baker

Your Rabbit: A Kid's Guide to Raising and Showing
By Nancy Searle

Songs and Rhymes

"Some Bunnies" (Sing to the tune of "My Bonnie Lies over the Ocean")
Some bunnies have bright shiny noses.
I'm telling you this as a friend.
The reason their noses are shiny–
Their powder puff's on the wrong end.
Wrong end, wrong end,
Their powder puff's on the wrong end, my friend.
Wrong end, wrong end,
Their powder puff's on the wrong end.

"Four Little Bunnies"
Four little bunnies went out to lunch.
They found carrots and took a bunch.
They ate the carrots with a crunch, crunch, crunch!
Four little bunnies went out to lunch.
They found some lettuce and took a bunch.
They ate the lettuce with a munch, munch, munch!

"Bunnies Surprise" (Sing to the tune of "Eensy Weensy Spider")
Once there was a bunny
Who hopped around the town.
He brought colored eggs
And laid them on the ground.

When the children woke up,
They had a big surprise.
Lots of pretty eggs
Right before their eyes!

"Easter Bunny Hops" (Sing to the tune of "Kookaburra")
Easter Bunny hops
All through the town,
Hiding eggs
So they can't be found.
Go Easter Bunny go!
Hide your eggs around!

"Here Comes a Bunny"
Here comes a bunny - hippity, hop, (Squat down and hop)
With ears so funny - floppity, flop. (Put index fingers on side of head and wiggle them
When in danger he -sniffity, sniffs, (Wiggle nose)
Then hides in his hole - jiffity, jiff! (Place hands over head to hide)

"A Rabbit"
Can you make a rabbit
With two ears, so very long (Hold up fingers)
And let him hop, hop, hop about (Hop)
On legs so small and strong?
He nibble, nibbles carrots (Pantomime nibbling)
For his dinner every day.
As soon as he has had enough
He scampers fast away! (Hop on all fours)

"A Bunny"
Once there was a bunny (Double left fist and extend two fingers for ears)
And a green, green cabbage head. (Double left fist on the right hand)
"I think I'll have some breakfast," the little bunny said. (Move bunny toward cabbage head)
So he nibbled and he nibbled (Move fingers on the left hand)
Then he turned around to say,
"I think this is the time I should be hopping on my way! (Make hopping movements with
the left hand)

"Easter Rabbits"
Five little Easter rabbits sitting by the door. (Hold up five fingers)
One hopped away, and then there were four. (Bend one finger)
REFRAIN (repeat after each verse)
Hop, hop, hop, hop! (Clap on each hop)
See how they run!
Ho, hop, hop, hop! (Clap on each hop)
They think it is great fun!
Four little Easter rabbits under a tree. (Hold up four fingers)
One hopped away, and then there were three. (Bend one finger)
Three little Easter rabbits looking at you. (Hold up three fingers)
One hopped away, and then there were two. (Bend one finger)
Two little Easter rabbits resting in the sun. (Hold up two fingers)
One hopped away, and there was one. (Bend one finger)
One little Easter rabbit left all alone. (Hold up one finger)
He hopped away, and then there were none. (Put hand behind back)
Hop, hop, hop, hop! (Clap on each hop)
All gone away!
Hop, hop, hop, hop! (Clap on each hop)
They'll come back some day.

THE BEAR

Websites

http://www.first-school.ws/theme/animals/wild/bear.htm

http://atozteacherstuff.com/Themes/Bears/

http://www.everythingpreschool.com/themes/bears/index.htm

http://www.showmomthemoney.com/bear-preschool-theme-crafts/

http://edtech.kennesaw.edu/web/bears.html

http://www.adaycare.com/PreschoolCurriculumSample1.html

http://stepbystepcc.com/animals/teddybear.html

http://www.teachingheart.net/teddybear.html

http://www.lindaslearninglinks.com/teddybears.html

http://www.preschooleducation.com/stbear.shtml

Picture Books

A Bear Called Paddington
By Michael Bond

Bear Feels Scared
By Karma Wilson

Bear Feels Sick
By Karma Wilson

Bear Stays Up for Christmas
By Karma Wilson

Bear Wants More
By Karma Wilson

Bear's New Friend
By Karma Wilson

Bears
By Ruth Krauss

Bears: Polar Bears, Black Bears and Grizzly Bears
By Deborah Hodge

The Berenstain Bears and the Truth
By Stan Berenstain and Jan Berenstain

The Biggest Bear
By Lynd Ward

A Birthday for Bear
By Bonny Becker

Black Bear: North America's Bear
By Stephen R. Swinburne

A Boy and a Bear: The Children's Relaxation Book
By Lori Lite

Brown Bear, Brown Bear, What Do You See?
By Bill Martin Jr.

Corduroy
By Don Freeman

Father Bear Comes Home
By Else Holmelund Minarik

Goldilocks and the Three Bears
By Candice Ransom

Good Night, Little Bear
By Patsy Scarry

The Grizzly Bear Family Book
By Michio Hoshino

How One Little Polar Bear Captivated the World
By Craig Hatkoff

Jesse Bear, What Will You Wear?
By Nancy White Carlstrom

A Kiss for Little Bear
By Else Holmelund Minarik

Little Bear
By Else Holmelund Minarik

Little Bear's Visit
By Else Holmelund Minarik

The Little Mouse, the Red Ripe Strawberry, and the Big Hungry Bear
By Don Wood

Old Bear
By Kevin Henkes

One True Bear
By Ted Dewan

Orange Pear Apple Bear
By Emily Gravett

Polar Bear, Polar Bear What Do You Hear?
By Bill Martin Jr.

The Teddy Bears' Picnic
By Jimmy Kennedy

The Three Bears
By Golden Books

The Three Snow Bears
By Jan Brett

Touching Spirit Bear
By Ben Mikaelsen

The Valentine Bears
By Eve Bunting

A Visitor for Bear
By Bonny Becker

We're Going on a Bear Hunt
By Michael Rosen

Wonder Bear
By Tao Nyeu

Songs and Rhymes

"Teddy Bear, Teddy Bear"
Teddy bear, teddy bear, turn around
Teddy bear, teddy bear, touch the ground
Teddy bear, teddy bear, dance on your toes

Teddy bear, teddy bear, touch your nose
Teddy bear, teddy bear, stand on your head
Teddy bear, teddy bear, go to bed.

"Three Bears with a Beat"
© Bobby Troup, Londontown Music/ASCAP, 1946
(Snap, clap or pat on the words in parenthesis)
(Once) upon a (time) in the (mid)dle of the (woods), there were (three) (Bears).
(One) was a (Pa)pa bear, (one) was a (Ma)ma bear, (one) was a (wee) bear. (clap clap
A(long) came the (girl) with the (gold)en curls. She (knocked) on the (door) but (no) one
was (there). So she (walked) right (in) 'cause she (did)n't care.
(Home), (home), (home), came the (Pa)pa bear,

(Home), (home), (home), came the (Ma)ma bear,

(Home), (home), (home), came the (wee) bear. (Clap clap)

(Change voice with each bear)
"(Some)one's been (eat)ing my (porr)idge!" (clap) said the (Pa)pa (bear). "Grrrrrrrr" (Hold
hands in front like sharp claws)
"(Some)one's been (eat)ing my (porr)idge!" (clap) said the (Ma)ma (bear). "Ahhhhhhh"
(Throw both hands up in surprise)
"(Hey)-baba-(ree)-bear," (said) the little (wee) bear, "(Some)one has (eat)en my (soup)!
"Hmmmmmph!" (Cross arms on chest and pout)
"(Some)one's been (sit)ting in (my) (chair)!" said the (Pa)pa (bear). "Grrrrrrrrr"
"(Some)one's been (sit)ting in (my) (chair)!" said the (Ma)ma (bear)!" "Ahhhhhhh"
"(Hey)-baba-(ree) bear," said the little (wee) bear, "(Some)one has (brok)en my (seat)!
Hmmmmmph!"
"(Some)one's been (sleep)ing in (my) (bed)!" said the (Pa)pa (bear)!"Grrrrrrrrr" "(Some)
one's been (sleep)ing in (my) (bed)!" said the (Ma)ma(bear)."Ahhhhhhhh"
"(Hey)-baba-(ree)-bear," (said) the little (wee) (bear), "(Some)one is (still) in my (bed)!
Hmmmmmph!"
(Change to a whisper) Just then Goldilocks woke up. (Scream, arms raised:)
"Aaaaahhhhhhhhh!"
She (jumped) out of (bed) and she (beat) it out of (there)! (Point with thumb)
"(Bye), (bye), (bye)," said the (Pa)pa bear. (Wave)
"(Bye), (bye), (bye)," said the (Ma)ma bear. (Wave)
"(Hey)-baba-(ree)-bear," (said) the little (wee) bear, "(This) is the (end) of our (tale).
Hmmmmmph!"

"Bear Song" (Sing to the tune of "Row, Row, Row Your Boat")

Hug, hug, hug your bear

Hug, hug, hug your bear

Squeeze him very tight

Hold him high

Help him fly

Then hug with all your might.

"You Are My Teddy Bear" (Sing to the tune of "You Are My Sunshine")

You are my teddy bear

My only teddy bear

You make me smile dear

You are my friend

You'll never know dear

How much I like you

I'm so glad you're my Teddy Bear today.

"Five Little Bears: Counting Up"

One little bear

Wondering what to do

Along came another

Then there were two!

Two little bears

Climbing up a tree

Along came another

Then there were three!

Three little bears

Ate an apple core

Along came another

Then there were four!

Four little honey bears

Found honey in a hive

Along came another

Then there were five!

"Five Little Bears: Counting Down"

Five little bears

Heard a loud roar

One ran away

Then there were four!
Four little bears
Climbing up a tree
One slid down
Then there were three!
Three little bears
Deciding what to do
One fell asleep
Then there were two!
Two little bears
Having lots of fun
One went home
Then there was one!
One little bear
Feeling all alone
Ran to his mother
Then there were none!

"Cinnamon Bear"
Cinnamon, Cinnamon, Cinnamon Bear,
Sitting on a kitchen chair.
Cinnamon sugar in a shaker
Shake, shake, shake it
Like a baker.
Sprinkle it on buttered toast.
It's the treat
You'll love the most.
Cinnamon, Cinnamon, Cinnamon Bear,
Do you think that we may share?

"The Bear" (Sing to the tune of "The Littlest Worm")
The other day (the other day),
I met a bear (I met a bear),
Away up there (away up there)
A great big bear (a great big bear)
The other day I met a bear,
A great big bear a way up there.
He looked at me (he looked at me)
I looked at him (I looked at him)

He sized up me (he sized up me)

I sized up him (I sized up him)

He looked at me, I looked at him,

He sized up me, I sized up him.

He said to me (he said to me)

"Why don't you run? (why don't you run?)

I see you don't (I see you don't)

Have any gun (have any gun)

He said to me, "Why don't you run? I see you don't have any gun."

And so I ran (and so I ran)

Away from there (away from there)

And right behind (and right behind)

Me was that bear (me was that bear)

And so I ran away from there,

And right behind me was that bear.

Ahead of me (ahead of me)

I saw a tree (I saw a tree)

A great big tree (a great big tree)

Oh, golly gee (oh, golly gee)

Ahead of me there was a tree,

A great big tree, oh, golly gee.

The lowest branch (the lowest branch)

Was ten feet up (was ten feet up)

I had to jump (I had to jump)

And trust my luck (and trust my luck)

The lowest branch was ten feet up,

I had to jump and trust my luck.

And so I jumped (and so I jumped)

Into the air (into the air)

And missed that branch (and missed that branch)

Away up there (away up there)

And so I jumped into the air,

And missed that branch away up there.

Now don't you fret (now don't you fret)

And don't you frown (and don't you frown)

I caught that branch (I caught that branch)

On the way back down (on the way back down)

Now don't you fret and don't you frown,

I caught that branch on the way back down.

That's all there is (that's all there is)

There is no more (there is no more)

Until I meet (until I meet)

That bear once more (that bear once more)

That's all there is, there is no more,

Until I meet that bear once more.

The end, the end (the end, the end)

The end, the end (the end, the end)

The end, the end (the end, the end)

The end, the end (the end, the end)

The end, the end, the end, the end,

This time it really is the end!

"The Bear Went Over the Mountain" (Sing to the tune of "For He's a Jolly Good Fellow")

The bear went over the mountain,

The bear went over the mountain,

The bear went over the mountain,

To see what he could see.

To see what he could see,

To see what he could see,

The other side of the mountain,

The other side of the mountain,

The other side of the mountain,

Was all that he could see.

Was all that he could see,

Was all that he could see,

The other side of the mountain,

Was all that he could see!

"Grizzly Bear"

I'm gonna tell y'a little story 'bout a grizzly bear,

Tell y'a little story 'bout a grizzly bear.

Well, a great big grizzly, grizzly bear,

A great big, grizzly, grizzly bear.

Well, my mama was a-scared of that grizzly bear,

My mama was a-scared on that grizzly bear.

So my Daddy went a-huntin' for that grizzly bear,

My Daddy went a-huntin' for that grizzly bear.

He had long, long hair that grizzly bear,
He had long, long hair that grizzly bear.
He had big, blue eyes that grizzly bear,
He had big, blue eyes that grizzly bear.
Well, he looked everywhere for that grizzly bear,
He looked everywhere for that grizzly bear.
But he couldn't find that great big grizzly bear,
He couldn't find that great big grizzly bear.
So my mama's not a-scared of that grizzly bear,
My mama's not a-scared of that grizzly bear.
That great big grizzly, grizzly bear,
That great big grizzly, grizzly bear.

"Teddy Was His Name-O" (Sing to the tune of "B-I-N-G-O")
There was a boy who had a bear, and Teddy was his name-O
T E D D Y, T E D D Y, T E D D Y and Teddy was his name-O.

"Bear Song" (Sing to the tune of "Row, row, row your boat")
Hug, hug, hug your bear
Squeeze him very tight
Hold him high
Help him fly
Then hug with all your might.

"Going on a Bear Hunt"
Going on a bear hunt,
Gonna catch a big one,
I'm not afraid. (Shake head no)
What's that up ahead? (Shade eyes with hand, look around)
A field. Can't go around it, can't go under it, can't go over it,
Gotta go through it. (Rub hands together)
A lake (Swimming motion)
A mud puddle (Cup hands together, suction sound)
A tree (Climbing motion)
A cave (Reaching out in the dark)
What's this? I feel something ... It has a nose, eyes, ears, fur ... It's a bear! RUN!!!
A cave (Reaching out in the dark)
A tree (Climbing motion)
A mud puddle (Cup hands together, suction sound)

A lake (Swimming motion)
A field (Rub hands together)
Whew! We're home! I'm not afraid!

THE MOUSE

Websites

http://www.first-school.ws/theme/animals/wild/mouse.htm

http://stepbystepcc.com/animals/mice.html

http://www.angelfire.com/dc/childsplay/mice_theme.htm

http://www.everythingpreschool.com/themes/mice/index.htm

http://www.preschooleducation.com/shousepets.shtml

Picture Books

Alexander and the Wind-Up Mouse
By Leo Lionni

Cat and Mouse in a Haunted House
By Geronimo Stilton

Happy Easter, Mouse!
By Laura Numeroff

Happy Valentine's Day, Mouse!
By Laura Numeroff

If You Give a Mouse a Cookie
By Laura Numeroff

If You Take a Mouse to the Movies
By Laura Numeroff

The Karate Mouse
By Geronimo Stilton

Library Mouse
By Daniel Kirk

The Lion and the Mouse
By Gail Herman

The Little Mouse, the Red Ripe Strawberry, and the Big Hungry Bear
By Don Wood

Mice Are Nice
By Charles Ghigna

Mice Squeak, We Speak
By Arnold Shapiro

A Mouse Called Wolf
By Dick King-Smith

Mouse Count
By Ellen Stoll Walsh

The Mouse Island Marathon
By Geronimo Stilton

Mouse Mess
By Linnea Asplind Riley

Mouse Paint
By Ellen Stoll Walsh

Mouse's First Spring
By Lauren Thompson

Mouse Shapes
By Ellen Stoll Walsh

Mouse Soup
By Arnold Lobel

Mouse Tales
By Arnold Lobel

Once a Mouse ...
By Marcia Brown

The Pop-Up Mice of Mr. Brice
By Dr. Seuss

Seven Blind Mice
By Ed Young

The Story of Jumping Mouse
By John Steptoe

There's a Mouse About the House!
By Richard Fowler

Time for School, Mouse!
By Laura Numeroff

Town Mouse, Country Mouse
By Jan Brett

Valentine Mice!
By Bethany Roberts

Whose Mouse Are You?
By Robert Kraus

Songs and Rhymes

"The Mouse" (Sing to the tune of "The Bear Went Over the Mountain")
The mouse ran around the room, (Make circling motions with arms)
The mouse ran around the room,
The mouse ran around the room,
And what do you think he saw?
He saw a great big cat, (Raise arms and make a large circle)
He saw a great big cat,
He saw a great big cat,
So what do you think he did?
The mouse ran into his hole, (Squat down)
The mouse ran into his hole,

The mouse ran into his hole,

Safe and sound at last. (Cover head with arms)

"Mice Are Nice"

We think mice are nice. Oh, we think mice are nice!

Mice have noses that twitch and sniff. We think mice are nice!

We think mice are nice. Oh, we think mice are nice!

Mice have whiskers that wiggle and jiggle. We think mice are nice!

We think mice are nice. Oh, we think mice are nice!

Mice have feet that hurry and scurry. We think mice are nice!

"Hickory Dickory Dock"

Hickory, dickory, dock,

The mouse ran up the clock.

The clock struck one,

The mouse ran down!

Hickory, dickory, dock

"Five Little Mice"

Five little mice came out to play

Gathering crumbs along the way

Out came pussycat sleek and fat

Four little mice go scampering back.

Four little mice came out to play

Gathering crumbs along the way

Out came pussycat sleek and fat

Three little mice go scampering back.

Three little mice came out to play

Gathering crumbs along the way

Out came pussycat sleek and fat

Two little mice go scampering back.

Two little mice came out to play

Gathering crumbs along the way

Out came pussycat sleek and fat

One little mouse goes scampering back.

One little mouse came out to play

Gathering crumbs along the way

Out came pussycat sleek and fat

No little mice go scampering back.

"Little Mousie"
Here's a little mousie
Peeking through a hole. (Poke index finger of one hand through fist of the other hand)
Peek to the left. (Wiggle finger to the left)
Peek to the right. (Wiggle finger to the right)
Pull your head back in, (Pull finger into fist)
There's a cat in sight!

THE MONKEY

Websites

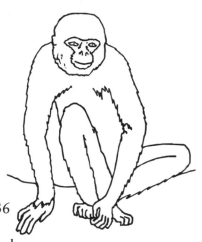

http://www.first-school.ws/activities/animals/wild/monkeys.htm

http://www.amug.org/~jbpratt/education/theme/animals/primate.html

http://www.thebestkidsbooksite.com/thispartictopic.cfm?BookTopic=236

http://www.printactivities.com/Theme-Printables/Monkey-Printables.html

http://www.dltk-kids.com/animals/jungle-monkeys.html

http://www.enchantedlearning.com/crafts/magnetanimals/

Picture Books

Apes and Monkeys (Our Wild World)
By Deborah Dennard

Apes and Monkeys (Science Kids)
By Barbara Taylor

Busy Monkeys
By John Schindel

Caps for Sale
By Esphyr Slobodkina

The Clever Monkey: A Folktale from West Africa
By Rob Cleveland

Curious George
By H. A. Rey

A Different Kind of Hero
By Leah Beth Evans

Eyewitness Books: Gorilla, Monkey & Ape
By Ian Redmond

Hand, Hand, Fingers, Thumb
By Al Perkins

I Am a Little Monkey
By François Crozat

I Love Monkey
By Suzanne Kaufman

I Love You, Little Monkey
By Alan Durant

It's Bedtime for Little Monkeys
By Susie Lee Jin

The Monkey and the Crocodile
By Paul Galdone

Monkey and the Engineer
By Jesse Fuller

Monkey Business (Brand New Readers)
By David Martin

Monkey Business: Stories from Around the World
By Shirley Climo

Monkey Do!
By Allan Ahlberg

Monkey, Monkey, Monkey
By Cathy MacLennan

Monkey See, Monkey Do
By Marc Gave

Monkey Trouble (Brand New Readers)
By David Martin

Monkey with a Tool Belt
By Chris Monroe

Monkey's Clever Tale
By Andrew Fusek-Peters

Monkeys (Our Wild World)
By Deborah Dennard

Monkeys (Science Emergent Readers)
By Susan Canizares

Monkeys and Other Primates
Rebecca Sjonger

Night Monkey Day Monkey
By Julia Donaldson

One Monkey Too Many
By Jackie French Koller

The Sassy Monkey
By Anne Cassidy

So Say the Little Monkeys
By Nancy Van Laan

The Three Monkey Brothers
By Dani Silberman

What Do Monkeys Do?
By Dee Phillips

When the Monkeys Came Back
By Kristine L. Franklin

Songs and Rhymes

"Five Little Monkeys"
Five little monkeys high up in the tree,
Teasing Mr. Alligator, "You can't catch me!"
Along comes Mr. Alligator quiet as can be,
SNAP! that monkey right out of that tree!
(Continue song, counting down to zero little monkeys.)

"Underneath The Monkey Tree" (Sing to the tune of "The Muffin Man")
Come and play a while with me
Underneath the monkey tree.
Monkey See and Monkey Do,
Just like monkeys in the zoo.
Swing your tail, one, two, three
Underneath the monkey tree.
Monkey See and Monkey Do,
Just like monkeys in the zoo.
Jump around and smile like me
Underneath the monkey tree.
Monkey See and Monkey Do,
Just like monkeys in the zoo.

"I'm a Little Monkey" (Sing to the tune of "I'm a Little Teapot")
I'm a little monkey in the tree,
Swinging by my tail so merrily.
I can leap and fly from tree to tree.
I have lots of fun you see.
I'm a little monkey, watch me play,
Munching on bananas every day.
Lots of monkey friends to play with me.
We have fun up the tree.

"Itsy Bitsy Monkey" (Sing to the tune of "Itsy Bitsy Spider")
The itsy bitsy monkey climbed up the coconut tree
Down came a coconut and hit him on his knee—
OWWWWW
Out came a lion a hanging his mighty mane—
ANNNNND
The itsy bitsy monkey climbed up the tree again.

"Monkey See, Monkey Do!"

Monkey see, monkey do!

Let's watch them in the zoo.

We stare in. (Put left hand up)

They look out. (Put right hand up; both hands face each other)

We eat popcorn. (Left hand fingers touch the thumb)

They eat popcorn. (Right hand fingers touch the thumb)

We eat fruit. (Right finger sways back and forth)

They eat fruit. (Left finger sways back and forth)

We stand up. (Left fingers up)

They stand up. (Right fingers up)

We sit down. (Left fingers down)

They sit down. (Right fingers down)

Monkey see, monkey do.

We do it first and they do it, too!

"5 Little Monkeys"

Five little monkeys jumping on the bed,

One fell off and bumped his head.

Momma called the doctor and the doctor said,

"No more monkeys jumping on the bed!"

Four little monkeys ...

Three little monkeys ...

Two little monkeys ...

One little monkey jumping on the bed,

He fell off and bumped his head.

Momma called the doctor and the doctor said,

"Put those monkeys back in bed!"

THE DOG

Websites

http://www.first-school.ws/theme/animals/pets/dog.htm

http://stepbystepcc.com/animals/dogs.html

http://www.mommynature.com/dogs-letter-Dd-preschool-theme.html

http://www.daniellesplace.com/HTML/dog_crafts.html

http://www.dltk-kids.com/animals/pets-dogs.htm

http://familycrafts.about.com/od/dogcrafts/Dog_Craft_Projects.htm

http://www.dog-paw-print.com/games-kids-can-play.html

http://www.preschooleducation.com/shousepets.shtml

Picture Books

Adventures of Fraser the Yellow Dog: Rescue on Snowmass Mountain
By Jill Sheeley

The Adventures of Taxi Dog
By Debra Barracca

Can an Old Dog Learn New Tricks? And Other Questions About Animals
By Buffy Silverman

Caring for Your Dog
By Jill Foran

Dog
By Matthew Van Fleet

Dog
By Clare Walters and Jane Kemp

The Dog That Dug for Dinosaurs
By Shirley-Raye Redmond

Dog's Colorful Day: A Messy Story About Colors and Counting
By Emma Dodd

A Dog's Life
By Nancy Dickmann

Dogs
By Emily Gravett

Dogs (Slim Goodbody's Inside Guide to Pets)
By Slim Goodbody

Dogs on the Job! True Stories of Phenomenal Dogs
By Christopher Farran

Dr. Dog
By Babette Cole

From Puppy to Dog: Following the Life Cycle
By Suzanne Slade

Go, Dog. Go!
By P. D. Eastman

Good Dog, Carl
By Alexandra Day

The Green Dog (Science Solves It!)
By Melinda Luke

Grouping at the Dog Show
By Simone T. Ribke

Having Fun with Your Dog
By Audrey Pavia and Jacque Lynn Schultz

How Dogs Came from Wolves and Other Explorations of Science in Action
By Jack Myers, Ph.D.

Is a Paw a Foot?
By Kris Hirschmann

Jack & Jill: The Miracle Dog with a Happy Tail to Tell
By Jill Rappaport

Living with a Dog (Keep It Simple Guides)
By Dr. Bruce Fogle

Marley: A Dog Like No Other
By John Grogan

May I Pet Your Dog? The How-to Guide for Kids Meeting Dogs (and Dogs Meeting Kids
By Stephanie Calmenson

Measuring at the Dog Show
By Amy Rauen

My Dog: A Book About a Special Pet
By Heather Feldman

National Geographic My First Pocket Guide: Dogs & Wild Dogs
By National Geographic

One Incredible Dog! Lady
By Chris Williams

Our Walk in the Woods
By Charity Nebbe

Puppies and Dogs (QED Know Your Pet)
By Michaela Miller

Rosie: A Visiting Dog's Story
By Stephanie Calmenson

Sesame Subjects: My First Book About Dogs
By Kama Einhorn

Sled Dogs (Dog Heroes)
By Lori Haskins

The Story of the Boxer (Dogs Throughout History)
By Martha Mulvany

Tiny the Snow Dog
By Cari Meister

Uncover a Dog
By Paul Beck

Understanding Man's Best Friend: Why Dogs Look and Act the Way They Do
By Dr. Ann Squire

What Is a Dog? (Science of Living Things)
By Bobbie Kalman and Hannelore Sotzek

Why Is Blue Dog Blue?
By George Rodrigue and Bruce Goldstone

Songs and Rhymes

"Five Little Puppies"
Five little puppies were playing in the sun. (Hold up hands, fingers extended)
This one saw a rabbit, and he began to run. (Bend first finger)
This one saw a butterfly, and he began to race. (Bend second finger)
This one saw a cat, and he began to chase. (Bend third finger)
This one tried to catch his tail, and he went round and round. (Bend fourth finger)
This one was so quiet that he never made a sound. (Bend thumb)

"Little Puppies"
Little puppy one fell asleep in the sun. (Pretend to sleep)
Little puppy two likes to play with my shoe. (Point to shoe)
Little puppy three always kisses me. (Point to cheek)
Little puppy four ran out the door. (Fingers run)
Little puppy five watched a crow dive. (Hands dive)
Little puppy six likes to do little tricks. (Pretend sit up like a dog)
Little puppy seven counted stars in heaven. (Count, looking at sky)
Little puppy eight jumped over the gate. (Fingers jump up)
Little puppy nine sat down to dine. (Pretend to eat)
Little puppy ten fell asleep in the den. (Pretend to sleep)
Can you count the puppies?
1,2,3,4,5,6,7,8,9,10.

"I Had a Little Poodle"
I had a little poodle.
His coat was silver grey.
One day I thought I'd bathe him
To wash the dirt away.
I washed my little poodle
Then dried him with a towel.
My poodle seemed to like his bath.
He didn't even growl.

"Doggie" (Sing to the Tune of "Teddy Bear, Teddy Bear")
Doggie, Doggie,
Turn around. (Spin around)
Doggie, Doggie,
Touch the ground. (Touch the floor)
Doggie, Doggie,
Shine your shoes. (Rub shoes)
Doggie, Doggie, Skidoo.
Doggie, Doggie,
Go upstairs. (Pretend to climb stairs)
Doggie, Doggie,
Say your prayers. (Fold hands, and pretend to pray)
Doggie, Doggie,
Turn out the light. (Pretend to pull string on light bulb)
Doggie, Doggie,
Say good night. (Fold hands next to cheek, and pretend to sleep)

"The Dog Went Over the Mountain" (Sing to the tune of "For He's a Jolly Good Fellow")
The dog went over the mountain,
The dog went over the mountain,
The dog went over the mountain,
To see what he could see.
To see what he could see,
To see what he could see,
The other side of the mountain,
The other side of the mountain,
The other side of the mountain,
Was all that he could see.
Was all that he could see,
Was all that he could see,
The other side of the mountain,
Was all that he could see!

"Bingo"
There was a farmer had a dog,
And Bingo was his name-o.
B-I-N-G-O!
B-I-N-G-O!
B-I-N-G-O!

And Bingo was his name-o!
There was a farmer had a dog,
And Bingo was his name-o.
(Clap)-I-N-G-O!
(Clap)-I-N-G-O!
(Clap)-I-N-G-O!
And Bingo was his name-o!
There was a farmer had a dog,
And Bingo was his name-o.
(Clap, clap)-N-G-O!
(Clap, clap)-N-G-O!
(Clap, clap)-N-G-O!
And Bingo was his name-o!
There was a farmer had a dog,
And Bingo was his name-o.
(Clap, clap, clap)-G-O!
(Clap, clap, clap)-G-O!
(Clap, clap, clap)-G-O!
And Bingo was his name-o!
There was a farmer had a dog,
And Bingo was his name-o.
(Clap, clap, clap, clap)-O!
(Clap, clap, clap, clap)-O!
(Clap, clap, clap, clap)-O!
And Bingo was his name-o!
There was a farmer had a dog,
And Bingo was his name-o.
(Clap, clap, clap, clap, clap)
(Clap, clap, clap, clap, clap)
(Clap, clap, clap, clap, clap)
And Bingo was his name-o!

Games

Dog Bone Jar – Version One
For older children, fill a small jar with dog bones. Ask each child to guess how many dog bones are in the jar. For younger children, limit the number of dog bones to less than ten. Record each child's guess. Count the dog bones.

Dog Bone Jar – Version Two

Provide three identical jars with pre-counted dog bones of 20, 30, and 40. Label these jars 20, 30 and 40. Place 20 to 40 dog bones in a fourth identical jar. Allow the children to examine all four jars before they guess. Record the children's guesses. Count the dog bones.

Musical Dogs

Cut out dog or bone shapes from colored paper. Laminate them, and cut them out. Place them on the floor. Play music, and have the children walk around the room. When the music stops, each child needs to find a shape to stand on. For younger children, use a lot of shapes, so they can easily find one to stand on.

Doggie Doggie, Where's Your Bone?

Children sit in a circle. The teacher chooses one child to be the "doggie." That child sits in the middle of the circle and hides his or her eyes. Then the teacher gives a toy to one child. That child hides the toy behind his or her back. The other children pretend to have the toy by holding their hands behind their backs.

The children then chant:
Doggie, doggie, where's your bone?
Somebody took it from your home.
Upstairs, downstairs, by the telephone,
Wake up doggie! Find your bone.

The child in the middle uncovers his or her eyes. This child guesses who has the toy by pointing to another child. That child shows his or her hands. After three guesses, the child in the middle goes back to his or her spot, whether he or she was correct or not. The child who has the toy sits in the middle, and the game continues.

THE HORSE

Websites

http://www.first-school.ws/activities/alpha/h/horse.htm

http://www.everythingpreschool.com/themes/horses/index.htm

http://www.everythingpreschool.com/themes/western/songs.htm

---

http://www.printactivities.com/Theme-Printables/Horse-Printables.html

http://www.suite101.com/content/horse-sock-puppet-a53283

http://www.busybeekidscrafts.com/Foot-Print-Horse.html

http://www.artistshelpingchildren.org/horsescraftsideasactivitieskids.html

Picture Books

101 Facts About Horses and Ponies
By Julia Barnes

1000 Things You Should Know About Horses
By Belinda Gallagher

Face to Face with Wild Horses
By Yva Momatiuk

A Field Full of Horses
By Peter Hansard

From Foal to Horse
By Robin Nelson

Galloping Across the U.S.A.: Horses in American Life
By Martin W. Sandler

Horse (Eyewitness Guides)
By Juliet Clutton-Brock

The Horse (My First Discoveries Series)
By Henri Galeron

Horse & Pony Care
By Sandy Ransford

Horse Crazy! 1001 Fun Facts, Ideas, Activities, Projects, Games, and Know-How for Horse-Loving Kids
By Jessie Haas

Horses
By Laura Driscoll

Horses (Crabapples)
By Tammy Everts and Bobbie Kalman

Horses and Ponies (Young Nature)
By Jo Litchfield

I Wonder Why Chestnuts Wear Shoes and Other Questions About Horses
By Jackie Gaff

The Kids' Horse Book
By Sylvia Funston

The Kingfisher Illustrated Horse and Pony Encyclopedia
By Sandy Ransford

Life on a Horse Farm
By Judy Wolfman

My First Horse and Pony Care Book
By Judith Draper

The Pebble First Guide to Horses
By Zachary Pitts

Race Horses
By Judith Janda Presnall

See How Horses and Ponies Grow
By Kathryn Walker

Welcome to the World of Wild Horses
By Diane Swanson

What Is a Horse?
By Bobbie Kalman and Heather Levigne

Where Horses Run Free: A Dream for the American Mustang
By Joy Cowley

Where the Wild Horses Roam
By Dorothy Hinshaw Patent

Why Do Horses Have Manes?
By Elizabeth MacLeod

The Wild Horse Family Book
By Sybille Kalas

Songs and Rhymes

"If I Were a Horse" (Sing to the tune of "Mr. Ed Theme Song" by Ray Evans and Jay Livingston)
If I were a horse,
A horse, a horse,
I'd like to be a (a color) horse, of course.
I'd like to be a (a color) horse,
And my name would be (child's name).

"I'm a Little Cowboy/Cowgirl" (Sing to the tune of "I'm a Little Tea Pot")
I'm a little cowboy/cowgirl. Here's my hat. (Point to hat)
Here are my spurs, and here are my chaps. (Point to foot and legs)
When I get up, I work all day, (Jump on work)
Get on my horse and ride away. (Galloping motion)

"Big Strong Cowboy/Cowgirl" (Sing to the tune of "I'm a Little Tea Pot")
I'm a cowboy/cowgirl big and strong. I ride horses all day long.
I carry a lasso and sing a song. I'm a cowboy big and strong.
Ai-yi-ya-yea-yippee-i-ay, ai-yi-ya-yea-yippee-i-ay, ai-yi-ya-yea-yippee-i-ay
I'm a cowboy/cowgirl big and strong!

"I Hop on my Horse"
I hop on my horse and go to town. (Pretend to hop on horse)
I ride up high, and I don't fall down. (Pretend to ride horse)
I wear a hat, so my hair won't blow, (Put hand on head)
And when I want to stop, I just say Ho! (Pretend to pull back on reins)

"Horsey, Horsey"
© 1938 by Paddy Roberts
Horsey, horsey on your way,

We've been together many a day.
So let your tail go swish,
And your wheels go 'round.
Giddy-up, we're homeward bound.

"If I Were a Horse"
If I were a horse, I'd neigh, of course.
I'd run and jump and leap, I'd have so much fun,
I'd never be done, if I were a horse, of course.
If I were a horse I'd stay all day
In the meadow so lovely and green.
I'd eat and eat and still stay lean,
If I were a horse, of course.

THE BIRDS

Websites

http://www.everythingpreschool.com/themes/birds/

http://www.amug.org/~jbpratt/education/theme/animals/bird.html

http://www.preschooleducation.com/bird.shtml

http://www.childcarelounge.com/Caregivers/bird.htm

http://www.daniellesplace.com/HTML/birdcrafts.html

Picture Books

About Birds: A Guide for Children
By Cathryn Sill

Are You My Mother?
By P. D. Eastman

Baby Einstein: Birds
By Julie Aigner-Clark

Backyard Birds
By Jonathan Latimer and Karen Stray Nolting

Backyard Birds of Winter
By Carol Lerner

Bird (DK Eyewitness Books)
By David Burnie

Bird, Butterfly, Eel
By James Prosek

Bird Eggs
By Helen Frost

Bird Families
By Helen Frost

Birds
By Kevin Henkes

Birds, Nests and Eggs
By Mel Boring

Birds of All Kinds
By Rebecca Sjonger and Bobbie Kalman

Bizarre Birds
By Sarah Swan Miller

Everything You Never Learned About Birds
By Rebecca Rupp

Grumpy Bird
By Jeremy Tankard

Have You Seen Birds?
By Joanne Oppenheim

How Birds Fly
By Bobbie Kalman

How Do Birds Find Their Way?
By Roma Gans

The Life Cycle of a Bird
By Bobbie Kalman and Kathryn Smithyman

The Mountain That Loved a Bird
By Alice McLerran

Our Yard Is Full of Birds
By Anne Rockwell

A Place for Birds
By Melissa Stewart

Raptors: Birds of Prey
By John Hendrickson

Smithsonian Bird-watcher
By David Burnie

Urban Roosts: Where Birds Nest in the City
By Barbara Bash

What Is a Bird?
By Bobbie Kalman

What Makes a Bird a Bird?
By May Garelick

What's That Bird?: Getting to Know the Birds Around You, Coast to Coast
By Joseph Choiniere and Claire Mowbray Golding

Wild Birds
By Joanne Ryder

Songs and Rhymes

"Two Little Birds"
Two little black birds sitting on a hill, (Hold up both index fingers)
One named Jack, one named Jill. (Wiggle one index finger, then the other)
Fly away Jack, fly away Jill. (Make index fingers "fly" behind your back)

Come back Jack, come back Jill. (Make index fingers "fly" back)
Two little bluebirds sitting on a hill, Hold up both index fingers)
One named Jack, one named Jill. (Wiggle one index finger, then the other)
Fly away Jack, fly away Jill. (Make index fingers "fly" behind your back)
Come back Jack, come back Jill. (Make index fingers "fly" back)
Two little red birds sitting on a hill, (Hold up both index fingers)
One named Jack, one named Jill. (Wiggle one index finger, then the other)
Fly away Jack, fly away Jill. (Make index fingers "fly" behind your back)
Come back Jack, come back Jill. (Make index fingers "fly" back)

"Robin in the Rain"
© Claire Senior Burke
Robin in the rain such a saucy fellow
Robin in the rain mind your spots of yellow
Running through the garden, on your nimble feet
Digging for your dinner with your long strong beak
Robin in the rain, you don't mind the weather showers
They always make you gay
But the worms wish you could stay at home on a rainy day

"Humming Birds"
Five humming birds flying in the air, (Hold up five fingers)
The first one landed in my hair. (Grab little finger)
The second and third were a pair. (Touch index finger and thumb together)
The fourth humming bird didn't care. (Grab ring finger)
The fifth humming bird hummed everywhere. (Touch middle finger and hum loudly)

"Robin Red Breast"
Way up high, little robin flying just so, (Put hands up as high as possible)
Quick down low for a worm he must go. (Put hands low, almost touching the floor)
With a wing on the left and a wing on the right, (Extend arms one at a time)
Fly to your nest for soon it will be night. (Flap arms like flying)

THE LIZARD

Websites

http://www.first-school.ws/theme/animals/reptiles.htm

http://www.amug.org/~jbpratt/education/theme/animals/reptile.html

http://deannasstuff.blogspot.com/2009/07/kids-crafts-lizard-climber.html

http://www.preschooleducation.com/areptile.shtml

oneminutecrafts.com/FoamLizard.html

http://www.craftsforkids.com/projects/lizard.htm

Picture Books

All About Lizards
By Jim Arnosky

Amazing Lizards!
By Fay Robinson

Beaded and Monitor Lizards
By Erik Daniel Stoops

Eyewitness: Reptile
By Colin McCarthy

Frogs, Toads, Lizards, and Salamanders
By Nancy Winslow Parker and Joan Richards Wright

Fun Facts About Lizards!
By Carmen Bredeson

Horned Lizards
By Lyn A. Sirota

The Iguana Brothers: A Tale of Two Lizards
By Tony Johnston

The Little Lazy Lizard
By Susan Denise

Little Skink's Tail
By Janet Halfmann

Lizard Sees the World
By Susan Tews

Lizards (Beginning Vivarium Systems)
By Russ Case

Lizards (Great Pets)
By Ruth Bjorklund

Lizards (Nature's Monsters: Reptiles & Amphibians)
By Brenda Ralph Lewis

Lizards (Our Wild World)
By Deborah Dennard

Lizards (Perfect Pets)
By Susan Schafer

Lizards (Scary Creatures)
By Gerard Cheshire

Lizards (True Books)
By Trudi Strain Trueit

Lizards, Frogs, and Polliwogs
By Douglas Florian

Lizards of the World
By Chris Mattison

Lizards Weird and Wonderful
By Margery Facklam

Lucas the Littlest Lizard
By Kathy Helidoniotis

Mongwis: A Tale of Luke's Lizard
By Beth Scussel

My Pet Lizards
By LeAnne Engfer

The Pebble First Guide to Lizards
By Zachary Pitts

Smithsonian Handbooks: Reptiles and Amphibians
By Mark O'Shea and Tim Halliday

Snakes & Lizards (A Golden Junior Guide)
By George S. Fichter

Snakes and Lizards
By Daniel Moreton and Pamela Chanko

Those Lively Lizards
By Marta Magellan

Songs and Rhymes

"Have You Ever Seen a Lizard?" (Sing to the tune "Did You Ever See a Lassie?")
Have you ever seen a lizard, a lizard, a lizard?
Have you ever seen a lizard all dressed up in pink?
With pink eyes, and pink nose,
And pink legs, and pink toes.
Have you ever seen a lizard all dressed up in pink?
Have you ever seen a lizard, a lizard, a lizard?
Have you ever seen a lizard all dressed up in white?
With white eyes, and white nose,
And white legs, and white toes.
Have you ever seen a lizard all dressed up in white?
Have you ever seen a lizard, a lizard, a lizard?
Have you ever seen a lizard all dressed up in purple?
With purple eyes, and purple nose,
And purple legs, and purple toes.
Have you ever seen a lizard all dressed up in purple?
Have you ever seen a lizard, a lizard, a lizard?

Have you ever seen a lizard all dressed up in blue?
With blue eyes, and blue nose,
And blue legs, and blue toes.
Have you ever seen a lizard all dressed up in blue?

"Lizards in a Log"
Five lizards live in a log. (Hold up five fingers and cover them with other hand)
One left to live with a frog. (Fold thumb down)
One left to live with a dog. (Fold index finger down)
Two left to live with a hog. (Fold middle and ring finger down)
One little lizard living in the bog. (Fold little finger)
Is a little lonely living in a log. (Make a sad face)

"Five Little Lizards in a Tree"
Five little lizards climbing in a tree,
Teasing the alligators, "You can't catch me! You can't catch me!"
Along came an alligator quiet as can be
And snapped that lizard right out of that tree!
Four little lizards climbing in a tree ...
Three little lizards climbing in a tree ...
Two little lizards climbing in a tree ...
One little lizard climbing in a tree ...
No little lizards climbing in a tree ...

"Lizard Fingerplay"
(Use the fist of one hand to represent the lizard. Move pointer finger in and out of fist quickly as the lizard's "tongue." Five fingers on the other hand are the "bugs" that "disappear" as the lizard's fast tongue "gets" them.)
Five little bugs on the forest floor ... Along came a sticky-tongued lizard ... SLURP!!! Now there are four.
Four little bugs on a kapok tree ... Along came a sticky-tongued lizard ... SLURP!!! Now there are three.
Three little bugs without a single clue ... Along came a sticky-tongued lizard ... SLURP!!! Now there are two.
Two little bugs soaking up the hot sun ... Along came a sticky-tongued lizard ... SLURP!!! Now there is one.
One little bug knew that he was done ... Along came a sticky-tongued lizard ... SLURP!!! Now there is none.

READ-ALOUD BOOKS

Additional resources are located at http://fhautism.com/arc.html that I call Read-Aloud-Books. They are short, four-to-five-page picture books that feature illustrations and scenarios similar to the ones on the worksheets. You can print out the books (minimal color was used, so you should be able to print them without using up your printer cartridges) and read them aloud to the class. This will allow the students to become more familiar with the illustrations and concepts without the pressure of the work, which might make the worksheets less stressful for students in the future. Hopefully it will promote questions, discussions, and maybe even a few laughs.

After finishing the picture books, I thought I may as well include them as coloring books too! You can print a book for each student, or one coloring page per student. Whatever works for you.

The text from each Read-Aloud Book is on the following pages, for quick reference, and the actual books are available at http://fhautism.com/arc.html for you to print out. Enjoy!

THE CAT

The cat has four legs, two ears, and a tail.

The cat can run, jump, and say meow.

The cat likes milk, cat food, and fish. And pizza!

The gray cat is drinking milk.

The milk is in the bowl.

The bowl is purple.

The orange cat is under the blue table.

The cat is eating pizza.

Hooray for the cat!

Items Available at http://fhautism.com/arc.html

**Read-Aloud
Picture Book**

**Read-Aloud
Coloring Book**

THE RABBIT

The rabbit has long ears, a nose, and a tail.
The rabbit can hop, run, and dig.
The rabbit likes carrots, leaves, and lettuce.
The pink rabbit is in the yellow basket.
The rabbit is eating a carrot.
The brown rabbit is eating lettuce.
The lettuce is in the bowl.
The bowl is pink.
Hooray for the rabbit!

Items Available at http://fhautism.com/arc.html

**Read-Aloud
Picture Book**

**Read-Aloud
Coloring Book**

THE BEAR

The bear has two eyes, claws, and fur.

The bear can walk, climb, and roar.

The bear likes honey, fish, and hamburgers.

The orange bear is eating a fish.

The fish is yellow.

The fish is on a plate.

The plate is red.

The brown bear is behind the boy.

The boy is wearing red pants.

The bear is eating a hamburger.

The boy feels scared.

Don't be scared! This bear is friendly.

Hooray for the bear!

Items Available at http://fhautism.com/arc.html

Read-Aloud Picture Book

Read-Aloud Coloring Book

THE MOUSE

The mouse has a long tail, two ears, and teeth.

The mouse can run, jump, and chew.

The mouse likes cheese, fruit, and seeds.

The pink mouse is on the brown cat.

The mouse is eating cheese.

The cat feels angry.

The pink mouse is running away from the brown cat!

The mouse is jumping over the ball.

The ball is green.

Go mouse, go!

Hooray for the mouse!

Items Available at http://fhautism.com/arc.html

**Read-Aloud
Picture Book**

**Read-Aloud
Coloring Book**

THE MONKEY

The monkey has a tail, fur, and two ears.
The monkey can climb, swing, and jump.
The monkey likes bananas, apples, and coconuts.
The brown monkey is outside the cage.
The monkey is eating a banana.
The zookeeper is inside the cage.
He is wearing a green jacket.
The zookeeper feels angry.
The orange monkey is swinging from a vine.
The vine is green.
The monkey is eating an apple. The apple is red.
Go, monkey go!
Hooray for the monkey!

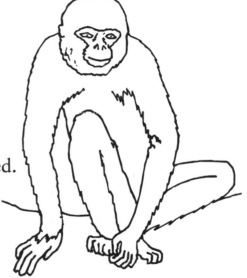

Items Available at http://fhautism.com/arc.html

**Read-Aloud
Picture Book**

**Read-Aloud
Coloring Book**

THE DOG

The dog has a tail, four legs, and teeth.
The dog can bark, wag his tail, run, and dig.
The dog likes dog food, bones, and hamburgers.
The brown dog is on the yellow couch.
The dog is eating a bone.
Mother is next to the couch.
She is wearing a pink dress.
Mother feels angry.
The brown dog is holding a bone.
The dog is next to his doghouse.
The doghouse is orange.
The ball is inside the doghouse. The ball is blue.
Hooray for the dog!

Items Available at http://fhautism.com/arc.html

**Read-Aloud
Picture Book**

**Read-Aloud
Coloring Book**

THE HORSE

The horse has four legs, a mane, and a tail.

The horse can gallop, run, and jump.

The horse likes apples, hay, and carrots.

The boy is in front of the brown horse.

The boy's shirt is orange.

The boy's hat is yellow.

The horse is eating a red apple.

The horse feels happy.

The boy is riding the orange horse.

The boy's hat is blue.

The boy's pants are green.

The horse is jumping over the fence. The fence is yellow.

Hooray for the horse!

Items Available at http://fhautism.com/arc.html

**Read-Aloud
Picture Book**

**Read-Aloud
Coloring Book**

THE BIRDS

The bird has wings, a beak, and feathers.
The bird can fly, chirp, and lay an egg.
The bird likes worms, bugs, and seeds.
There are three birds in the nest.
They are eating pink worms.
The left bird is red.
The middle bird is yellow.
The right bird is blue.
The red bird is standing on the branch.
He is eating a brown worm.
The yellow flying bird is chirping.
The blue sitting bird is laying an egg.
Hooray for the bird!

Items Available at http://fhautism.com/arc.html

**Read-Aloud
Picture Book**

**Read-Aloud
Coloring Book**

THE LIZARD

The lizard has four legs, a long tail, and a tongue.

The lizard can climb, run, and lie in the sun.

The lizard likes leaves, bugs, and worms.

The green lizard is on the gray rock.

The lizard is eating birthday cake!

The cake is pink.

The lizard feels happy.

The lizard is holding a blue balloon.

The orange lizard is climbing up the tree.

The tree is green.

The leaves are yellow.

The lizard likes to eat leaves.

The lizard caught a bug with his long tongue. The bug is red.

Hooray for the lizard!

Items Available at http://fhautism.com/arc.html

Read-Aloud Picture Book

Read-Aloud Coloring Book

DATA-COLLECTION SHEETS

Even though the lessons in this book are designed for whole group instruction, individual assessment of each student's progress is essential—especially in a special needs classroom, where every student comes with an IEP and a set of goals that need to be addressed. That process involves identifying which goals are worthwhile and relevant for each individual student, how to facilitate progress towards that goal, and then finally, how to assess and gather evidence on said progress.

This is a lot of work, I know, and precisely why I wanted to do what I could to simplify the process. So I identified the goals that are automatically addressed, just by teaching the lessons contained in this book, and created data-collection sheets for each one of these goals. All you have to do now is figure out which goal is appropriate for which student, make a copy of the corresponding data-collection sheet, give that collection sheet to a classroom aide, and proceed to teach the lesson. The aide will sit by the student they are assigned to and observe the student during the lesson, recording that student's progress.

I hope this added element will help to streamline your teaching duties.

Goal #1 (Objective #1):

RECOGNITION OF VOWELS/CONSONANTS

Data Collection Sheet—40 Observations

(Enough for up to three times a week in a typical school year calendar, for a third of the school year. This is the duration of the data collection for the first objective, or one-third of the total, annual goal.)

	A	E	I	O	U	B	C	D	F	G	H	J	K	L	M	N	P	Q	R	S	T	V	W	X	Y	Z
1																										
2																										
3																										
4																										
5																										
6																										
7																										
8																										
9																										
10																										
11																										
12																										
13																										
14																										
15																										
16																										
17																										
18																										
19																										
20																										
21																										
22																										
23																										
24																										
25																										
26																										
27																										
28																										
29																										
30																										
31																										
32																										
33																										
34																										
35																										
36																										
37																										
38																										
39																										
40																										

If student successfully identifies the given letter, fill in the corresponding square. If not, leave it blank. Highlight as many vowels and letters covered under this objective.

Goal #1 (Objective #2):

RECOGNITION OF VOWELS/CONSONANTS

Data Collection Sheet—40 Observations

(Enough for up to three times a week in a typical school year calendar, for a third of the school year. This is the duration of the data collection for the first objective, or one-third of the total, annual goal.)

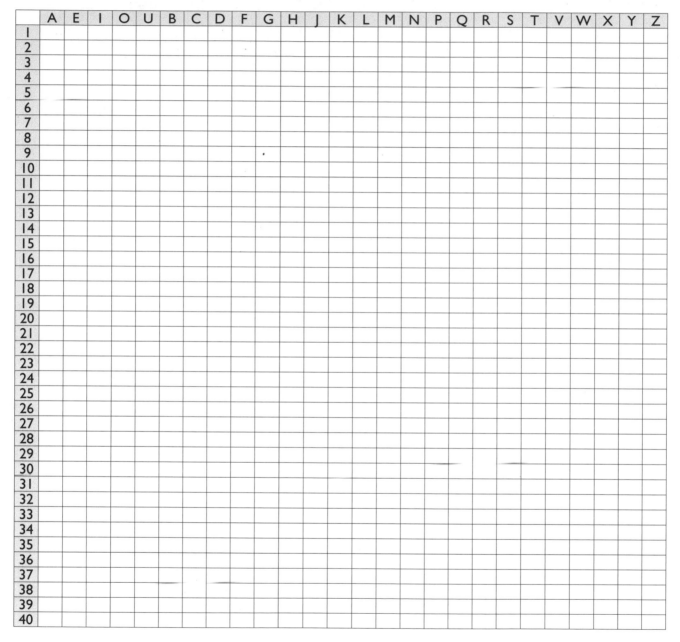

If student successfully identifies the given letter, fill in the corresponding square. If not, leave it blank. Highlight as many vowels and letters covered under this objective.

Goal #1 (Final Report):

RECOGNITION OF VOWELS/CONSONANTS

Data Collection Sheet—40 Observations

(Enough for up to three times a week in a typical school year calendar, for a third of the school year. This is the duration of the data collection for the first objective, or one-third of the total, annual goal.)

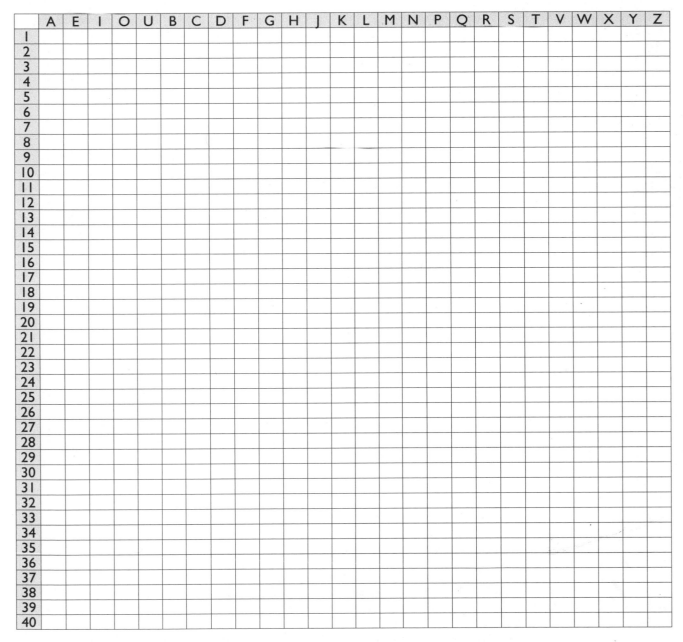

If student successfully identifies the given letter, fill in the corresponding square. If not, leave it blank. Highlight as many vowels and letters covered under this objective.

Goal #2 (Objective #1):

RECOGNITION OF VOWELS/CONSONANTS

Data Collection Sheet—40 Observations

(Enough for up to three times a week in a typical school year calendar, for a third of the school year. This is the duration of the data collection for the first objective, or one-third of the total, annual goal.)

	A	E	I	O	U	B	C	D	F	G	H	J	K	L	M	N	P	Q	R	S	T	V	W	X	Y	Z
1																										
2																										
3																										
4																										
5																										
6																										
7																										
8																										
9																										
10																										
11																										
12																										
13																										
14																										
15																										
16																										
17																										
18																										
19																										
20																										
21																										
22																										
23																										
24																										
25																										
26																										
27																										
28																										
29																										
30																										
31																										
32																										
33																										
34																										
35																										
36																										
37																										
38																										
39																										
40																										

If student successfully identifies the given letter, fill in the corresponding square. If not, leave it blank. Highlight as many vowels and letters covered under this objective.

Goal #2 (Objective #2):

RECOGNITION OF VOWELS/CONSONANTS

Data Collection Sheet—40 Observations

(Enough for up to three times a week in a typical school year calendar, for a third of the school year. This is the duration of the data collection for the first objective, or one-third of the total, annual goal.)

	A	E	I	O	U	B	C	D	F	G	H	J	K	L	M	N	P	Q	R	S	T	V	W	X	Y	Z
1																										
2																										
3																										
4																										
5																										
6																										
7																										
8																										
9																										
10																										
11																										
12																										
13																										
14																										
15																										
16																										
17																										
18																										
19																										
20																										
21																										
22																										
23																										
24																										
25																										
26																										
27																										
28																										
29																										
30																										
31																										
32																										
33																										
34																										
35																										
36																										
37																										
38																										
39																										
40																										

If student successfully identifies the given letter, fill in the corresponding square. If not, leave it blank. Highlight as many vowels and letters covered under this objective.

Goal #2 (Final Report):

RECOGNITION OF VOWELS/CONSONANTS

Data Collection Sheet—40 Observations

(Enough for up to three times a week in a typical school year calendar, for a third of the school year. This is the duration of the data collection for the first objective, or one-third of the total, annual goal.)

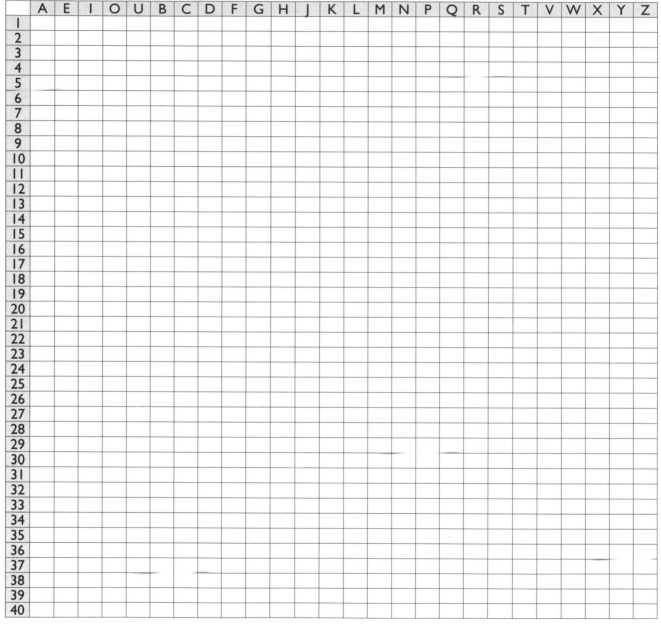

	A	E	I	O	U	B	C	D	F	G	H	J	K	L	M	N	P	Q	R	S	T	V	W	X	Y	Z
1																										
2																										
3																										
4																										
5																										
6																										
7																										
8																										
9																										
10																										
11																										
12																										
13																										
14																										
15																										
16																										
17																										
18																										
19																										
20																										
21																										
22																										
23																										
24																										
25																										
26																										
27																										
28																										
29																										
30																										
31																										
32																										
33																										
34																										
35																										
36																										
37																										
38																										
39																										
40																										

If student successfully identifies the given letter, fill in the corresponding square. If not, leave it blank. Highlight as many vowels and letters covered under this objective.

Goal #3 (Objective #1):

DEMONSTRATION OF COLOR IDENTIFICATION

Data Collection Sheet—40 Observations

(Enough for up to three times a week in a typical school year calendar, for a third of the school year. This is the duration of the data collection for the first objective, or one-third of the total, annual goal.)

	BLUE	RED	GREEN	ORANGE	YELLOW	BLACK	BROWN	PURPLE	PINK
1									
2									
3									
4									
5									
6									
7									
8									
9									
10									
11									
12									
13									
14									
15									
16									
17									
18									
19									
20									
21									
22									
23									
24									
25									
26									
27									
28									
29									
30									
31									
32									
33									
34									
35									
36									
37									
38									
39									
40									

If student successfully identifies the given color, fill in the corresponding square. If not, leave it blank. Highlight as many colors covered under this objective.

Goal #3 (Objective #2):

DEMONSTRATION OF COLOR IDENTIFICATION

Data Collection Sheet—40 Observations

(Enough for up to three times a week in a typical school year calendar, for a third of the school year. This is the duration of the data collection for the first objective, or one-third of the total, annual goal.)

	BLUE	RED	GREEN	ORANGE	YELLOW	BLACK	BROWN	PURPLE	PINK
1									
2									
3									
4									
5									
6									
7									
8									
9									
10									
11									
12									
13									
14									
15									
16									
17									
18									
19									
20									
21									
22									
23									
24									
25									
26									
27									
28									
29									
30									
31									
32									
33									
34									
35									
36									
37									
38									
39									
40									

If student successfully identifies the given color, fill in the corresponding square. If not, leave it blank. Highlight as many colors covered under this objective.

Goal #3 (Final Report):

DEMONSTRATION OF COLOR IDENTIFICATION

Data Collection Sheet—40 Observations

(Enough for up to three times a week in a typical school year calendar, for a third of the school year. This is the duration of the data collection for the first objective, or one-third of the total, annual goal.)

	BLUE	RED	GREEN	ORANGE	YELLOW	BLACK	BROWN	PURPLE	PINK
1									
2									
3									
4									
5									
6									
7									
8									
9									
10									
11									
12									
13									
14									
15									
16									
17									
18									
19									
20									
21									
22									
23									
24									
25									
26									
27									
28									
29									
30									
31									
32									
33									
34									
35									
36									
37									
38									
39									
40									

If student successfully identifies the given color, fill in the corresponding square. If not, leave it blank. Highlight as many colors covered under this objective.

Goal #4 (Objective #1):

FOLLOWING ONE- AND TWO-STEP DIRECTIONS

Data Collection Sheet—40 Observations

	Take out two crayons	Take out two crayons/ place on table	Take out pencil	Take out pencil/ write name	Other one-step direction	Other two-step direction
1						
2						
3						
4						
5						
6						
7						
8						
9						
10						
11						
12						
13						
14						
15						
16						
17						
18						
19						
20						
21						
22						
23						
24						
25						
26						
27						
28						
29						
30						
31						
32						
33						
34						
35						
36						
37						
38						
39						
40						

If student successfully follows the directions, fill in the corresponding square. If not, leave it blank. Highlight the one and/or two-step direction(s) being covered under this objective.

Goal #4 (Objective #2):

FOLLOWING ONE- AND TWO-STEP DIRECTIONS

Data Collection Sheet—40 Observations

	Take out two crayons	Take out two crayons/ place on table	Take out pencil	Take out pencil/ write name	Other one-step direction	Other two-step direction
1						
2						
3						
4						
5						
6						
7						
8						
9						
10						
11						
12						
13						
14						
15						
16						
17						
18						
19						
20						
21						
22						
23						
24						
25						
26						
27						
28						
29						
30						
31						
32						
33						
34						
35						
36						
37						
38						
39						
40						

If student successfully follows the directions, fill in the corresponding square. If not, leave it blank. Highlight the one and/or two-step direction(s) being covered under this objective.

Goal #4 (Final Report):

FOLLOWING ONE- AND TWO-STEP DIRECTIONS

Data Collection Sheet—40 Observations

	Take out two crayons	Take out two crayons/ place on table	Take out pencil	Take out pencil/ write name	Other one-step direction	Other two-step direction
1						
2						
3						
4						
5						
6						
7						
8						
9						
10						
11						
12						
13						
14						
15						
16						
17						
18						
19						
20						
21						
22						
23						
24						
25						
26						
27						
28						
29						
30						
31						
32						
33						
34						
35						
36						
37						
38						
39						
40						

If student successfully follows the directions, fill in the corresponding square. If not, leave it blank. Highlight the one and/or two-step direction(s) being covered under this objective.

REFERENCES

Chiang, H., Lin, Y. (2007). Reading comprehension instruction for students with autism spectrum disorder: A review of the literature. *Focus on Autism and Other Developmental Disabilities,* Volume 22, 259-267.

Frith, U., & Snowling, M. (1983). Reading for meaning and reading for sound in autistic and dyslexic children. *British Journal of Developmental Psychology, 1,* 329–342.

Healey, J. M. (1982). The enigma of hyperlexia. *Reading Research Quarterly, 17,* 319–338.

Kluth, P. (2005). Tell me about the story: Comprehension strategies for students with autism. Retrieved from http://www.paulakluth.com/articles/comprehension.html.

Lovett, M. W., Borden, S. L., Warren-Chaplin, P. M., Lacerenza, L., DeLuca, T., & Giovinazzo, R. (1996). Text comprehension training for disabled readers: An evaluation of reciprocal teaching and text analysis training programs. *Brain and Language, 54,* 447–480.

O'Connor, I.M., Klein, P.D. (2004). Exploration of strategies for facilitating the reading comprehension of high-functioning students with autism spectrum disorders. *Journal of Autism and Developmental Disorders,* Volume 34, 115-127.

Plaisted, J. (1999). Hierarchical attention shifting in children with autism. *Journal of Autism and Developmental Disorders, 29,* 29–47.

Quill, K. A. (1997). Instructional considerations for young children with autism: the rationale for visually cued instruction. *Journal of Autism and Developmental Disorders, 27,* 697–714.

Whitehouse, D., Harris, J. (1984). Hyperlexia in infantile autism. *Journal of Autism and Developmental Disorder, Vol. 14,* 281-289.

INDEX